Changing the Way
We Manage Change

Changing the Way We Manage Change

EDITED BY
RONALD R. SIMS

QUORUM BOOKS
Westport, Connecticut • London

Library of Congress Cataloging-in-Publication Data

Changing the way we manage change / edited by Ronald R. Sims.
    p.   cm.
    Includes bibliographical references and index.
    ISBN 1–56720–461–9 (alk. paper)
    1. Organizational change.   I. Sims, Ronald R.
  HD58.8C463   2002
  658.4'06—dc21   2001057868

British Library Cataloguing in Publication Data is available.

Library of Congress Catalog Card Number: 2001057868
ISBN: 1–56720–461–9

First published in 2002

Quorum Books, 88 Post Road West, Westport, CT 06881
An imprint of Greenwood Publishing Group, Inc.
www.quorumbooks.com

Printed in the United States of America

∞™

The paper used in this book complies with the
Permanent Paper Standard issued by the National
Information Standards Organization (Z39.48–1984).

10 9 8 7 6 5 4 3 2 1

Copyright Acknowledgments

The author and publisher are grateful for permission to reproduce the following copyrighted
material:

Figures 4.1–4.3, 4.5, and 4.6 from Gilley, J.W., Quatro, S.A., Hoekstra, E., et al. 2001. *The
Manager as Change Agent*. Cambridge, MA: Perseus Publishing.

Figure 7.3 courtesy of E. Curtis Alexander, Ph.D.

Contents

Preface

No matter which way they turn, organizations are increasingly expected to find better and faster ways of responding to the change challenges presented by the revolution in information technology, increased globalization, smarter customers, and a constantly changing employee base. Are organizations successfully responding to these challenges, or are they crippled by their inability to bring about the necessary changes? How effective are organizations in managing change? Are the change management or organizational development (OD) theories, models, interventions, and change agent skills proving to be of value to organizations in their efforts to change? If so, how can we improve on them? If not, then what should we be doing differently? These were some of the questions that inspired me to create *Changing the Way We Manage Change*.

The book you are reading reveals the collective thoughts of individuals committed to change management and OD. *Changing the Way We Manage Change* brings together change agents with extensive experience from various vantage points in managing change, allowing you to understand the way we are managing change now and what changes in the way we manage change may need to be made to improve change management success.

Although no book can address every potential manifestation of change management, this book is an attempt to look clearly without flinching at the ways we manage change, what we can learn from the way we manage change, and new ways of managing change. The good and not so good change management habits we can learn from this book will prove useful—even critical—for change success, not only in increasingly complex environments but also in an increasingly demanding and unforgiving world.

I wish to thank my blue-ribbon group of authors who have crafted their array of skills both on the firing line and from various other change management vantage points. They represent a group of individuals who have contributed in their own unique way to the still emerging discipline of change management and organizational development. They have contributed generously of their time and energy to *Changing the Way We Manage Change* to share their collective ideas for how we can better manage change.

Once again, a very special thanks goes to Herrington Bryce, who continues to serve as a colleague, mentor, and valued friend. The administrative support of Larry Pulley, Dean of the School of Business Administration at the College of William & Mary, is also acknowledged. I am also indebted to Eric Valentine, publisher at Quorum Books, who still continues to provide an outlet for my ideas.

My thanks and appreciation as usual also goes to my wife, Serbrenia, and the rest of the gang, Nandi, Dangaia, Sieya and Kani, who have supported me during one of those times when it seemed as if all I ever did was read and sit in front of the computer. A special thanks goes out to Ronald, Jr., Marchet, Vellice, Shelley, and Sharisse.

The book is dedicated posthumously to Phyllis Viands, former receptionist and secretary at the School of Business Administration at the College of William & Mary, who is sadly missed but fondly remembered as a warm and kind friend.

Changing the Way
We Manage Change

Chapter 1

General Introduction and Overview of the Book

Ronald R. Sims

As the twenty-first century begins, the world is in a constant state of change, and no organization, in the United States or elsewhere, can escape the effects of operating in a continually dynamic, evolving landscape. The forces of change are so great that the future success, indeed the very survival, of thousands of organizations depends on how well they respond to change or, optimally, whether they can actually stay ahead of change.

It is widely acknowledged that change—from such forces as globalization, relentless technological advances, unprecedented competition, political upheaval, and the opening of new markets—exerts constant pressure on organizations of all sizes and types. As a result, these organizations are beginning to shift their own gears in response to evolving developments in the world. But all is not rosy, given the disturbing reality of the poor batting average posted by organizations that have sincerely dedicated themselves to change.

Effective change management appears to be in short supply these days, given that the landscape is filled with failed attempts to manage. Although a handful of organizations have scored admirable successes, the majority of them have failed to find the magic new mode or style that is needed to survive and thrive in the new economy and the volatile macroenvionment. The degree of failures should not be surprising when one considers that according to a recent report only 51% of the companies surveyed rated their leaders as excellent or good in their capabilities to meet business challenges. Included among these challenges were executing aggressive new growth strategies, attracting and retaining employees in increasingly competitive markets, coping with high rates of uncertainty and change, competing in a global economy, and implementing mergers and acquisitions. All of these challenges require organizational changes.

In response to the large number of failed change efforts and the challenges of the new economy, books, articles, seminars, and workshops on leadership and change management have flooded the market offering the latest and greatest answers intended to increase organizational and change agent effectiveness and improve change success rates. No matter where one looks there are more and more advertised remedies purporting to address the change failure rate and the challenge of today's new economy. They have ranged from the easily recognizable: learning organizations, flat organizations, reengineering, team-based organizations, and on and on. With all of our collective responses to address change failures still not showing the return needed, it is clear that there is a need to rethink the way we manage change and where appropriate change the way we manage change. And rethinking the way we manage change is what the contributors in this book will focus on.

THE FOCUS OF THIS BOOK

Why is it that it seems as if we are experiencing déjà vu in feeling that we have been through this rethinking the way we manage change process before and that we still have a long way to go if we are going to improve our change success rate, especially given the demands for change in this new economy? How can we improve not only the prescriptions but also the changes to change in our efforts to help organizations meet the demands of a much different marketplace and environment in the new economy?

There is no simple answer, just like there is no one-size-fits-all solution for leading or successfully managing change. The competencies, beliefs, and values that change agents need depend on the organization's strategy and organizational context.

There are an endless number of change-related questions that need answers. For example:

- How can we better manage change?
- Do we need to change the way we manage change?
- What kind of change agent(s) or change management program(s) are needed to increase successful organization change?
- What are the most effective approaches to change for today's new organizational context?
- What traditional change management methodologies and interventions work in the new economy?
- What are the roles of internal and external change agents in today's organizational change efforts?
- What skills or competencies are important to change agent success?
- What can organizations do to ensure that their change efforts are successfully implemented?

- How can an organization create an environment in which every employee is a change agent?

A basic premise of this book is that searching to find answers to questions like these will allow us to better navigate the challenges of the new economy and better manage change overall. Readers will find that there are a variety of responses to these questions and a variety of solutions for better managing change. For example, for many who are in the managing change business or grappling with change every day, the answers to meeting today's challenges involve continuing to strive to better redefine and align strategies, mission, operations, and people. For others, the answer lies in simply improving organizational relationships between management and employees so that both parties accept the value of working together. The fundamental organizing principle for this new relationship is maximizing employee involvement before, during, and after any organizational change initiative, creating new conversations, and better preparing the "new breed" of today's change agents. And for still others the answer is seen as discarding the term "organizational development" in favor of a new one called "change management. See for example, the recent point-counterpoint-rejoinder taking place in the *Journal of Applied Behavioral Science* among Worren, Ruddle, and Moore (1999, 2000), Farias and Johnson (2000), and Hornstein (2001). Regardless of whether someone feels the answers are already there, right around the corner, or will never be within our reach, we must continue to search for answers to these and other questions. And, that is the reason for this book!

This book is titled *Changing the Way We Manage Change* because it begins from the premise that "managing change" is not a problem or process that will ever go away but rather an opportunity to develop greater individual and organizational effectiveness by continuously rethinking the way we manage change. This book is written for those individuals and organizations who are in the midst of grappling with the challenges of managing change. In this book, the contributors, as change agents, discuss their views on how we may or may not need to change the way we manage change to increase the change success rate. In offering their views on changing the way we manage change the contributors critique traditional change management theories, models, interventions, and change processes while arguing in some cases that well-meaning change prescriptions are no longer suitable for handling the degree of change that is necessary in the new organizational context. In presenting their views about changes in the way we manage change, the contributors discuss what they view as the major challenges in managing change and offer suggestions for improving the way we manage change.

In some instances the contributors will offer very new and unique road maps for changing the way we manage change, while in other instances they will simply refocus our attention on the roads that have always been there or offer suggestions on how to redirect the roads. The contributors sketch the route that must be taken toward changing the way we manage change and denote some milestones, turns, stop signs, red lights, yellow caution lights, and the sensing devices that keep all stakeholders on the main road. But *Changing the Way We Manage Change* does not set down rigid approaches. In line with the underlying premise of this book that organizations must always be adaptable, flexible, and nimble, the ideas presented in the following pages stress the possible alterations for changing the way we manage change.

Changing the Way We Manage Change is intended to be a practical, action-oriented document that contributes to the never ending dialogue on how we can change the way we manage change. Its contents can be used to view the whole change management process any organization might go through to determine how to improve individual change.

There is still much that we can learn and do in the area of change management, and it is our hope that the collective ideas presented in this book will get us a little closer than we are now to better managing change. Like others who have and are currently contributing to the dialogue on managing change, I thank and applaud the contributors to this book, who are willing to share their experiences and ideas on change management.

Part I: The Process and People of Change

The four chapters in Part I of this book introduce us to the process and people of change. In Chapter 2, "Unleashing the Power of Self-Directed Learning," Richard E. Boyatzis suggests the self-directed learning process as a possible road map for how to increase the effectiveness of change and learning efforts. The chapter provides a look at individuals and their capacity to grow, develop, or simply change as a result of self-directed learning. Self-directed learning is defined as an intentional change in an aspect of who one is (i.e., the Real) or who one wants to be (i.e., the Ideal), or both. Self-directed learning is self-directed change in which individuals are aware of the change and understand the process of change. This understanding provides them with firsthand and personal experience as a change agent, allowing them to be in a better position to understand and contribute to organizational change. The model presented by Boyatzis is built on the premise that experiencing discontinuity, a part of the process that may not and often does not occur as a smooth, linear event, is a key component of self-directed learning. The chapter describes five discontinuities that begin the process of self-directed learning: "Catching Your Dreams, Engaging Your Passion," "Am I a Boiling Frog?," "Mindfulness through a Learning Agenda," "Metamorphosis," and "Relationships That Enable Us to Learn."

In Chapter 3, "Employee Involvement Is Still the Key to Successfully Managing Change," Serbrenia J. Sims and Ronald R. Sims take a look at change failures and argue that the key to improving our change management record is to find ways to maximize employee involvement at every opportunity before, during, and after any change initiative. Maximizing employee involvement is offered as the only guaranteed way an organization can develop a cadre of internal change agents—change agents who understand their roles and responsibilities because they are involved in every way with the organization. The authors also offer insights into a number of misconceptions about employee involvement that have contributed to the failure to maximize employee involvement in change initiatives. Characteristics of high-involvement organizations (HIOs) are reviewed and offered as a vehicle for establishing an organizational foundation for maximizing employee involvement. Sims and Sims also provide suggestions for smoothing the change process and easing employees' pain during change initiation.

In Chapter 4, "Holistic Model for Change Agent Excellence: Core Roles and Competencies for Successful Change Agency," Scott A. Quatro, Erik Hoekstra, and Jerry W. Gilley provide a framework to address two of the most frequent criticisms of change agents: (1) being too fragmented in their approach to change agency and (2) insufficient emphasis on the key competencies required of change agents that drive change engagements. Quatro, Hoekstra, and Gilley suggest that change agents must approach their change efforts holistically with brain, heart, courage, and vision. The model presents contemporary change agents with an overview of the core roles (i.e., business partner, servant leader, change champion, future shaper) that they must be willing to fulfill in order to holistically engage their clients and the personal competencies that they must develop in order to be capable of doing so.

In Chapter 5, "The Changing Roles and Responsibilities of Change Agents," Ronald R. Sims builds on the people and change agent theme offered in the first three chapters. Sims discusses change agent roles and responsibilities that he believes must be filled by all internal (i.e, boards of directors, senior leaders, middle managers, nonmanagers) and external change agents (customers and external change management consultants) in order to bring about successful change. The basic premise underlying the ideas presented in this chapter is in line with the view that everyone in today's organizations must become intentional change agents and be more aware of options to help their organizations adapt to today's new environment. Similarly, the author suggests that external change agents must rethink their roles and responsibilities in working with client organizations if they are going to be able to play an active role in collaboratively working with the organization's internal change agents.

Part II: Global Views and Experiences of Change

The two chapters in Part II of this book take a look at changing the way we manage change from the perspective of the international change agent. The authors offer insights on change challenges presented by working in our increasingly global world and on ways to increase change success in these environments.

In Chapter 6, "Why the Bridge Hasn't Been Built and Other Profound Questions in Multicultural Organizational Development," Terry R. Armstrong discusses his experiences in undertaking multicultural organizational development (OD) projects. Using examples based on his own international work with several clients, the author offers a firsthand look at his own development as an OD consultant engaged in cross-cultural OD. Based on his years of experience in working with very different organizations and individuals throughout the world, Armstrong offers the reader a better opportunity to understand the challenges faced in promoting cross-cultural change. Armstrong's revelations about how his experiences have helped shaped his view of what is important in successful multicultural change work provides a fresh way of understanding the development of a change agent. The chapter provides a number of concepts and tools for cross-cultural analysis of human behavior as well as lessons learned that can be helpful to others who are interested in multicultural OD.

In Chapter 7, "Reconciling the Dynamic of Symbols and Symptoms in Bringing about International Change," Edgar J. Ridley suggests that productivity and other improvements have not taken place on a global scale consistent with our technological advancements because business leaders continue to make decisions from a mythological framework that renders technological advances impotent. A cornerstone of Ridley's arguments is that today's change consultants must bring new tools to the table in order to challenge the status quo and a world built on myths and symbol systems. The concept of symptomatic thought process (STP) is introduced as a replacement for the symbolic thought process, which in Ridley's view has been a standard behind many traditional models and tools used by change consultants.

Part III: Change Cases

Part III of this book provides four chapters that illustrate current and future issues for change agents in more technologically oriented environments. While these chapters do not focus on specific change cases they illustrate the change challenges that change agents must be aware of in specific situations.

In Chapter 8, "Change Management Methods in an Exciting New World of Business-to-Business Commerce," Ronald R. Sims and William J. Mea begin the discussion of specific change issues as they focus on the background, context, and suggestions for change management specialists who wish to consult effectively in business-to-business (B2B) and business-to-portal (B2P) commerce. The authors suggest the need for new focus areas for change management specialists interested in working with these new organizations. In addition to describing current and future challenges these new organizations pose for change management specialists, the chapter also offers a look at future trends and considerations of which change management specialists must be aware. Best practices for change management specialists, which are based on the experiences of the authors and their colleagues in working with these new organizations, are also presented for the reader's consideration.

In Chapter 9, "Privatization of Public Utilities Drives Change in Consulting Firms," Kathi Mestayer suggests that the trend toward privatization of public services has engendered a series of changes in public utility (water and waste-water) organizations. Based on this suggestion, Mestayer describes how those organizations have been impacted, how their consultants have attempted to meet their changing needs, and how those attempts are, in turn, requiring the consulting firms to manage their own change processes. The chapter discusses how two industries (utilities and engineering firms) are trying to change, with the latter trying to change into change consultants.

In Chapter 10, "Data Processing to Knowledge Management: Are Information Technology Professionals Still Addressing the Same Change Management Issues?" Gigi G. Kelly discusses the challenges the unpredictable business environment presents to people responsible for delivering information technology (IT) solutions. The chapter offers answers to questions like "Has anything really changed in the IT profession during the past 20 years?" and "Are IT professionals still trying to gather requirements, develop programs, and implement systems that meet the end user's expectations despite the chaotic and often unpredicatable business environment?" In offering answers to these and other questions the chapter takes a look at the past and the present and ponders the future of IT within the business environment. Issues including knowledge management, collaborative technologies, and creating and implementing new IT solutions such as enterprise-wide resource planning (ERP) systems are discussed and analyzed to provide the reader with an understanding of corresponding change agent challenges. Examples from a variety of IT projects are used as the backdrop to further investigate the changing, or not-so-changing, world of information technology.

In Chapter 11, "The Balanced Scorecard: New Strategy Applications in Business-to-Business Commerce," William J. Mea, Theodore L. Robinson III, and James W. Handlon update concepts from the balanced scorecard and apply them to the corporate context in the digital economy. The chapter offers an examination of a number of basic strategy issues to be considered when applying the balanced scorecard technique to companies, especially those engaged in B2B and B2P commerce. The chapter proposes new scorecard perspective options intended to help consultants assist companies to build more stable e-business organization models and provide a more innovative approach to building and implementing strategy.

Part IV: New Approaches and Models for Change

Part IV includes four chapters that describe new approaches or models for change and change agent development. Each of these chapters makes a contribution to the need to look for alternative or nontraditional ways of managing change and changing the way we manage change. As in previous chapters, readers are asked to think about roles, values, assumptions, and change interventions in new ways. After all, thinking about what we do in managing change can only maximize our learning and our ability to change the way we manage change.

In Chapter 12, "Changing How Organizations Manage Change from the Inside Out," Andrea B. Bear and Kathleen A. Brehony explore the relationship between change, consciousness, and the ways in which vibrant organizations passionately respond to change and use their power as an opportunity for growth, fulfillment, and the actualization of full potential. The authors describe the importance of individual and organizational consciousness to increased self-awareness and organizational knowledge and change. The concept of corporate consciousness is introduced, and the authors discuss the power of consciousness and change, suggesting a model ("C-Model") as a mechanism for building conscious organizations.

In Chapter 13, "Change: Build It In, Just Like Quality!" William I. Sauser, Jr. and Lane D. Sauser discuss the reasons why we can no longer consider organizational change as a project or event—with a beginning and an end—to be managed and why we must consider change management as an ongoing aspect of the leader's job. The implications of this viewpoint for the way we teach change management in our colleges of business and in our continuing professional education programs are described. In an effort to provide further support for why we need to view organizational change in a different light, the authors examine questions like "How can we refocus ourselves to consider change as the natural state of things and thus an element of our environment to which we must continually adapt?" and "How might we inculcate this viewpoint into those we are preparing to lead our organizations in the future?"

In Chapter 14, "Creating a New Kind of Conversation: A Consultant's Role in Building Sustainable Change in the New Economy," Ann C. Baker focuses on the importance of quality conversations among different stakeholders to achieve sustainable change in the new economy. Baker calls for a new kind of conversation—conversational learning—used by consultants in their work with organizations and in communities. Conversational learning and reframing of two primary ideas—change and differences—are defined and their applicability to an actual consulting situation is described in the chapter.

In Chapter 15, "Restorying and Postmodern Organization Theater: Consultation to the Storytelling Organization," Grace Ann Rosile and David M. Boje describe the use of narrative and theatrics for organizational development. Rosile and Boje view organizational life as a story and organizational development as a means of changing that story or "restorying." The chapter describes a seven-step process to guide individuals, groups, and organizations in their own restorying process. The authors explain their change management methods through a series of organizational consultation case studies. Rosile and Boje provide detailed descriptions of specific structured intervention activities to demonstrate the use of narrative and theatrics in bringing about change or organizational development.

REFERENCES

Farias, G., & Johnson, H. 2000. Organizational development and change management: Setting the record straight. *The Journal of Applied Behavioral Science*, 36(3): 327–379.

Hornstein, H. 2001. Organizational development and change management: Don't throw the baby out with the bath water. *The Journal of Applied Behavioral Science*, 37(2): 223–226.

Worren, N.A., Ruddle, K., & Moore, K. 1999. From organizational development to change management: The emergence of a new profession. *The Journal of Behavioral Science*, 35(3): 273–286.

Worren, N.A., Ruddle, K., & Moore, K. 2000. Response to Farias and Johnson's commentary. *The Journal of Behavioral Science*, 36(3): 380–381.

Part I

The Process and People of Change

Chapter 2

Unleashing the Power of
Self-Directed Learning

Richard E. Boyatzis

INTRODUCTION

The new economy is not about technology, it is about a change in the basic assumptions about the nature of work. Contributing to this are several demographic factors. Worldwide, the work force is aging. In the United States in 1999, 19% of the work force was 70 or older. By 2050, the average age of the U.S. population will increase to 40 (from 36 in 1995). By that same year, the number of retirees in Europe will be greater than the number of people in the work force ("Europe's demographic time bomb," 2001). The work force and population are becoming increasingly ethnically and racially diverse. By 2050, 24% of the work force (about 97 million people) in the United States will be Hispanic. Women are filling more positions of power in organizations each year. Slowing population growth and resettlement patterns are changing the human resource picture in entire countries. For example, by 2050, without extraordinary immigrations, the populations of Spain and Italy will shrink by 25%.

Technology has changed the design of work and the rhythm of our lives. We are engaged by it everywhere—shopping, conversations, information acquisition, medical advice, learning, and so on—yet we still fail to comprehend the magnitude of this change. For example, current U.S. high school graduates are the first generation to never have touched a typewriter. Their basic assumptions about how to work, live, and learn are different from previous generations' as a result of technology.

At the same time, right-sizing, acquisitions, dot com exuberance, and changing values have led to dramatically different relationships between people and the organizations within which they work. People are more individualistic in the way they view their careers and commitment to organizations. Organizations have done little to encourage any other perspective, viewing people as a tradable and expendable human resources. People today want increasing work/life balance and an holistic approach to life. Among those with skills and better educations, many believe that there are plentiful opportunities available for work, especially for the most talented.

It is no wonder that organizations face a war for talent (see studies by McKinsey in 1998 and 2000, reported in *Fast Company* [Anders, 2001]). Finding the right people and keeping them has become a major problem for organizations. This occurs even when they are simultaneously laying others off and restructuring their work force. There is almost full employment in the industrial and knowledge industry sections of many countries. The CEO of Hewlett-Packard, Carly Fiorina, has developed a mantra that describes her approach to this dilemma, "Capture their hearts, their minds will follow."

The current relationship or psychological contract between a person and an organization seems best characterized by the concept of free agency. Like free agents in sports, people feel that they can and should look for the best offer, one that suits their individual needs and career aspirations each year, or sooner if opportunities come along.

The emerging forms of organizations will depend on free agency more and more. For the longest period of human history, the primary form of social organization was a hunting and gathering society. They were mobile groups of 50 to 100 people who adapted continuously to climate, food sources, and external threats. They lasted at least 50,000 years, and were organic. When agricultural forms came into being about 4,000–5,000 years ago and then spread, hunting and gathering societies began to fade. Agricultural societies became the predominant form of social organization beyond the family for about 3,000 years.

Then we developed bureaucratic forms of organization—military, feudal system, and churches (which lasted for about 1,000 or so years). These forms of social organization featured a command and control system. Then science paved the way for the industrial revolution that lasted about 200 years. Money was the key resource, but we were separated from our completed products and customers. Functional and even matrix forms were popular.

But this form of organization began to fade with the emergence of fluid organizations. Fed by the information revolution and knowledge economy, especially evident in professional services and technology but spreading to many types of organization, we have seen the growth of fluid organizations in the last 10 years or so. They are adaptive systems using self-organizing principles described by complexity theory. Fluid organizations have fuzzy boundaries, alliances, and communities of practice. Information and people are the key resource. Velocity is vital as we pursue e-business, e-learning, and e-relationships. These emerging forms are organic and tribal.

This reminds us of and may in fact lead us back to hunting and gathering societies. In fluid or hunting and gathering societies, any person can leave with an hour. Kevin Kelly says in *New Rules for the New Economy* (1998), that adaptability will replace productivity as the key measure of organizational performance in the coming years. He was talking about adapting to clients, markets, technology, the work force, and so forth. In fluid organizations, free agency is the primary form of psychological contract.

"How do the 'best companies to work for' maintain an edge in this environment? One word: culture!" (Levering & Moskowitz, 2001, p. 149). The desired culture is one that is exciting and viewed as a great place to grow and develop. This has been shown in surveys of the managerial and professional work force in the United States since the mid-1980s.

CAN PEOPLE GROW AND DEVELOP THEIR TALENTS?

Decades of research on the effects of psychotherapy (Hubble, Duncan, & Miller, 1999), self-help programs (Kanfer & Goldstein, 1991), cognitive behavior therapy (Barlow, 1988), training programs (Morrow, Jarrett, & Rupinski, 1997), and education (Pascarella & Terenzini, 1991; Winter, McClelland, & Stewart, 1981) have shown that people can change their behavior, moods, and self-image. But most of the studies focused on a single characteristic, like maintenance of sobriety, reduction in a specific anxiety, or a set of characteristics often determined by the assessment instrument, such as the scales of the Minnesota Multiphasic Personality Index (MMPI). For example, the impact of Achievement Motivation Training was a dramatic increase in small business success, with people who had the training creating more new jobs, starting more new businesses, and paying more taxes than comparison groups (McClelland & Winter, 1969; Miron & McClelland, 1979). The impact of Power Motivation Training was improved maintenance of sobriety (Cutter, Boyatzis, & Clancy, 1977).

A series of longitudinal studies under way at the Weatherhead School of Management of Case Western Reserve University have shown that people can change on the complex set of competencies that distinguish outstanding performers in management and professions. In contrast to the honeymoon effect of most training, education, and development programs, the behavioral improvements did not fade away after three weeks or three months. They lasted for years. A visual comparison of different samples is shown in Figure 2.1.

Up to two years after going through the change process—compared to when they first entered the course—they showed 47% improvement on self-awareness competencies such as self-confidence and on self-management competencies such as the drive to achieve and adaptability. When it came to social awareness and relationship management skills, improvements were even greater: 75% on competencies such as empathy and team leadership.

These gains stand in stark contrast to those from standard MBA programs, where there is no attempt to enhance emotional intelligence abilities. The best data here comes from a project by a research committee of the American

Figure 2.1
Percentage Improvement of Emotional Intelligence Competencies of Different Groups of MBA Graduates Taking the Self-Directed Learning Course

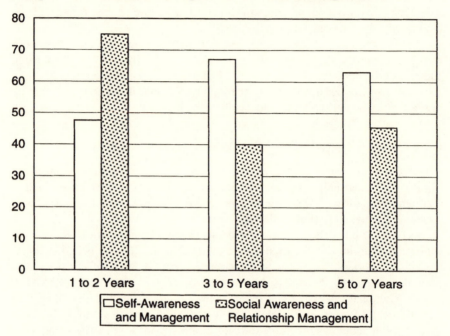

Assembly of Collegiate Schools of Business. They found that graduating students from two highly ranked business schools showed improvements of only 2% in the skills of emotional intelligence compared to their levels when they began their MBA training. In fact, when students from four other high-ranking MBA programs were assessed on a more thorough range of tests, they showed a gain of 4% in self-awareness and self-management abilities, but a *decrease* of 3% in social awareness and relationship management.

The dramatic gains from the new program did not end at two years. When looking at part-time MBA students going through the course based on self-directed learning theory, the dramatic gains were found again in these students who typically take three to five years to graduate. These groups showed 67% improvement in self-awareness and self-management competencies and 40% improvement in social awareness and social skills competencies by the end of their MBA program.

That's not all. Jane Wheeler tracked down groups of these part-timers two years *after* they had graduated. Even all that time later, they still showed improvements in the same range: 36% on the self-awareness and self-management competencies, and 45% on the social awareness and relationship management competencies (Wheeler, 1999). These are remarkable results, the first to demonstrate gains sustained over so many years in the emotional intelligence building blocks of resonant leadership.

The "honeymoon effect" of typical training might start at 30% to 40% improvement immediately following the training, but within one to three months it would drop to about 10% and stay there.

To be more specific, MBA students, whose average age at entry into the program was 27 years old, showed dramatic changes on videotaped and audiotaped behavioral samples and questionnaire measures of these competencies as a result of the competency-based, outcome-oriented MBA program implemented in 1990 (Boyatzis, Baker, Leonard, Rhee, & Thompson, 1995; Boyatzis, Leonard, Rhee, & Wheeler, 1996; Boyatzis, Wheeler, & Wright, in press). These results are summarized in Figures 2.2 and 2.3.

Four cadres of full-time MBA students graduating in 1992, 1993, 1994, and 1995 showed improvement on 100% (7) of the competencies in the Self-Management cluster (e.g., Efficiency Orientation, Initiative, Flexibility) and 100% (8) of the competencies in the Social Awareness and Management cluster (e.g., Empathy, Networking, Group Management). Meanwhile the part-time MBA students graduating in 1994, 1995, and 1996 showed improvement on 86% (6 of 7) of the competencies in the Self-Management cluster and 100% (8) of the competencies in the Social Awareness and Management cluster. In a follow-up study of two of these graduating classes of part-time students, Wheeler (1999) showed that during the two years following graduation their continued improvement was statistically significant on an audiotaped, behavioral measure of two competencies in the Social Awareness and Management cluster (i.e., Empathy and Persuasiveness).

This is in contrast to MBA graduates of the 1988 and 1989 traditional full-time program of the Weatherhead School of Management, who showed strong improvement in only 80% of the competencies in the Self-Management cluster, and part-time graduates of those two years, who showed improvement in only 40% of these competencies. With regard to the competencies in the Social Awareness and Management cluster, the full-time MBAs showed improvement in only 38% of the competencies in the Social Awareness and Management cluster, while part-time graduates of those two years showed improvement in only 25% of these competencies.

In a longitudinal study of four classes completing the Professional Fellows Program (i.e., an executive education program at the Weatherhead School of Management), Ballou, Bowers, Boyatzis, and Kolb (1999) showed that there was statistically significant improvement in 45- to 55-year-old professionals and executives on Self-confidence, Leadership, Helping, Goal Setting, and Action skills. These were 67% of the emotional intelligence competencies assessed in this study.

Figure 2.2
Value-Added to Full-Time Students from the Old vs. the New MBA Programs

Evidence of Value-Added	Old Program			New Program		
	Self-Management	Social Awareness and Management	Analytic Reasoning	Self-Management	Social Awareness and Management	Analytic Reasoning
STRONG EVIDENCE	Self-Confidence		Use of Concepts Systems Thinking Quantitative Analysis Use of Technology Written Communication	Efficiency Orientation Planning Initiative Flexibility Self-Confidence	Social Objectives Networking Oral Communication Empathy Group Management	Use of Concepts Systems Thinking Pattern Recognition Written Communication Quantitative Analysis Use of Technology
SOME EVIDENCE	Efficiency Orientation Initiative Flexibility	Empathy Networking Social Objectives		Self-Control Attention to Detail	Developing Others Persuasiveness Negotiating	
NO EVIDENCE	Planning (Attention to Detail and Self-Control were not coded)	Persuasiveness Negotiating Group Management Developing Others Oral Communication				
NEGATIVE EVIDENCE			Pattern Recognition (verbal)			

Figure 2.3
Value-Added to Part-Time Students from the Old vs. the New MBA Programs

Evidence of Value-Added	Old Program			New Program		
	Self-Management	Social Awareness and Management	Analytic Reasoning	Self-Management	Social Awareness and Management	Analytic Reasoning
STRONG EVIDENCE	Flexibility		Systems Thinking Quantitative Analysis	Efficiency Orientation Initiative Flexibility Attention to Detail Self-Confidence	Group Management Social Objectives Networking Oral Communication Developing Others Negotiating	Use of Concepts Written Communication Use of Technology Pattern Recognition Quantitative Analysis Systems Thinking
SOME EVIDENCE	Efficiency Orientation	Negotiating Social Objectives	Written Communication	Planning	Empathy Persuasiveness	
NO EVIDENCE	Self-Confidence Planning Initiative (Attention to Detail and Self-Control were not coded)	Persuasiveness Oral Communication Networking Group Management Developing Others	Use of Concepts Pattern Recognition	Self-Control		
NEGATIVE EVIDENCE		Empathy	Use of Technology			

SELF-DIRECTED LEARNING

What these studies have shown is that adults learn what they want to learn. Other things, even if acquired temporarily (e.g., for a test), are soon forgotten (Specht & Sandlin, 1991). Students, children, patients, clients, and subordinates may act as if they care about learning something and go through the motions, but they proceed to disregard it or forget it unless it is something they want to learn. Even in situations where a person is under threat or coercion, a behavioral change will typically extinguish or revert to its original form once the threat is removed. This does not include changes induced, willingly or not, by chemical or hormonal changes in one's body. But even in such situations, the interpretation of the changes and behavioral comportment following it will be affected by the person's will, values, and motivations.

In this way, it appears that most, if not all, sustainable behavioral change is intentional. *Self-directed change is an intentional change in an aspect of who you are (i.e., the Real) or who you want to be (i.e., the Ideal), or both. Self-directed learning is self-directed change in which you are aware of the change and understand the process of change.*

The process of self-directed learning is graphically shown in Figure 2.4 (Boyatzis, 1999, 2001; Goleman, Boyatzis, & McKee, 2002). This is an enhancement of the earlier models developed by Kolb, Winter, and Berlew (1968), Boyatzis and Kolb (1969), Kolb and Boyatzis (1970a, 1970b), and Kolb (1971). The description and explanation of the process in this chapter is organized in five sections. Each section starts with a point of discontinuity—that is, a part of the process that may not and often does not occur as a smooth, linear event but rather as a surprise. The person's behavior may seem to be stuck for long periods of time, and then a change appears quite suddenly. This is a discontinuity. A person might begin the process of self-directed learning at any point in the process, but it will often begin when the person experiences a discontinuity, the associated epiphany, or a moment of awareness and a sense of urgency.

This model describes the process as it was designed into a required course and the elements of the MBA and executive programs implemented in 1990 at the Weatherhead School of Management. Experimentation and research into the various components have resulted in refinement of these components and the model as discussed in this chapter. For a detailed description of the course, read Boyatzis (1994, 1995).

THE FIRST DISCONTINUITY: CATCHING YOUR DREAMS, ENGAGING YOUR PASSION

The first discontinuity and potential starting point for the process of self-directed learning is the discovery of who you want to be. Our Ideal Self is an image of the person we want to be. It emerges from our ego ideal, dreams, and

Figure 2.4
Boyatzis' Theory of Self-Directed Learning

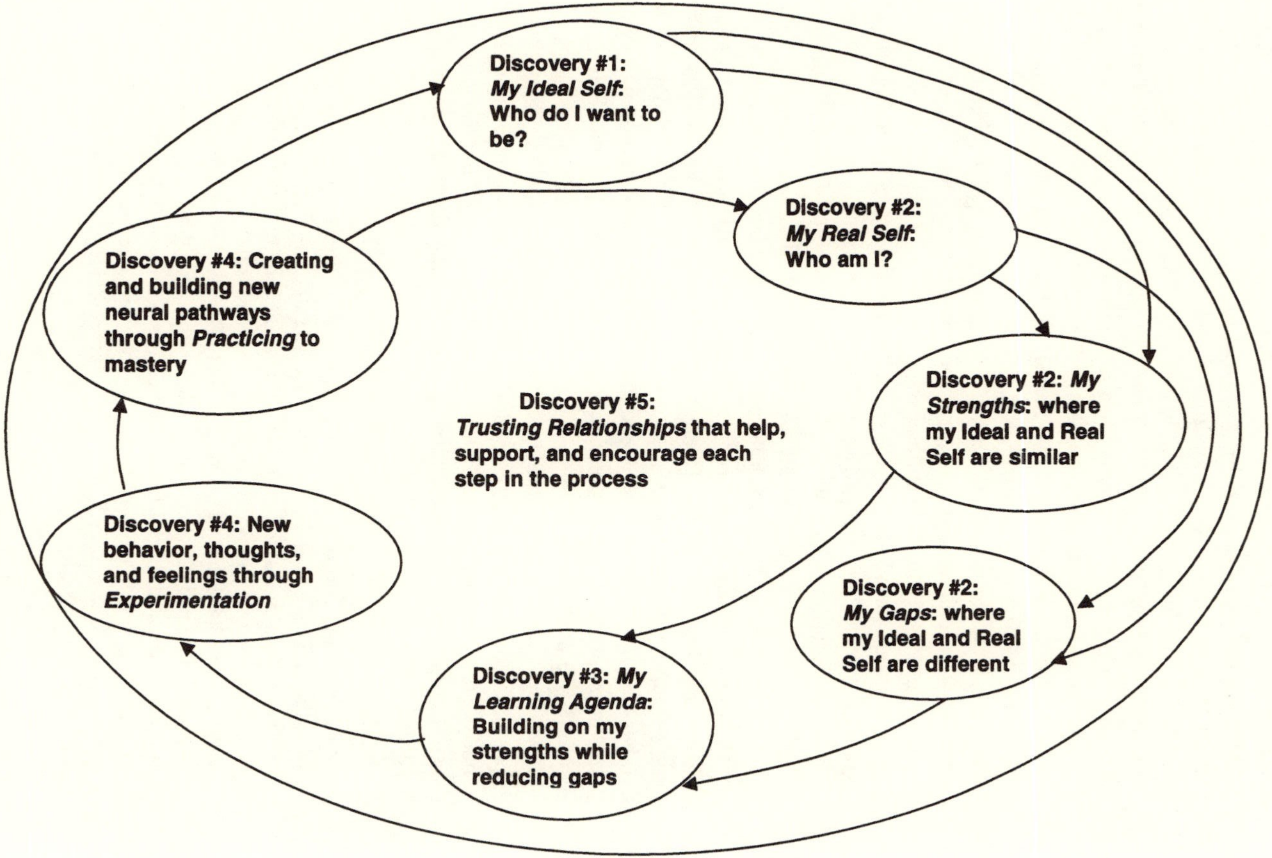

Discovery #1:
My Ideal Self:
Who do I want to be?

Discovery #2:
My Real Self:
Who am I?

Discovery #2: *My Strengths*: where my Ideal and Real Self are similar

Discovery #2:
My Gaps: where my Ideal and Real Self are different

Discovery #5:
Trusting Relationships that help, support, and encourage each step in the process

Discovery #3: *My Learning Agenda:* Building on my strengths while reducing gaps

Discovery #4: Creating and building new neural pathways through *Practicing* to mastery

Discovery #4: New behavior, thoughts, and feelings through *Experimentation* aspirations. The last 20 years have revealed literature supporting the power of positive imaging or visioning in sports psychology, appreciative inquiry (Cooperrider, 1990), meditation and biofeedback research, and other psychophysiological research. It is believed that the potency of focusing one's thoughts on the desired end state of condition is driven by the emotional components of the brain (Goleman, 1995). The Ideal Self is a reflection of the person's intrinsic drives. Numerous studies have shown that intrinsic motives have more enduring impact on a person's behavior than extrinsic motives (Deci & Ryan, 1985).

Our aspirations, dreams, and desired states are shaped by our values, philosophies (Boyatzis, Murphy, & Wheeler, 2000), life and career stages (Boyatzis & Kolb, 1999), motives (McClelland, 1985), role models, and other factors. This research indicates that we can access and engage deep emotional commitment and psychic energy if we engage our passions and conceptually catch our dreams in the image of our Ideal Self.

It is an anomaly that we know the importance of considering the Ideal Self, and yet often when engaged in a change or learning process, we skip over the clear formulation or articulation of our Ideal Self. If a parent, spouse, boss, or teacher tells us something should be different, they are giving us *their* version of our Ideal Self. They are telling us about the person *they* want us to be. The extent to which we believe or accept this image determines that extent to which it becomes part of our Ideal Self. Our reluctance to accept others' expectations or wishes for us to change is one of many reasons why we may not live up to others' expectations or wishes and not change or learn according to their agenda! In current psychology, others' versions of what our Ideal Self should be is referred to as the "Ought Self."

We may be victims of the expectations of others and the seductive power of popularized images from the media, celebrities, and our reference groups. In his book, *The Hungry Spirit: Beyond Capitalism, A Quest for Purpose in the Modern World*, Charles Handy (1997) describes the difficulty of determining his ideal.

I spent the early part of my life trying hard to be someone else. At school I wanted to be a great athlete, at university an admired socialite, afterwards a businessman and, later, the head of a great institution. It did not take me long to discover that I was not destined to be successful in any of these guises, but that did not prevent me from trying, and being perpetually disappointed with myself. The problem was that in trying to be someone else I neglected to concentrate on the person I could be. That idea was too frightening to contemplate at the time. I was happier going along with the conventions of the time, measuring success in terms of money and position, climbing ladders which others placed in my way, collecting things and contacts rather than giving expression to my own beliefs and personality. (p. 86)

In this way, we allow ourselves to be anesthetized to our dreams and lose sight of our deeply felt Ideal Self.

THE SECOND DISCONTINUITY: AM I A BOILING FROG?

The awareness of the current self, the person that others see and with whom they interact, is elusive. For normal reasons, the human psyche protects itself from the automatic "intake" and conscious realization of all information about ourselves. These ego-defense mechanisms serve to protect us. They also conspire to delude us into an image of who we are that feeds on itself, becomes self-perpetuating, and eventually may become dysfunctional (Goleman, 1985).

The "boiling frog syndrome" applies here. It is said that if one drops a frog into a pot of boiling water, it will jump out with an instinctive defense mechanism. But if you place a frog in a pot of cool water and gradually increase the temperature, the frog will sit in the water until it is boiled to death. These slow adjustments to changes are acceptable, but the same change made dramatically is not tolerated.

The greatest challenge to an accurate current self-image (i.e., seeing yourself as others see you and consistent with other internal states, beliefs, emotions, and so forth) is the boiling frog syndrome. Several factors contribute to it. First, people around you may not let you see a change. They may not give you feedback or information about how they see it. Also, they may be victims of the boiling frog syndrome themselves as they adjust their perception on a daily basis. For example, when seeing a friend's child after two years, you may gasp at the child's growth. Meanwhile, the parent is aware of the child's growth only when having to buy new shoes or clothes, or when there is a sudden change in the child's hormonal balance leading to previously unlikely behavior.

Second, enablers—those who forgive the change, are frightened of it, or do not care—may allow it to pass unnoticed. Our relationships and interpersonal contexts mediate and interpret cues from the environment. They help us interpret what things mean. You ask a friend, "Am I getting fat?" To which she responds, "No, you look great!" Whether this is reassuring to the listener or not, it is confusing and may not be providing feedback to the question asked. Of course, if she had said, "No, it is just the spread of age or normal effects of gravity," you may not have more useful information either.

In counseling sessions with effective CEOs and managing directors of not-for-profits, I have often been surprised by their inability to see themselves as leaders even though others may see them as leaders. Sometimes humility blocks this perception. Sometimes, it is the interpersonal or cultural context. On the planet Krypton, Superman was just another citizen without "supernatural" power. This lack of admitting that which is obvious to others to yourself can also occur when you have prolonged spiritual blackouts, losing sight of your core values and your philosophy.

Some organizational cultures will, as mentioned earlier, encourage a preoccupation with the "gaps." Some individuals have philosophies, or value orientations, that push them to focus on areas of improvement (i.e., a pragmatic value orientation or philosophy [Boyatzis et. al., 2000] or a dominant underlying motive of the need for achievement [McClelland, 1985]). Some individuals have such a low level of self-confidence or self-esteem that they assume they are unworthy, distrust positive feedback, and focus on negative issues and the gaps.

To truly consider changing a part of yourself, you must have a sense of what you value and want to keep. Likewise, to consider what you want to preserve about yourself involves admitting aspects of yourself that you wish to change or adapt in some manner. Being aware of these two and exploring them exist in the context of each other.

All too often, people explore growth or development by focusing on the "gaps" or deficiencies. Organizational training programs and managers conducting annual "reviews" often commit the same mistake. There is an assumption that we can "leave well enough alone" and get to the areas that need work. It is no wonder that many of these programs or procedures intended to help a person develop result in the individual feeling battered, beleaguered, and bruised rather than not helped, encouraged, motivated, or guided. The gaps may get your attention because they disrupt progress or flow (Fry, 1993).

Exploration of yourself in the context of your environment (How am I fitting into this setting? How am I doing in the view of others? Am I part of this group or organization or family?) and examination of your Real Self in the context of your Ideal Self both involve comparative and evaluative judgements. A comprehensive view includes both strengths and weaknesses. That is, to contemplate change, one must contemplate stability. To identify and commit to changing parts of yourself you must identify those parts you want to keep and possibly enhance. In this way, adaptation does not imply or require "death" but rather evolution of the self.

There are four major "learning points" from the first two discontinuities in the self-directed learning process:

1. Engage your passion and create your dreams;

2. Know yourself;

3. Identify or articulate both your strengths (those aspects of yourself you want to preserve) and the gaps or discrepancies in your Real Self and Ideal Self (those aspects of yourself you want to adapt or change); and

4. Keep your attention on both characteristics, forces, or factors—do not let one become the preoccupation.

All of these learning points can be achieved by finding and using multiple sources for feedback about your Ideal Self, Real Self, strengths, and gaps.

The sources of insight into your Real Self can include systematically collecting information from others, such as 360-degree feedback, currently considered fashionable in organizations. Other sources of insight into your Real Self, strengths, and gaps may come from behavioral feedback through videotaped or audiotaped interactions, such as collected in assessment centers. Various psychological tests can help you determine or make explicit inner aspects of your Real Self, such as values, philosophy, traits, motives, and so forth.

Sources for insight into your Ideal Self are more personal and more elusive than those for the Real Self. Various exercises and tests can help by making explicit various dreams or aspirations you have for the future. Talking with close friends or mentors can help. Allowing yourself to think about your desired future, not merely your prediction of your most likely future, is the biggest obstacle. These conversations and explorations must take place in psychologically safe surroundings. Often, the implicit norms of one's immediate social groups and work groups do not allow or encourage such discussion. In this case, you may want to search for groups of individuals who are considering changing their lives in an academic program, career development workshop, or personal growth experience.

THE THIRD DISCONTINUITY: MINDFULNESS THROUGH A LEARNING AGENDA

The third discontinuity in self-directed learning is development of an agenda and focusing on the desired future. A learning orientation will replace a performance orientation for those organizations that thrive in the coming decades. While performance at work or happiness in life may be the eventual consequence of our efforts, a learning agenda focuses on development. Individuals with a learning agenda are more adaptive and oriented toward development. In one study, a learning agenda resulted in dramatically better presentations, whereas a performance agenda resulted in people becoming defensive, not wanting to fail or not wanting to look bad, and did not result in increased performance (Brett & VandeWalle, 1999). A learning orientation arouses a positive belief in one's capability and the hope of improvement. A learning agenda helps a person focus on what they want to become. This results in people setting personal standards of performance, rather than "normative" standards that merely mimic what others have done (Beaubien & Payne, 1999). Meanwhile, a performance orientation evokes anxiety and doubts about whether or not we can change (Chen, Gully, Whiteman, & Kilcullen, 2000). A performance agenda focuses on success, producing proof of our capability, and getting praise. Performance goals arouse the wrong parts of our brain for development. In studying sales achieved in a three-month promotion in the medical supply distribution business, a learning goal orientation predicted sales volume, a performance goal orientation did not.

As part of one of the longitudinal studies at the Weatherhead School of Management, Leonard (1996) showed that MBAs who set goals desiring to change on certain competencies, changed significantly on those competencies as compared to other MBAs. Previous goal-setting literature had shown how goals affected certain changes on specific competencies (Locke & Latham, 1990) but had not established evidence of behavioral change on a comprehensive set of competencies that constitute emotional intelligence.

The major learning point from this section crucial in self-directed learning is: *Create your own, personal learning agenda!*

Others cannot tell you how you should change. They may tell you, but it will not help you engage in the change process. Parents, teachers, spouses, bosses, and sometimes even your children will try to impose goals for change or learning. People only learn what they want to learn!

The late 1960s and early 1970s witnessed a widespread program in organizations called management by objectives. It was so popular that it spread to other arenas—you could find books and workshops on learning by objectives, teaching by objectives, and so on and so forth. In all of these programs, there was one and only one approach to goal setting and planning taught. It specified development of behavior specific, observable, time-phased, and challenging goals (i.e., involved moderate risk). Unfortunately, the one-size-fits-all approach lacked a credible alternative until McCaskey (1974) suggested that some people plan by "domain and direction setting." Later, as part of the Weatherhead longitudinal studies, McKee (1991) studied how MBA graduates planned personal improvement. She discovered four different styles of planning: objectives-oriented planning; domain and direction planning; task- (or activity-) oriented planning; and "present-oriented" planning. The latter appeared as an existential orientation to one's involvement in developmental activities, and could be considered a non-planning style.

A major threat to effective goal setting and planning is that people are already busy and cannot add anything else to their lives. In such cases, the only success with self-directed change and learning occurs if people can determine what to say "no" to and stop some current activities in their lives to make room for new activities.

Another potential challenge or threat is the development of a plan that calls for a person to engage in activities different from their preferred learning style or learning flexibility (Boyatzis, 1994; Kolb, 1984). In such cases, a person commits to activities, or action steps in a plan, that require a learning style which is not their preference or not within their flexibility. When this occurs, a person becomes demotivated and often stops the activities or becomes impatient and decides that the goals are not worth the effort.

THE FOURTH DISCONTINUITY: METAMORPHOSIS

The fourth discontinuity and potential start of self-directed learning is to experiment and practice desired changes. Acting on the plan and toward the goals involves numerous activities. These are often made in the context of experimenting with new behavior. Typically following a period of experimentation, the person practices the new behaviors in actual settings within which they wish to use them, such as at work or at home. During this part of the process, self-directed change and learning begins to look like a "continuous improvement" process.

To develop or learn new behavior, the person must find ways to learn more from current, or ongoing experiences. That is, the experimentation and practice does not always require attending "courses" or a new activity. It may involve trying something different in a current setting, reflecting on what occurs, and experimenting further in this setting. Sometimes, this part of the process requires finding and using opportunities to learn and change. People may not even think they have changed until they have tried new behavior in a work or "real-world" setting. Rhee (1997) studied full-time MBA students in one of the Weatherhead cadres over a two-year period. He interviewed, tested, and videotaped and audiotaped them about every six to eight weeks. Even though he found evidence of significant improvements on numerous interpersonal abilities by the end of the second semester of their program, the MBA students did not perceive that they had changed or improved on these abilities until after they returned from their summer internships.

Dreyfus (1990) studied managers of scientists and engineers who were considered superior performers. Once she documented that they used considerably more of certain abilities than their less effective counterparts, she pursued how they developed some of those abilities. One of the distinguishing abilities was group management, also called team building. She found that many of these middle-aged managers had first experimented with team building skills in high school and college, in sports, clubs, and living groups. Later, when they became "bench scientists and engineers" working on problems in relative isolation, they still used this ability in activities outside of work. They practiced team building and group management in social and community organizations, such as 4-H clubs, and in professional associations for planning conferences and so forth.

The experimentation and practice are most effective when they occur in conditions in which the person feels safe (Kolb & Boyatzis, 1970b). This sense of psychological safety creates an atmosphere in which the person can try new behavior, perceptions, and thoughts with relatively less risk of shame, embarrassment, or serious consequences of failure.

THE FIFTH DISCONTINUITY: RELATIONSHIPS THAT ENABLE US TO LEARN

Our relationships are an essential part of our environment. The most crucial relationships are often with groups that have particular importance to us. These relationships and groups give us a sense of identity, guide us toward appropriate and "good" behavior, and provide feedback on our behavior. In sociology, they are called reference groups. These relationships create a "context" within which we interpret our progress on desired changes and the utility of new learning, and even contribute significant input to formulation of the Ideal (Kram,

1996). In this sense, our relationships are mediators, moderators, interpreters, sources of feedback, sources of support, and sources of permission for change and learning! They may also be the most important source of protection from relapses or returning to our earlier forms of behavior. Wheeler (1999) analyzed the extent to which MBA graduates worked on their goals in multiple "life spheres" (i.e., work, family, recreational groups, etc.). In a two-year follow-up study of two of the graduating classes of part-time MBA students, she found those who worked on their goals and plans in multiple sets of relationships improved the most and more than those working on goals in only one setting, such as work or within one relationship.

In a study on the impact of the year-long executive development program for doctors, lawyers, professors, engineers, and other professionals mentioned earlier, Ballou et. al. (1999) found that participants gained self-confidence during the program. Even at the beginning of the program, others would say these participants were very high in self-confidence. It was a curious finding! The best explanation came from follow-up questions to the graduates of the program. They explained the evident increase in self-confidence as an increase in the confidence to change. Their existing reference groups (i.e., family, groups at work, professional groups, community groups) all had an investment in them staying the same, meanwhile the person wanted to change. The Professional Fellows Program allowed them to develop a new reference group that encouraged change!

Based on social identity, reference group, and now relational theories, our relationships both meditate and moderate our sense of who we are and who we want to be. We develop or elaborate our Ideal Self from these contexts. We label and interpret our Real Self from these contexts. We interpret and value strengths (i.e., aspects considered our core that we wish to preserve) from these contexts. We interpret and value gaps (i.e., aspects considered weaknesses or things we wish to change) from these contexts.

The major learning points from the fourth and fifth discontinuities critical in the self-directed learning process are:

1. Experiment and practice, and try to learn more from your experiences;
2. Find settings in which you feel psychologically safe within which to experiment and practice; and
3. Develop and use your relationships as part of your change and learning process.

SIGNPOSTS ON THE PATH TO CHANGE AND LEARNING

In guiding yourself or others through the self-directed learning process, the learning points below can be used as signposts, or benchmarks. If you do not feel that you have addressed each learning point in turn, do not bother attempting to move forward. The process needs to slow down and either wait for the person to reach the learning point or try another way to help the person. Please remember, people do not gain these discoveries or experience the epiphany of the discontinuity in a smooth manner. One person may take minutes to achieve a breakthrough of one discovery, and yet another discovery may take several days, weeks, months, or even years.

The signposts on the path to self-directed learning are:

1. Has the person engaged their passion and dreams? Can they describe the person they want to be, the life and work they want to have in the future? Can they describe their Ideal Self?
2. Does the person know himself or herself? Do they have a sense of their Real Self?
3. Can the person articulate both their strengths (those aspects he/she wants to preserve) and gaps or discrepancies (those aspects he/she wants to adapt or change) between their Real Self and Ideal Self?
4. Has the person held their attention on both strengths and gaps—not letting one become the preoccupation?
5. Does the person have his/her own personal learning agenda? Is it really his/her own? Can the elements of the plan fit into the structure of his/her life and work? Do the actions fit with his/her learning style and flexibility?
6. Is the person experimenting and practicing new habits and actions? Is the person using a learning plan to learn more from the experiences?
7. Has the person found settings in which to experiment and practice in which he/she feels psychologically safe?
8. Is the person developing and utilizing his/her relationships as part of the learning process? Does the person have coaches, mentors, friends, and others with whom he/she can discuss progress on the learning agenda? Does he/she have relationships with people with whom it is possible to explore new behaviors and habits, new Ideal Self, new Real Self, and new strengths and gaps as the process unfolds?
9. Is the person helping others engage in a self-directed learning process?

CONCLUSION

Our future may not be entirely within our control, but most of what we become is within our power to create. The self-directed learning process described in this chapter can provide a road map and guidance for how to increase the effectiveness of change and learning efforts. As a concluding thought, I offer a few lines from the 1835 John Anster translation of Goethe's *Faustus: A Dramatic Mystery*. In the Prologue to the Theater, he says:

> What you can do, or dream you can, begin it,
> Boldness has genius, power and magic in it!

REFERENCES

Anders, G. 2001. War for talent. *Fast Company*, 41 (January): 95–99.

Ballou, R., Bowers, D., Boyatzis, R.E., & Kolb, D.A. 1999. Fellowship in lifelong learning: An executive development program for advanced professionals. *Journal of Management Education*, 23(4): 338–354.

Barlow, D.H. 1988. *Anxiety and disorders: The nature and treatment of anxiety and panic*. New York: The Guilford Press.

Beaubien, J.M., & Payne, S.C. 1999. Individual goal orientation as a predictor of job and academic performance: A meta-analytic review and integration. Paper presented at the meeting of the Society for Industrial and Organizational Psychology, Atlanta, GA, April.

Boyatzis, R.E. 1994. Stimulating self-directed change: A required MBA course called managerial assessment and development. *Journal of Management Education*, 18(3): 304–323.

Boyatzis, R.E. 1995. Cornerstones of change: Building the path for self-directed learning. In R.E. Boyatzis, S.S. Cowen, & D.A. Kolb (eds.), *Innovations in professional education: Steps on a journey from teaching to learning*. San Francisco: Jossey-Bass, pp. 50–91.

Boyatzis, R.E. 1999. Self-directed change and learning as a necessary meta-competency for success and effectiveness in the 21st century. In R. Sims & J.G. Veres III (eds.), *Keys to employee success in coming decades*. Westport, CT: Quorum Books, pp. 15–32.

Boyatzis, R.E. 2001. Developing emotional intelligence. In D. Goleman & C. Cherniss (eds.), *Research and theoretical advances in emotional intelligence*, Vol. 1. San Francisco: Jossey-Bass.

Boyatzis, R.E., Baker, A., Leonard, D., Rhee, K., & Thompson, L. 1995. Will it make a difference? Assessing a value-based, outcome oriented, competency-based professional program. In R.E. Boyatzis, S.S. Cowen, & D.A. Kolb (eds.), *Innovations in professional education: Steps on a journey from teaching to learning*. San Francisco: Jossey-Bass, pp. 167–202.

Boyatzis, R.E., Cowen, S.C., & Kolb, D.A. 1995. *Innovations in professional education: Steps on a journey from teaching to learning*. San Francisco: Jossey-Bass.

Boyatzis, R.E., & Kolb, D.A. 1969. *Feedback and self-directed behavior change*. Unpublished Working Paper #394–69, Sloan School of Management, Massachusetts Institute of Technology.

Boyatzis, R.E., & Kolb, D.A. 1999. Performance, learning, and development as modes of growth and adaptation throughout our lives and careers. In M. Peiperl, M.B. Arthur, R. Coffee, & T. Morris (eds.), *Career frontiers: New conceptions of working lives*. London: Oxford University Press, pp. 76–98.

Boyatzis, R.E., Leonard, D., Rhee, K., & Wheeler, J.V. 1996. Competencies can be developed, but not the way we thought. *Capability*, 2(2): 25–41.

Boyatzis, R.E., Murphy, A.J., & Wheeler, J.V. 2000. Philosophy as a missing link between values and behavior. *Psychological Reports*, 86: 47–64.

Boyatzis, R.E., Wheeler, J., & Wright, R. (in press). Competency development in graduate education: A longitudinal perspective. In *Proceedings of the first world conference on self-directed learning*. Montreal: GIRAT.

Brett, J.F., & VandeWalle, D. 1999. Goal orientation and goal content as predictors of performance in a training program. *Journal of Applied Psychology*, 84(6): 863–873.

Chen, G., Gully, S.M., Whiteman, J.A., & Kilcullen, R.N. 2000. Examination of relationships among trait-like individual differences, state-like individual differences, and learning performance. *Journal of Applied Psychology*, 85(6): 835–847.

Cooperrider, D.L. 1990. Positive image, positive action: The affirmative basis of organizing. In S. Srivastva et al. (eds.), *Appreciative management and leadership*. San Francisco: Jossey-Bass, pp. 91–125.

Cutter, H., Boyatzis, R.E., & Clancy, D. 1977. The effectiveness of power motivation training for rehabilitating alcoholics. *Journal of Studies on Alcohol*, 38(1): 131–141.

Deci, E.L., & Ryan, R.M. 1985. *Intrinsic motivation and self-determination in human behavior*. New York: Plenum Press.

Dreyfus, C. 1990. *The characteristics of high performing managers of scientists and engineers*. Doctoral dissertation, Case Western Reserve University.

Europe's demographic time bomb. 2001. *New York Times*, January 7, p. 8.

Fry, R. 1993. Change and continuity in organizational growth. In S. Srivastva et al. (eds.), *Executive change and continuity*. San Fransciso: Jossey-Bass, pp. 1–34.

Goleman, D. 1985. *Vital lies, simple truths: The psychology of self-deception*. New York: Simon and Schuster.

Goleman, D. 1995. *Emotional intelligence*. New York: Bantam Books.

Goleman, D. 1998. *Working with emotional intelligence*. New York: Bantam Books.

Goleman, D., Boyatzis, R.E., & McKee, A. 2002. *Leadership and emotional intelligence*. Boston: Harvard Business School Press.

Handy, C. 1997. *The hungry spirit: Beyond capitalism, a quest for purpose in the modern world*. London: Hutchinson.

Hubble, M.A., Duncan, B.L., & Miller, S.D. (eds.). 1999. *The heart and soul of change: What works in therapy*. Washington DC: American Psychological Association.

Kanfer, F.H., & Goldstein, A.P. (eds.). 1991. *Helping people change: A textbook of methods*, 4th ed. Boston: Allyn and Bacon.

Kelly, K. 1998. *New rules for the new economy*. New York: Penguin Books.

Kolb, D.A. 1971. *A cybernetic model of human change and growth*. Unpublished Working Paper #526–71, Sloan School of Management, Massachusetts Institute of Technology.

Kolb, D.A. 1984. *Experiential learning: Experience as the source of learning and development*. Englewood Cliffs, NJ: Prentice Hall.

Kolb, D.A., & Boyatzis, R.E. 1970a. On the dynamics of the helping relationship. *Journal of Applied Behavioral Science*, 6(3): 267–289.

Kolb, D.A., & Boyatzis, R.E. 1970b. Goal-setting and self-directed behavior change. *Human Relations*, 23(5): 439–457.

Kolb, D.A., Winter, S.K., & Berlew, D.E. 1968. Self-directed change: Two studies. *Journal of Applied Behavioral Science*, 6(3): 453–471.

Kram, K.E. 1996. A relational approach to careers. In D.T. Hall (ed.), *The career is dead: Long live the career*. San Francisco: Jossey-Bass, pp. 132–157.

Leonard, D. 1996. *The impact of learning goals on self-directed change in management development and education*. Doctoral dissertation, Case Western Reserve University.

Levering, R., & Moskowitz, M. 2001. The 100 best companies to work for. *Fortune*, January 8, pp. 148–162.

Locke, E.A., & Latham, G.P. 1990. *A theory of goal setting and task performance.* Englewood Cliffs, NJ: Prentice Hall.

McCaskey, M.B. 1974. A contingency approach to planning: Planning with goals and without goals. *Academy of Management Journal*, 17(2): 281–291.

McClelland, D.C. 1985. *Human motivation.* Glenview, IL: Scott, Foresman.

McClelland, D.C., & Winter, D.G. 1969. *Motivating economic achievement.* New York: Free Press.

McKee (London), A. 1991. *Individual differences in planning for the future.* Doctoral dissertation, Case Western Reserve University.

Miron, D., & McClelland, D.C. 1979. The impact of achievement motivation training on small business. *California Management Review*, 21(4): 13–28.

Morrow, C.C., Jarrett, M.Q., & Rupinski, M.T. 1997. An investigation of the effect and economic utility of corporate-wide training. *Personnel Psychology*, 50: 91–119.

Pascarella, E.T., & Terenzini, P.T. 1991. *How college affects students: Findings and insights from twenty years of research.* San Francisco: Jossey-Bass.

Rhee, K. 1997. *Journey of discovery: A longitudinal study of learning during a graduate professional program.* Doctoral dissertation, Case Western Reserve University.

Specht, L., & Sandlin, P. 1991. The differential effects of experiential learning activities and traditional lecture classes in accounting. *Simulations and Gaming*, 22(2): 196–210.

Wheeler, J.V. 1999. *The impact of social environments on self-directed change and learning.* Doctoral dissertation, Case Western Reserve University.

Winter, D.G., McClelland, D.C., & Stewart, A.J. 1981. *A new case for the liberal arts: Assessing institutional goals and student development.* San Francisco: Jossey-Bass.

Chapter 3

Employee Involvement Is Still the Key to Successfully Managing Change

Serbrenia J. Sims and Ronald R. Sims

> We live in a moment in history where change is so speeded up that we begin to see the present only when it is already disappearing.
> —R.D. Laing, *The Politics of Experience*

INTRODUCTION

Talk to anyone in an organization today and they will tell you that it seems like everything in our world is changing faster and faster, and leading or managing change is an increasingly important issue in this rapidly shifting environment, or new economy. This environment demands that we all learn new skills for fulfilling our roles and working with others in managing change, and it requires new frameworks to meet the demands placed on us.

Change for today's organizations is now different in nature and greater in extent than ever before. In most instances, the changes facing organizations and change agents (both internal and external) are unknown and unquantifiable. This simple acknowledgment frees us in some ways to better manage the necessary organizational changes. We can't predict what will happen or how it will affect organizations or their products and services. In a sense a case can be made that we shouldn't even try to anticipate specific changes. It is the premise of this chapter that an opportunity exists for us to expand employee involvement in change efforts even more than we have in recent years. For many organizations this means becoming high-involvement organizations (HIOs).

An organization's employees have always been and always will be the most important single resource in change management. If we are to change the way we manage change in any way, then we must find ways to maximize employee involvement at every opportunity before, during, and after any change initiative. In the first part of this chapter, we briefly look at change failures and some factors contributing to these failures. Next, we take a more specific look at obstacles that must be overcome to decrease change failures. Then, we focus on the importance of maximizing employee involvement in today's change efforts. The misconceptions of employee involvement are addressed next. Our discussion then turns to a closer look at the characteristics of HIOs. We then discuss strategies for smoothing the change process. A description of strategies for easing your own pain during the change process concludes the chapter.

CHANGE IN THE NEW ECONOMY

By all accounts, the new economy will continue to see an accelerated rate of change that will be driven principally by the exponential growth and global availability of information, technologies, and technology-based infrastructure as well as the improving global transportation infrastructure. How well organizations are prepared to change, survive, and thrive is a fundamental issue. Part of the answer to successfully surviving and thriving and thereby achieving competitiveness and success will be earned through continually managing change in order to provide the products and services that the customer will buy. Success will also be earned through rapidly responding to abrupt changes driven by:

• Technology
• Global economy
• Knowledge management
• Culture
• Increased capability
• Legislation
• Social pressures
• New markets

Today's and tomorrow's organizations will evolve, not through random mutation but through purposeful strategies designed to lead and manage change initiatives that are predictable and respond effectively to unpredictable and shifting marketplace demands. Changing the way we manage change means that more and more of an organization's people will need to be involved in helping organizations rethink old assumptions about what it takes to succeed in the new economy. And they will have to do it "on the fly." They will need to help organizations improve the quality of their discussions and the speed with which they make decisions. Decisions will have to be made in a business environment that is in large part unique. Perhaps the best place to begin understanding why organizations need to do more to get their employees involved in bringing about needed change is to look at change failures.

CHANGE FAILURES

In efforts to respond to the new economy, organizations are structuring and managing themselves differently from the traditional approaches of the past. An organization is now challenged to be a quality organization, to be a learning organization, to be customer focused, to be at the forefront of the technology revolution and yet to be a flatter and leaner organization. The environmental rules have changed and so have the design of organizations, management philosophies, and the techniques used to manage in this new environment. In short, there have been and continue to be a number of organizational change efforts.

If history is a guide, no more than a third of today's major corporations will survive and thrive in an important way over the next 25 years. Those that do not survive will die a Hindu death of transformation as they are acquired or merged with part of a larger, stronger organization. The demise of these companies will come from a lack of competitive adaptiveness. To be blunt, most of these companies will die or be bought out and absorbed because they are too slow to keep pace with change in the marketplace. By 2020, more than three-quarters of the Standard & Poors (S&P) 500 will consist of companies we don't know today—new companies drawn into the maelstrom of economic activity from the periphery, springing from insights unrecognized today.

The assumption of continuity, on which most of our leading corporations have been based for years, no longer holds. Discontinuity dominates. The 100 or so companies in the current S&P 500 that survive into the 2020s will be unlike the corporate survivors today. They will have to be masters of creative destruction, built for discontinuity, remade like the market ("Change management," 2001). But, an important question for these and other organizations is: If the need to be able to change rapidly to survive and thrive and be masters of creative destruction, built for discontinuity, is so great in today's new economy, then how will this happen given our change record to date?

Over recent years many change failures have been reported. William Schienmann points out in his article "Why Change Fails" (1992) that fewer than half the changes undertaken by *Fortune* 500 companies are successful and that the chief reason for failure is resistance to the change. Michael Hammer and James Champy point out in their book *Reengineering the Corporation* (1994) that more than 50% of all the massive restructuring and reengineering projects fail. More recently, one estimate suggests that only 30% of all change programs implemented by a sample of *Fortune* 100 companies since 1980 produced improvement in bottomline results that exceeded the company's cost of capital (Day, 2000). Wolfsmith, Kaiser, Adams, and Johnson (2000) noted that the success rate of large-scale change averages around 50%.

A Standish Group report indicates that 91% of all the information technology projects undertaken in large corporations fail. Over 30% of the projects studied were canceled before completion (Harrington, Conner, & Horney, 2000).

In a study performed by MIT in 1992, researchers reported that the banking industry was more productive in 1981 than in 1991, despite the billions of dollars that companies spent on information technology. This was primarily because information technology was used as a driver rather than as an enabler and because the organizations were inadequately prepared to accept the new technology.

An increasing number of articles in magazines such as *Business Week* and *Fortune* point out that failures of total quality management (TQM) projects are extensive. The estimate of failed TQM projects runs between 60% to 75% of the total number of attempts.

Moran, Lathan, Hogeveen, and Russ-Eft reported in *Winning Competitive Advantage* (1994) that 75% of the resistance to the quality improvement programs came from middle managers and 63% came from first-line managers and supervisors.

A criticism (Church, Burke, Javitch, Burke, & Waclawski, 1996, p. 400) notes that many "popular trends in management organizational consulting" such as "business process re-engineering, total quality management and the learning organization represent systematic methods . . . for responding to and channelling effectively the forces for change. Unfortunately, the vast majority of improvement initiatives undertaken by organizations, even with the best of intentions, are destined to have little impact," with success rates in some industries being as low as 10%. Muehrcke (1999) recently noted that more than two-thirds of change efforts collapse.

The failure of many programs has been linked to a variety of factors, such as lack of vision and commitment from senior management, limited integration with other systems and processes in the organization, and ill-conceived implementation plans (Church et al., 1996). Garvin (1993) has argued that failure of TQM programs results mainly from organizations failing to understand that TQM requires a commitment to learning. Others have argued that "Like ISO 9000, TQM has been oversold as a stand-alone package, and the high level of failed programs has led to a search for the 'missing ingredients' and to some disenchantment with TQM" (Chelsom, 1997, p. 140).

Perhaps Anderson and Anderson (2001) sum up best what we know about change failures when they note:

Organizations' track records at change are not very good. The vast majority of today's change efforts are failing to produce their intended business results. These struggling efforts are producing huge cost to budgets, time, people, customers, and faith in leadership. Organizations are spending tens of millions of dollars on change efforts such as reengineering and informational technology installations, yet not obtaining their intended return on investment. Furthermore, the very methods used in these failed efforts are causing tremendous resistance and burnout in people, loss of employee morale, and turmoil in the cultures of organizations. Put simply, organizational leaders are falling short in their efforts to lead change successfully. (pp. 1–2)

Granville (1996) has also pointed out that "Unfortunately, failed programs far outnumber successes, and improvement rates remain distressingly low. Working on style, improving communications and the like still do not seem to be getting anybody anywhere. Is it surprising that people get a bit cynical about all these quick-fix solutions and flavors of the month?" (p. 39).

One should not be surprised by the reasons. Reductions in lead time, attempts to enhance services, cost minimization, value creation, and stock reduction "are all enticing business goals" (Granville, 1996, p. 39) of increasingly efficient and lean production. But these require new arrangements, which ultimately means that such companies can only develop by reducing labor to "half or less of the human effort, time and overall cost" (Granville, 1996, p. 39). Interestingly, failure to achieve the desired performance is often seen as a failure of the task itself, thus requiring some new, previously unrecognized activity. It is rarely seen as a deeper change management problem requiring entirely different solutions of maximum employee (and other) participation and involvement. For example:

Good as these experiences may be, they should have made us realize that applying lean techniques to discrete activities is not the end of the road. If individual breakthroughs can be linked up and down the value chain to form a continuous value stream, the performance of the whole can be raised to a dramatically higher level. (Granville, 1996, p. 39)

One of the problems in looking at what is written and reported about failed change efforts is that most of these reported initiatives tend to be programmed content approaches to change that lacked both the analytical depth and the processes (contracting, data collection, diagnosis, feedback, design/action, change interventions and change evaluation) of action research. In reviewing these kinds of programmatic changes in the healthcare industry, Edmonstone (1995) has pointed out that "Most change which has taken place in healthcare has been 'programmatic,' that is, it has been episodic, project-based and with a clear and distinct beginning, middle, and end" (p. 16). However, if the healthcare industry is typical of failed programmatic change cited in the literature, it tends to reflect older change management thinking of top-down information flows cascaded in a procedural manner through layers of managers operating at the level of strategies:

Change programs and projects have been seen to be distinctively different from the ongoing process of managerial life. "Bracketing-off," a problematic aspect of management into a change program with different management arrangements, has been seen as the conventional wisdom. Taking place in large public bureaucracies, it has embodied and enacted many bureaucratic assumptions. Thus, change has proceeded typically in

"Cascade" from top management to middle management, through junior management and then to the workforce. It has also focused on "infrastructure" matters (policies, structures and systems). Finally, it has assumed (in a good democratic tradition) that change is best brought about by "normative/re-educative" strategies, whereby individuals (most usually through education and training experiences) are encouraged to re-examine their values and attitudes, change them and hence modify their behavior at work. (Edmonstone, 1995, p. 16)

According to Edmonstone, various assumptions are made about employees' problematic behavior. These include assumptions that:

- Individual problematic behavior can be "isolated" and "changed";
- The primary target for change should be the content of ideas and attitudes;
- Behavior can be influenced by altering formal structures and systems; and
- Promulgating organizationwide change programs such as mission statements, TQM, and culture change programs, etc.

As a result, Edmonstone criticizes these change efforts by arguing that:

1. They tend, for example, to focus on global and longer-term issues that are not always perceived to be in the short-term "critical path" of the organization.
2. They rely heavily on education and training methods that encourage representational learning (through acquiring a new management language, complete with jargon, catchphrases, etc.) rather than behavioral learning (through doing).
3. They are too often driven by an exclusive core group which is seen to be the sole or main owner of the problem (and therefore of its solution).
4. Such groups are often insensitive to the history, culture, and priorities of subparts of the organization (among the masses that really must be brought on board any change).
5. All this serves to set up a tension between "rhetoric" and the "reality."

Another way of viewing the problem with many change efforts to date is to note the failure of the responsible change agents to integrate content, people, and process. "Content" refers to those elements of the organization that need to change, elements usually found in the external domain, such as strategy, structure, systems, processes, technology, and work processes. "People" refers to the behaviors, emotions, minds, and spirits of the human beings who are designing, implementing, supporting, or being impacted by the change (mostly internal domains). "Process" refers to how the content and people changes will be planned for, designed, and implemented. In other words, process denotes the actions that will produce both the external (content) and internal (people) changes (Anderson & Anderson, 2001). The failure of change efforts to achieve their objectives to date suggests a number of obstacles that must be overcome if we are going to improve our change record.

OBSTACLES TO OVERCOME

As noted thus far in this chapter, there is considerable evidence that most change programs don't achieve their objectives. Post-audits of failed efforts have identified a variety of potential problems, as described below.

Absence of Clear Change Leadership

Nothing will derail a program faster than absence of leadership. If the presumptive leaders lack credibility or credentials, demand politically acceptable solutions, or can't bring the rest of the management team to consensus, the whole effort is likely to be futile.

Change Initiative Burnout

A daunting obstacle is the weariness that settles on organizations that have been forced to change more or less continuously as strategic priorities change. Some employees will have seen five or six widely heralded change initiatives in their time with the company, each promising salvation and each soon supplanted by yet another initiative. This leads to a bewildering mix of approaches with distinct methods, vocabularies, deliverables, and teams of outside consultants, and these compete for a shrinking share of the organizational mind. When this syndrome prevails the cynics refer dismissively to the "fad of the month" and conclude that if they just wait patiently the latest one will soon pass. The beleaguered cartoon character "Dilbert" is a master at this passive resistance.

Stifling Organizational Cultures

Cultures in which managers and employees are suspicious of ideas outside the status quo can quickly derail a change process. Often the rules of conduct and practice thought to be behind an organization's earlier success are codified into rigid operating standards and styles. A more subtle form of resistance arises when the employees or middle managers think they are doing well and regard the new program as an implicit criticism of their efforts.

Top Management Turmoil

Too many initiatives have stalled or failed during turmoil in management's ranks. Not only is the champion of the change program gone, but the new team may not have accepted the initiative or may want to make their mark by doing something different. If there is a lot of turnover at the top, no one can remember why various initiatives were started, and the organization becomes progressively more confused and disenchanted. These signals strengthen the status quo. Those clinging to the past are encouraged by inconsistencies in the picture of the future.

They are further encouraged when the picture changes rapidly and for no apparent reason.

Lack of Urgency

If managers and employees don't feel the change is urgently needed, other more pressing concerns (such as immediate sales results) will push it aside. This lack of urgency leads to the argument that "We're too busy now and can't possibly spare the time." Others may protest that "We're already doing it," or "This is a waste of money," or "We already know our customers and competitors, which should be obvious since we're doing well right now."

Poor Implementation

Implementation problems range from not allocating enough resources or time to the benefits and goals not being clearly understood by employees. It is also very hard to sustain enthusiasm if there is a lack of early success or if successes aren't celebrated properly. If early encouraging results do not occur, it is important not to allow impatience to short-circuit key steps in building support or putting systems in place.

These obstacles or conditions provide some clarity about why the success rate of change efforts is so bad. Regardless of the reasons why change efforts fail and whether or not things have changed or are still as bad, when it comes to managing change, the reality is that even if only 50% or 25% of future change efforts were to fail, we would still need to seriously rethink the way we manage change.

We believe the change failure statistics are especially alarming because organizations survive and thrive only by constantly transforming themselves. We must do everything possible to try to understand and reduce the reasons for these failures. Our clients will continue to expect better results for the money they invest in these change efforts. The bar is being raised dramatically, and the latest, already-faltering, fad-based change techniques being used today or thought up for tomorrow will certainly fail unless we can figure out what we need to do differently. The key in our view is to move away from what appears to be a common practice of separating content change and people change to better integrating the two. It is our premise that this integration is best achieved by an increased emphasis on maximizing employee involvement in organizational change initiatives. However, before moving on to this discussion, we suggest why, based on our own experiences, change initiatives often fail to meet objectives.

In our experience the failure of change initiatives can be attributed to factors found in the change process itself and its misuse. Thus, we believe the following factors, all of which can be directly tied back to insufficient employee involvement, contribute to the ineffectiveness of change efforts:

• Relying on the few versus the many.
• Not eliminating the "us" versus "them" mentality between organizational leaders and other members.
• Failing to link the various steps of the change process (i.e., design, implementation, evaluation).
• Failing to institutionalize the values of the parallel organization.
• Cultural shifts that are secondary to process improvements.
• Incongruency in the change process itself.

Many of our previous efforts to manage change may no longer be appropriate for the needs of today's complex and rapidly changing environment. Change agents must find new ways to address employee cynicism and resistance and increase employee involvement in organizational change efforts. The next section offers a closer look at several principles that we believe can help address employee cynicism and resistance and increase their involvement in change management within their organizations.

FOCUS ON EMPLOYEE INVOLVEMENT

A brief review of the literature on why change efforts often do not live up to their initial promises invariably uncovers answers that run the gamut from the change champion or change agent team got the strategy wrong to the change agents were unable to develop sufficient employee (or organizational) support for the intended changes. In a number of these instances it appears that the change agents failed to recognize that the way they were trying to bring about change (i.e., the process they employed) was the root cause of the problem. Too often, the change management team fails to fully involve the very people whose support is essential to success. Unfortunately, many change agents, failing to recognize that the change process (or paradigms) they are using is the problem, redouble their efforts to make it work, resulting in increased frustration on their part and increased alienation on the part of most of the organization's employees. In order to change the way we manage change as internal and external change agents we need to recognize and address the frustration of employees, who often don't believe that their voices count.

As noted in other chapters in this book, today's organizations, leaders, managers, and other employees are under tremendous pressure from markets, customers, and competition to bring needed changes to their organizations (see for example Sims' chapter on change agent roles). It has been our experience that an organization's change agents do not intentionally go about creating more frustration for their employees. They desperately want to involve people in the increasing number of change issues that are vital to the organization's success. They want other employees to be willing partners rather than resistant or cynical. They want employees who are ready to put themselves wholeheartedly into the effort to bring about the required changes rather than employees who sit back or on the sidelines and take the attitude of "this too shall pass."

We all have participated in change situations where individuals or groups describe their experience by saying, "Wouldn't it be good if every other employee in the organization could have this same kind of positive change experience?" or "Wouldn't it be great if everyone could have learned what we learned about successful change?" These comments provide some key insights into how to change the way we manage change. That is, we must manage change in a way that decreases the likelihood of change failure and employee resistance and cynicism. This involves the application of the following principles:

1. Establish the extent of employee involvement in change efforts as a measure of change success.
2. Link employees to each other.
3. Create change communities.
4. Embrace open dialogue.

Establish Employee Involvement as a Measure of Change Success

Simply getting employee buy-in has been the keystone of most change efforts to date. Change agents must move toward deeply involving employees in the change process itself, creating a critical mass of highly energetic employees who help design, sell, implement, evaluate, resell, and support change in the organization. Increasing employee involvement means going beyond the one or two handfuls of individuals that are typically involved as change agents and involving hundreds, even thousands, of employees, suppliers, customers, and so on. In practical terms, increasing involvement means expanding the notion of who is expected (and actually gets) to participate in every phase of the change process. One way of increasing involvement is to make an informed, upfront effort to include new and different voices. Another way is by expanding the number of employees in order to create a critical mass for change so that the few change agents are no longer left in the position of deciding for the many, which is what typically happens in many change efforts. In addition to creating a critical mass for change, achieving "maximum" employee involvement also enhances innovation, adaptation, learning, and a change agent "mind-set" within the organization's employees. In the end, by inviting and building in employee involvement, employees are able to influence the needed changes and make things happen.

Link Employees to Each Other

When employees forge links with each other, ideas, creativity, and action are ensured. Barriers are lowered in the flow of information important for change, organization success, and new ideas. Work that is dependent upon ongoing change flows more smoothly because employees are more open and willing to learn how what they do fits into the larger whole and how to draw upon the needed resources for successful individual, group, and organizational change.

When employees feel linked with each other, they move beyond the familiar to really learning to trust and know one another. They stop being roles, functions, or just "differents" and become colleagues who share the same issues and concerns, employees who are doing the best they can to get the job done together. Fellow employees with unique talents recognize the value that each individual and the collective work contribute to their own success and to the organization's success during times of rapid change. They get to know one another as colleagues who have joint responsibility as change agents in helping their organization meet the challenges posed by the new economy.

Create Change Communities

As has always been the case, successfully addressing organizational challenges cannot be accomplished by any one employee (or change agent) single-handedly. We need a change community of employees who willingly provide their talents and insights to address increasingly complex issues. A change community is important because no one person has all the answers. Answers reside in all of us.

When we create a change community, we move beyond a group of employees who may have personal links with one another to a group of linked employees who have both the will and willingness to work together to accomplish a change goal that has meaning for them. Creating a sense of change community in organizations is not an easy task because the requirements of mechanistic structures run contrary to what it takes to build a change community. Nevertheless, we cannot ignore this task.

Embrace Open Dialogue

Open dialogue is the best way to get employees to come together, discuss and resolve issues, and act. It is through open dialogue that issues of self-interest versus the common good and minority versus majority opinion are dealt with in a way that ensures support and follow-through for any organizational course of action. Given increased globalization and today's e-marketplace there is a greater need for interaction and information sharing as well as a greater need for expression than there has ever been. In this new world and economy, imposed change is no longer acceptable. Change grounded in open dialogue has the best chance for success.

Open dialogue provides an ethical foundation and a moral fiber for any change effort. Open dialogue produces trust and confidence in both the change process and those responsible for managing and leading the change. Open dialogue, the desire to involve all, the desire to have a say, and the desire to be an active participant in shaping one's own and the organization's destiny is key to changing the way we manage change. (See Baker's chapter for more discussion on dialogue and conversational learning.)

The principles offered above are important to changing the way we manage change. While building on the wisdom of the traditional approach to managing change, the increased emphasis on involving employees in the change process provides a framework for developing not only employee support but also the enthusiastic involvement of the entire organization. We believe change agents can expect the following results when they incorporate these principles into their change initiatives:

- Organizational members increasingly grasp the issues, become aligned around a common purpose, and collectively create new change directions because they understand both the opportunities and challenges.
- Collective organizational urgency and energy are produced to create a new future.
- Open dialogue, free flowing information, and cooperation replace organizational barriers because employees are linked to the change issues and to one another.
- Improved productivity and employee and customer satisfaction result from broad employee participation, which quickly identifies performance gaps and change solutions.
- The contribution of creative high-quality ideas from employees, customers, suppliers, and important others increases.
- Change capacity increases as employees continuously develop the skills and processes to meet not just current challenges but the increasingly demanding challenges of the new economy as well.

So how do we do a better job of incorporating these principles into organizational change initiatives? We believe the place to start is with some of the misconceptions about employee involvement.

MISCONCEPTIONS OF EMPLOYEE INVOLVEMENT

There appear to be a consistent set of misconceptions about employee involvement in change management efforts. These misconceptions keep change agents holding on to familiar ways of managing change and prevent them and their organizations from moving to maximum employee involvement.

The first misconception is that increasing employee involvement requires organizational leaders to let go and trust more than they are comfortable doing.

As organizational leaders contemplate increasing employee involvement and embracing open dialogue, they sometimes believe that these principles will require them to abdicate their responsibility, authority, and ability to provide and control input based on their change knowledge and experience. Nothing could be further from the truth. Striving for maximum employee involvement is critical to change success. Paradoxically, increasing employee involvement requires more involvement from other employees or change agents than traditional and even more recent programmatic content change management models suggest. In our view, change agents from all levels of the organization must play crucial roles throughout the change process.

What does shift is the organizational leader's role as a change agent. Instead of being responsible for identifying the change challenge, problem, and solution, they are now expected to be jointly responsible for identifying the issues, purposes, and boundary constraints and applying the principles of increased employee involvement to better engage employees in this dialogue. Throughout the change process, change agents should concern themselves with the following questions:

- What needs to change and why?
- What needs to be different in the organization, in each group, and in each individual as a result of the organizational work and the demands of the new economy?
- What boundaries or barriers must we be cognizant of?
- Whose voice needs to be heard (and why)?
- Who else must be heard and why? How do we build the necessary links between employees and change ideas?
- How will we create a change community of employees who are ready and willing to be proactive?
- How will we ensure open dialogue throughout the change process?

One of the challenges confronting many senior change agents at the inception of change efforts is how to handle the concern that if they fully and visibly participate in a change process, employees will not speak out or will blindly accept what the leaders have to say. Similarly, employees often worry that if organizational leaders have already laid down the change gauntlet, they will not listen to their concerns. We believe these are important issues that must be addressed. As is always the case in any change effort, change agents must get leaders and employees to learn to work in an atmosphere in which there is give-and-take and ideas can be freely exchanged.

Both old and new economies require that change agents, regardless of their level in the organization, must get employees and organizational leaders to work together in addressing issues because each group has vital information the other does not have. Traditionally, organizational leaders have a view of what is happening in the outside world and employees have information about what is going on each day within the organization. With the advent of open-book management and with employees needing to take more responsibility for managing their careers by being better informed about what "happens in the business," the boundaries of these information sources have blurred. In any case, both sets of information are necessary to address today's systemic change issues. When organizations and their organizational leaders are committed to maximum employee involvement, they create situations in which this kind of information sharing is possible. And the information that is necessary for successful change is based on the ideas of the many versus those of the few.

Changing the way we manage change also means that organizations must continue to eliminate boundaries or barriers between themselves and outside stakeholders (i.e., suppliers, customers, and community members). In the new economy organizations must be more sensitive to the reality that these "outsiders" (and more and more insiders) care about the way the organization operates. Often accompanying the employee involvement misconception is the fear that if outsiders are included in the need to change or in the change process, the organization will be airing its dirty laundry in public, thus alienating some of the very people who are necessary to its success. Like others in the change management arena, we have experienced exactly the opposite.

Just as inclusion in change builds ownership and commitment within an organization, it also builds ownership and commitment among those outside the organization who in many instances have an increased stake in the organization's efforts to continuously change (i.e., note the increased number of new partnerships and organizational structures in recent years between various stakeholders). Organizational members are increasingly expected to get customers and suppliers to work with their host organization to build a future. These outside stakeholders are more heavily invested in the organization's success now that they have become true partners in the change process, having moved from making demands to offering ideas for mutual gain. Today's and tomorrow's change agents will increasingly find that it is common for customers and suppliers to be able to offer ideas about how they can help reduce costs or improve processes as a result of their investment in organizational and change outcomes. In many instances their involvement will be a given, meaning that they will need to be involved before, during, and after any organizational change effort.

The next misconception is that productivity will suffer if larger numbers of employees are involved in the change process. While some organizations routinely include hundreds of employees in their change efforts, others still rely on the same 10 employees who go off site for two or three days at a time to plan the "next" change. Contrary to the belief that productivity suffers when hundreds of employees are involved in change efforts, it has been our experience that productivity does not suffer. In fact, often it actually improves. This means that it may be well worth the cost of involving the maximum number of employees in such change steps in off-site retreats, for example. Old or new economy, when employees are involved in change processes, they put forth more effort when they believe their ideas count.

The final misconception is that it is more cost-effective to put the change process in the hands of external change agents or consultants (and pair them with the "best and brightest" from the organization) than to put the change process in the hands of the many. Certainly, it is costly to increase employee involvement, both emotionally and financially. The entire change process instantly becomes more visible and the stakes become higher. But what is the cost of not striving for maximum employee involvement? What is the cost of brilliant strategies that never get implemented? What is the cost of change processes that increase resistance and cynicism and provide new material for Scott Adams' "Dilbert" cartoons? What is the cost of all those employees we didn't want to lose from the company but actually did because they believed that their voices did not count?

Making a real commitment to increasing employee involvement in the way we manage change is not business as usual. It is not for the fainthearted change agent, and it is not for everyone. Maximizing employee involvement in change efforts is hard work that requires courage, risk taking, and perseverance. The reward for these efforts is an organization that is flexible, energetic, innovative, linked, and responsive enough to meet the demands of a constantly changing and new business environment. In the end, changing the way we manage change means giving "voice" to all.

HIGH-INVOLVEMENT ORGANIZATIONS

Perhaps the best way to get organizations to envision what we believe is needed in the way of employee involvement is to simply get all of its employees, and especially its senior leaders and middle managers, to ask themselves if they are a "high-involvement organization" (HIO) (Cummings & Worley, 2001). HIOs have altered all their organizational features through the joint efforts of management and other employees to promote high levels of involvement and performance. Organizational features that have been altered include structure, work designs, information and control systems, physical layout, human resources management policies, and reward systems.

In HIOs, employees are indeed empowered and have considerable responsibility for influencing and making decisions. HIOs have a decentralized philosophy. Employees receive extensive training in problem-solving and decision-making techniques, operation of the organization, and organizational policies. All organizational information is shared widely and is easily obtained by employees. Rewards are tied closely to unit or team performance as well as to knowledge and skill levels. HIOs make sure that these disparate aspects of the organization are mutually reinforcing and form a coherent pattern that contributes to employee involvement.

In determining whether or not an organization is an HIO one should consider the several elements which characterize HIOs. Most HIOs include several, if not all, of the following features (Cummings & Worley, 2001; Lawler, 1986):

- Flat, lean organization structures contribute to involvement by pushing the scheduling, planning, and controlling functions typically performed by management and staff groups toward the shop floor. Team-based structures are oriented to a common purpose or outcome. Participative structures, such as work councils and union-management committees, are used so that workers can influence the direction and policies of the organization.

- Job designs that provide employees with high levels of discretion, task variety, and meaningful feedback are used to enhance involvement. Self-managed teams are used to encourage employee responsibility by providing cross-training and job rotation, which give employees a chance to learn about the different functions contributing to organizational performance.

- Open information systems that are tied to jobs or work teams are used to provide the necessary information for employees to participate meaningfully in decision making. Goals and standards of performance are set participatively to provide employees with a sense of commitment and motivation for achieving those objectives.

- Career systems that provide different tracks for advancement and counseling to help employees choose appropriate paths are used to help employees plan and prepare for long-term development within the organization. Every effort is made to make employees aware of jobs that can further their development.

- Selection of employees emphasizes the use of realistic job previews to provide information to people about what it will be like to work in high-involvement organizations or situations. Teams are heavily involved in assessing potential and process skills of recruits as a means of facilitating a participative climate.

- Training employees for the necessary knowledge and skills to participate effectively in decision making is a commitment made by HIOs. Employee training includes peer training and emphasizes education on the economic side of the organization as well as interpersonal skill development.

- Reward systems information is open to employees, and rewards are based on acquiring new skills as well as on sharing gains from improved performance. Employees can choose from different fringe benefits, and reward distinctions among people from different hierarchical levels are minimized.

- Personnel policies are participatively set by employees to encourage stability of employment and a strong sense of commitment to the organization.

- Physical layouts or designs of the organization support team structures, and every effort is made to reduce status differences among employees to reinforce an egalitarian climate of employee participation.

These HIO designs are mutually reinforcing (Cummings & Worley, 2001). "They all send a message to people in the organization that says they are important, respected, valued, capable of growing, and trusted and that their understanding of and involvement in the total organization is desirable and expected" (Lawler, 1982, p. 299; Walton, 1985). Moreover, these design components tend to motivate and focus organizational behavior in a strategic direction and thus can lead to superior effectiveness and competitive advantage, particularly in contrast to more traditionally designed organizations (Cummings & Worley, 2001; Lawler, 1992).

Organizational success in the new economy depends on maximizing employee involvement. And this means that organizations must become HIOs to do just this. For many organizations achieving HIO status will require a major change initiative. However, we believe such a change is necessary to create a cadre of internal change agents who are committed to the organization's success.

In concluding this chapter we first suggest several change strategies that can be used to improve employee involvement in the change process and prevent negative effects. We then offer some suggestions on how employees can ease the pain and smooth the way for themselves, one another, and the entire organization during these times of unprecedented change.

STRATEGIES FOR SMOOTHING THE CHANGE PROCESS

There are a number of strategies that we think are appropriate for helping organization's and their employees have a smoother ride on the "change" train. For HIOs these strategies are a part of their everyday functioning. They are as follows:

• Build a climate for change.
• Improve communication.
• Encourage employee involvement.
• Share benefits.
• Avoid trivial change.
• Incorporate the five essential laws of change into every change effort.

Build a Climate for Change

Successful change in the new economy will result from a climate that welcomes, initiates, and manages change. In such a climate, risk is accepted as a natural part of doing business. A premium must be placed on innovation and creativity. Employees have to be encouraged to try new and different approaches to the job and other work processes.

Improve Communication

This will always be the most important strategy. It will do more to overcome resistance and contribute to maximum employee involvement than anything else an organization might do. Employees need more and more information—not only on *what* is going to happen but also *why*. The right kind and amount of information must be gathered and communicated throughout the organization, and it must be done in such a way that the facts will be clearly understood.

Encourage Employee Involvement

Today's employees have a strong desire to be involved in making the decisions that affect them. They are increasingly confident that they know the critical operational problems, and they want to share their insights. The organization must have mechanisms in place to tap this source of help. Employee involvement in making decisions helps those involved to understand the situation, assures them that managers and leaders are not trying to bamboozle them, and makes use of the contributions of those who must implement and live with the change.

Share Benefits

Another strategy is to make sure that employees share in the economic and nonfinancial benefits derived from successful organizational change and response to the demands of the new economy. Profit-sharing and production-sharing plans are examples. Where changes make everybody's job easier, less stressful, or less time consuming, today's organizations show that they are concerned about the total work environment.

Avoid Trivial Change

People have always been able to tolerate just so much change, and in today's rapidly changing and demanding world of work, organizations must do everything they can to avoid peppering employees with many irritating small changes. Organizations must strike a balance between excessive change, which results in organizational instability, and insufficient change, which causes organizational stagnation and possible death in the new economy. Organizations must encourage support for change by preventing trivial and unnecessary change.

Recognize and Incorporate the Five Essential Laws of Change into Every Change Effort

The first is that a change always takes longer to complete satisfactorily than anticipated. The second is that it always costs more than estimated. The third is that the process of change is stressful. The fourth law of change management: We cannot manage change itself, but we can manage our response to it. And, the fifth law is that any organization wishing to successfully manage change must involve and help its people move through it.

We especially like the last two. It has been our experience that no one can control the internal and external factors causing a change to take place, but we all have the ability to control how we deal with it. And it is the responsibility of those making any changes to supply their employees, colleagues, and even their family members with the tools they need to navigate successfully through today's uncharted waters. However, there are still too many top organizational leaders who decide that change must occur without involving and supporting those charged with making it happen and most affected by it.

STRATEGIES FOR EASING YOUR OWN PAIN

Grappling with change continues to be a challenge today as it has been in the past. We believe you should embrace change, thrive on it, and learn something new from it every day. But we are still trying to figure out how to do it ourselves. Consider the following suggestions, many of which have been around for years, for easing the pain of change:

• Expect, accept, and embrace change . . . and be a change agent.
• Control your attitude.
• Be tolerant of others' mistakes.
• Develop courage.
• See the inevitable changes as an opportunity for growth.
• Keep doing your job.

Expect, Accept, and Embrace Change . . . and Be a Change Agent

Let go of the old ways and recognize that change is an inevitable part of the new economy. Be prepared for it by being flexible. Accept the fact that you're going to have to adapt to new policies, procedures, operations, people, and so forth. Acknowledge that there is more than one way for the organization to be successful. Don't be an observer. Get involved in the change. Make suggestions. Be a change agent.

Control Your Attitude

Don't let negative attitudes develop. Try to find the positive potential in the change. Get involved. Don't wait to be asked. Seek opportunities to be helpful to those employees ultimately responsible for implementing the change. Maintain your composure even when the going gets tough.

Be Tolerant of Others' Mistakes

Be sympathetic, supportive, and helpful to your boss, other managers, and co-workers. Always give others the benefit of the doubt. Constantly exercise restraint. Always be a part of the solution rather than a part of the problem.

Develop Courage

Develop the courage to think and judge independently as a basis for responding to change. Acquire the protective "armor" that will buffer you from the stress of never-ending change. Through armoring yourself, you will be able to develop a certain amount of resiliency, ego strength, perseverance, backbone, toughness, and strength of conviction to be reenergized by the demands for change. (Note: See Bear and Brehony's chapter for further discussion on courage.)

See the Inevitable Changes as Opportunities for Growth

Use the changes to get a fresh start. Rethink your values, goals, and priorities. Take a hard look at your job performance, your strengths, and your deficiencies. Regularly set personal goals and objectives.

Keep Doing Your Job

Try harder. Work smarter. Use all the resources that are available to you. Don't let up on your work, and don't become passive. Invest yourself totally in your work and your assigned mission. Be a "beginner" of ideas, not an "aginner."

CONCLUSION

All organizations are being affected by change and they are all feeling the force of the new economy—a new economy that includes, for example, rapid and unpredictable change, increasing customer demand for quality and value, and the need to satisfy multiple constituencies. New management methods must continue to be tested, new organizational and human resources management policies and structures must be put in place, new production methods must be implemented, new customer service approaches must be used, and new change agents must be continuously developed and empowered.

Empowering new change agents means nothing more than maximizing employee involvement in every part of the organization. Employee involvement increases each employee's responsibilities as a change agent. In our opinion, this responsibility has to date been assumed by too few, thus contributing to the significant number of change effort failures. When employees take responsibility for change, they help organizations better address the obstacles that need to be overcome if we are to increase the success rate of change efforts.

Changing the way we manage change may simply mean making a greater commitment to incorporating employee involvement in a change as a metric of the change success. Gaining organizational support for this should not be that difficult, since there is a great deal of research that indicates that participation generally leads to commitment, not just compliance. People support what they help create, and involvement is a method of getting people to help in the creation of something new. Such an effort does not mean that middle managers and more senior leaders abdicate their responsibilities for decision making. We believe they actually gain power by asking all the organization's employees what they think.

As organizations struggle and move into the future, they must embrace the principle of "sustainability," which flies in the face of our current infatuation with fleeting "virtual" organizations and misses an important truth: Organizations will not be able to survive and thrive if they have no life beyond the next project or contract. Only with the loyalty and involvement of employees will change happen. In our experience, employee loyalty and involvement often translates into feelings of joy and passion in the work. The harnessing of employees' passion will continue to be the hallmark of an excellent organization.

Today's organizations must better learn how to involve and engage their employees while maintaining the flexibility they require. They can do this by recognizing that committed employees are at the heart of building organizations that last regardless of the economy (old or new). The goal must be one of keeping employees involved and engaged in the organization's future. Organizations have no choice but to become high-involvement organizations that value employee participation, move organizational decision making downward, and share information, knowledge, skills, and rewards will all levels of employees.

Acknowledging the contributions employees can make to proactively address the need for change, identify new metrics, contribute to the development of plans that support necessary organizational shifts, and help the organization move rapidly to better understand customers and competition should enhance the future prosperity of the organization. Failing to do so will pose severe limitations on growth and prosperity. The time to start rethinking the way we manage change is now. Like time and tides, the new economy will not have the patience to wait. Although this all may seem confusing at times, the reality is that while the only constant may be change, dealing with it hasn't changed much.

REFERENCES

Anderson D., & Anderson, L.A. 2001. *Beyond change management*. San Francisco: Jossey-Bass/Pfeiffer.
Change management. 2001. *The Journal of Business Strategy* (March–April): 5.

Chelsom, J.V. 1997. Total quality through empowered training? *Training for Quality*, 5(4): 140.

Church, A.H., Burke, W.W., Javitch, M., Burke, W., & Waclawski, J. 1996. Managing organizational change: What you don't know might hurt you. *Career Development International*, 1(2): 25–30.

Cummings, T.G., & Worley, C.G. 2001. *Organization development and change*, 7th ed. Cincinnati, OH: South-Western College Publishing.

Day, G.S. 2000. The market driven organization. *Direct Marketing* (January): 32–37.

Edmonstone, J. 1995. Managing change: An emerging new consensus. *Health Manpower Management*, 2(1): 16.

Garvin, D.A. 1993. Building the learning organization. *Harvard Business Review*, 71(4): 78–91.

Granville, D. 1996. Developing logistics potential through people. *Logistics Information Management*, 9(1): 39.

Hammer, M., & Champy, J. 1994. *Reengineering the corporation*. New York: HarperCollins.

Harrington, H.J., Conner, D.R., & Horney, N.L. 2000. *Project change management: Applying change management to improvement projects*. New York: McGraw-Hill.

Laing, R.D. 1967. *The politics of experience*. New York: Pantheon.

Lawler, E.E. III. 1982. Increasing worker involvement to enhance organizational effectiveness. In P. Goodman (ed.), *Change in organizations*. San Francisco: Jossey-Bass.

Lawler, E.E. III. 1986. *High-involvement management*. San Francisco: Jossey-Bass.

Lawler, E.E. III 1992. *The ultimate advantage*. San Francisco: Jossey-Bass.

Moran, L., Latham, J., Hogeveen, J., & Russ-Eft, D. 1994. *Winning competitive advantage*. San Jose, CA: Zenger Miller.

Muehrcke, J. 1999. Meeting the test of time. *Nonprofit World*, 17(6): 2–3.

Schienmann, W. 1992. Why change fails. *Across the Board* (April): 53–54.

Walton, R. 1985. From control to commitment in the workplace. *Harvard Business Review*, 63: 76–84.

Wolfsmith, H., Kaiser, M., Adams, M., & Johnson, H. 2000. Transferring learning from one change project to another. Unpublished manuscript, Loyola University, Chicago.

Chapter 4

Holistic Model for Change Agent Excellence: Core Roles and Competencies for Successful Change Agency

Scott A. Quatro, Erik Hoekstra, and Jerry W. Gilley

INTRODUCTION

Traditionally, change agents have been derided for being too fragmented in their approach to change agency. For example, they have been viewed as being too focused on the bottom line, or perhaps overly sensitive to the people impact associated with the change initiative at hand. Or worse yet, they have been regarded as unrealistic and overly optimistic rebels who enthusiastically drive change for change's sake. Even Jack Welch, perhaps the most successful corporate change agent of the twentieth century, was criticized early in his tenure at General Electric for being too insensitive to the people in his organization, earning him the nickname "Neutron Jack."

Moreover, the traditional emphasis within change management circles has been on the development of methodologies and theories to guide the change process itself, with little emphasis on the key competencies required of the change agents who ultimately drive change engagements. In short, the overriding focus within the change management academy has been on the process (change management), as opposed to the human resource (change agents) component of the equation.

The Holistic Model for Change Agent Excellence provides a framework to address both of these issues. The model presents contemporary change agents with an overview of the core roles that they must be willing to fulfill in order to holistically engage their clients, and the personal competencies that they must develop in order to be capable of doing so.

THE CORE ROLES OF A CHANGE AGENT

Today's change agents must develop the personal competencies necessary to holistically approach their change efforts with the *brains* to understand and intellectually influence their client organizations, the *heart* to meaningfully connect with the people in their client organizations, the *courage* to proactively change their client organizations, and the *vision* to define what their client organizations should look like in the future. Each of these—*brain*, *heart*, *courage*, and *vision*—are personal sources that must be collectively drawn upon by change agents as they operate within the following four *core roles*:

1. *Business Partner*—master your client's business and the tools of your profession.
2. *Servant Leader*—selflessly serve your client's needs, both personally and professionally.
3. *Change Champion*—exhort your client to strive for excellence throughout the change process.
4. *Future Shaper*—assist your client in defining the long-term future of the organization.

Each of these core roles is independent of one another, yet *interdependent* at the same time. That is, each provides change agents with a *decidedly different* platform from which to drive change, and yet by intentionally progressing through each of the core roles change agents operate in an increasingly broad sphere of influence.

THE CORE ROLES AS SPHERES OF INFLUENCE

The Business Partner Sphere of Influence

The *brain* must serve as the initial source of credibility for change agents as they strive to build internal and external client networks. Without first establishing this "brain-powered" credibility, the efforts of change agents are doomed to failure. Without it, change agents are regarded as "empty suits" with "soft" hearts, unnecessary change missions, and misguided visions of the future.

The Servant Leader Sphere of Influence

Once a credible business partnership is established, the *heart* becomes the source of selflessness necessary for change agents to gain the full commitment and trust of their clients. The change agent's main goal as Servant Leader is to demonstrate wholeness in approaching organizational life and work—a wholeness that compels clients to fully engage (hands, mind, heart, and spirit) in the effort at hand and to trust that the change agent is committed, first and foremost, to their (the client's) success.

The Change Champion Sphere of Influence

Garnering the commitment and trust of their client groups through selflessness earns change agents the right to employ *courage* and champion change throughout the client organization. Based on credible business analysis conducted within the Business Partner sphere, change agents can now proactively address organizational dysfunction and manage change efforts to improve organizational performance.

The Future Shaper Sphere of Influence

This final and broadest sphere of influence allows change agents to leverage *vision* and become a major driver of long-term strategic direction for client organizations. In order to operate in this sphere of influence, change agents need to demonstrate a proven track record of results over a significant period of time within their client organizations.

It is important to note that while change agents must *initially* progress through each of the four core roles successively to achieve increased breadth of influence, operating in one sphere does not mutually exclude the others. For example, once change agents have operated effectively in the Business Partner sphere they will continually "regress" as needed to operate within that sphere; or, at times, they will concurrently operate in any combination of the four spheres. This dynamic is clearly demonstrated in Figure 4.1, which portrays the core roles as increasingly broad, but not mutually exclusive, spheres of influence.

PERFORMING THE CORE ROLES: REQUIRED PERSONAL COMPETENCIES

Associated with each of the core roles are five personal competencies or keys to success that change agents must master in their quest for excellence. Each competency is a sine qua non of personal success as a change agent. *None* can be excluded from a change agent's toolkit if their goal is holistic client engagement. These "building blocks" are laid out in the unified model (Figure 4.2), and a discussion of each follows.

OPERATING IN THE FIRST CORE ROLE: BUSINESS PARTNER

> Without first establishing a business partnership, change agents are regarded as "empty suits" with "soft" hearts, unnecessary change missions, and misguided visions of the future.

Many change agents have the desire to make their organization a better place but lack the frontline skills to gain credibility. Thus, they lack the competencies for establishing a true *business partnership*. Gaining credibility as a change agent in any organization requires the ability to reach into a business toolkit for the knowledge, skills, and abilities the organization will take seriously.

Such a toolkit is, then, an absolute prerequisite for change agents who want to work with their stakeholders as Business Partners to solve problems, create

Figure 4.1
Change Agent Core Roles as Spheres of Influence

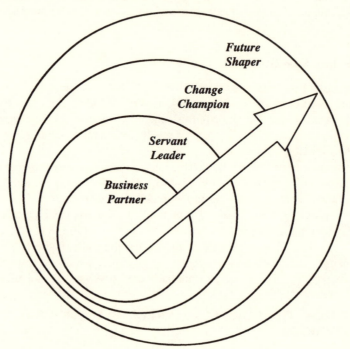

Source: Gilley, Quatro, Hoekstra et al., 2001.

opportunities, capitalize on strategic windows, and leverage organizational strengths. Without something to offer the partnership, promising change agents never get to first base, are never considered players, and are forced to stay on the bench while the real work of the organization happens around them. The following specific skills are essential for a promising change agent to become a driving force within an organization.

Stakeholder Relationship Skills

Participating in change initiatives requires the ability to work with people and to be recognized as someone who will add value to the organization. While it would be nice for stakeholders to view the relationship between themselves and change agents as a partnership, it seldom happens (Robinson & Robinson, 1996). Consequently, change agents face difficult challenges in developing stakeholder relationships.

Listen, Keep Your Eyes Open, and Empathize

Listening, observing, and empathizing are skills that are extremely important for change agents. Too often change agents seek to be the one listened to, instead

Figure 4.2
Holistic Model for Change Agent Excellence

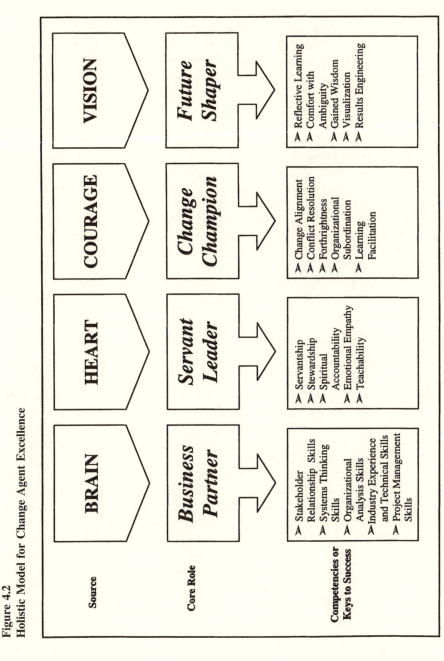

Source: Gilley, Quatro, Hoekstra et al., 2001.

of the one doing the listening. Change agents must strive to really hear what others are saying and to pick up on what is "between the lines" of a message. The first rule in relationship building with a stakeholder must be listening, truly hearing what stakeholders are saying, both verbally and nonverbally.

Similarly, too often change agents want to be the one being watched instead of the one watching. Change agents must be vigilant in order to develop an accurate idea of the situation confronting them. Only then will they be able to identify where the leverage points are in the client organization, what the norms of behavior are, how the organization gets things done, and most importantly, how they can position themselves to add value to the organization's change efforts.

People in organizations long to be understood. Although this process begins when change agents pay attention to others so they feel as if they are being "heard," it is most powerfully unleashed when an effort is made to walk in someone else's shoes. Clients have a desire for change agents to make a connection to their reality in a very real and tangible way. The real question that must be answered is "Do your clients truly believe you can relate to them and help them with their problem?" Developing the reflective skills of watching and listening are key to developing empathy, which translates into greater participation and greater influence in most organizations, as discussed in detail in the section on the core role of Servant Leader.

Systems Thinking Skills

Change agents must have the ability to identify gaps between what is (current state) and what should be (desired future state) in their client organization's interactions with the external environment. To do so requires that change agents develop an understanding of the characteristics and dynamics of open systems. These characteristics form a framework for appraising an organization's internal environment, isolating performance problems, and identifying relationships critical to organizational effectiveness.

At its core, viewing and understanding an organization as an open system requires that a change agent have detailed knowledge of the inputs, throughputs, and outputs of that organization as well as the critical connections and *disconnections* existent therein. This is true both for the current state as well as the evolving state of the client organization. The input-throughput-output cycle flows "smoothly" (albeit dysfunctionally at times) as long as the organization maintains its current processes and procedures. However, the change process itself will cause further breakdowns or disconnections that must be addressed as the organizational evolves toward the desired future state. Successful change agents determine how existing organizational policies and procedures help to preserve order, and they are able to identify which policy and procedure changes are necessary to adapt to or anticipate changing external and internal environmental conditions. In short, change agents must keep the "macro-level" issues facing their client organizations squarely in focus while concurrently remaining connected to the "micro-level" workings of the same organizations. Put another way, change agents must learn the art of seeing both the forest and the trees (Senge, 1990). This challenge is only becoming taller as organizations become increasingly more complex.

Organizational Analysis Skills

Change agents must think of organizational analysis as a process, not an event. It involves all key decision makers, stakeholders, and employees, and should be influenced by a clear understanding of the organization's performance and business needs as well as its strategic goals and objectives. As a process, organizational analysis is used to examine every aspect of organizational life.

Organizational analysis must be perceived as a daily philosophy and practice. As such, organizational analysis is an everyday process for change agents. Most importantly, when uncertain of usefulness, effectiveness, or credibility, change agents must conduct the appropriate analyses. Then and only then are they able to determine the viability and utility of their activities, initiatives, interventions, and processes.

Industry Experience and Technical Skills

Effective change agents ensure that they have significant industry-specific or technical training in their toolkit. Specialized change agents are needed in a variety of roles and functional areas, including process analysis and redesign, performance management, leadership development, information systems design and implementation, and more. However, change agents cannot expect to be taken seriously in any of these fields without first having cut their teeth in a related field of experience with significant responsibility. Thus, change agents must build their experience base around appropriate areas of technical and industry expertise. For example, a change agent who has developed expertise in merchandise buying and distribution process analysis and redesign within the retail industry is much more likely to be embraced by client stakeholders at a firm like Sears or Wal-Mart than is a less specialized change agent.

Despite this relative depth of technical expertise, successful change agents avoid using jargon when explaining performance problems, instead relying on straightforward language to describe processes and approaches to solving them. Successful change agents understand the functional and industry-specific language that other executives and senior managers use every day. "Talking their language" allows change agents to establish joint partnerships. Going back to the previous example, the successful change agent will connect merchandise buying and distribution process analysis and redesign project with critical retail performance measures such as same-store sales or sales per square foot, thereby employing the language of the client.

To aid in this effort change agents must take the initiative to remain current. This includes reading trade journals, popular business press articles, and press releases relevant to their client organizations, and reviewing organizational documents such as annual reports that provide information about the firm's vision, mission, strategic goals, and performance.

Project Management Skills

One of a change agent's most basic responsibilities is that of project management. However, many change agents have very little idea of what a project is and how to manage a project to its successful completion—a dangerous state of affairs, considering the fact that the overlap between project management skills and the skills required to be a change agent are among the most critical and significant (Fuller & Farrington, 1999).

What Is Project Management?

Above all else, project management is a way of thinking; a process of keeping desired results in focus. Project management involves planning and identifying objectives and activities that produce a desired result. It also includes organizing people to get the job done and directing them by keeping them focused on achieving the results. Project management requires change agents to measure the project team's progress and give them feedback to keep the project moving ahead, constantly monitoring progress toward, and deviation from, the project's goals. This monitoring activity allows change agents to make decisions that redirect the project and provide corrective action to narrow the discrepancy between stakeholder expectations and actual performance.

Project Management Pitfalls

No matter how experienced or efficient change agents are at project management, it is impossible to run any project perfectly. Some of the most common project management pitfalls faced by change agents are described below.

Project Scope Changes

Changes in scope of the project occur for several reasons including:

- *Icebergs*—as the project proceeds, new information requiring shifts or expansions in the project plan are discovered "below the surface."
- *Technology changes*—state-of-the-art changes develop as a result of innovations in the market or can be created by the project itself. A vendor or project team may need to design new technology specifically for the project.
- *Project member changes*—team members may resign, be transferred, be promoted, or be terminated, which changes the rhythm of the work plan and the dynamics of the team.

• *External forces*—changes in the marketplace, state or federal regulations, or even "acts of God" can change the scope of a project.

Although many of these changes are difficult to predict, they can be anticipated and accounted for by developing contingency plans that address each of these potentialities.

Scope Creep

Much more dangerous than mere changes in project scope is the disaster known as "scope creep," which refers to an ever-evolving change in focus by stakeholders. This makes it difficult, if not impossible, to set a concrete project goal and control costs, and is often the primary reason that a project fails. Change agents must insist that project scope boundaries are unambiguously documented at the beginning of the engagement, and all stakeholders must publicly agree on the scope of the project. Any changes in scope must be documented in detail and communicated to everyone affected by them.

Too Many People on the Project Team

Any experienced change agent can provide examples of projects that have failed because too many people were involved. Rarely do projects fail solely because there were not enough people involved. Each time a staff member is added to the project, the number of interpersonal relationships affecting the project is increased. Three members require three relationships, five members require 10 relationships, while 10 members require 45 relationships, as illustrated in Figure 4.3.

Each time a member is added to the project the relationships increase geometrically. The solution is to involve only the people who are vital to project success on the team and avoid including people for political or business etiquette reasons. Others can always be brought in briefly as subject matter experts for their specific expertise without being permanent project members.

OPERATING IN THE SECOND CORE ROLE: SERVANT LEADER

> The change agent's main goal as Servant Leader is to demonstrate wholeness in their approach to organizational life and work—a wholeness that compels clients to fully engage (hands, mind, heart, and spirit) in the effort at hand and to trust that the change agent is committed, first and foremost, to their (the client's) success.

Accessing the hearts of others is what enables change agents to bring about true individual and organizational transformation. But accessing the hearts of others requires change agents to selflessly humble themselves. Therefore, change agents must become Servant Leaders, focused first and foremost on the success

Figure 4.3
Project Team Size and Interpersonal Relationships

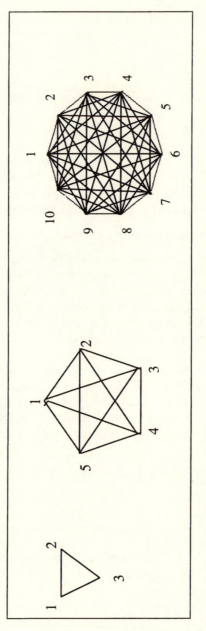

Source: Gilley, Quatro, Hoekstra et al., 2001.

of those around them, recognizing that their clients' successes are ultimately their own successes.

Make no mistake about it—this is not a "soft" issue with no real connection to the "bottom line" of a change initiative. This is an imperative for change agents to truly gain the trust and commitment of their clients, which of course is one of the most important goals of change agency. Operating in the core role of Servant Leader requires change agents to internalize and model the following five personal competencies: servantship, stewardship, spiritual accountability, emotional empathy, and teachability.

Servantship

In his seminal work on leadership and power, Robert Greenleaf (1970) introduced the American corporate world to the idea of leadership as servantship. To be sure, Greenleaf's message initially fell mostly on deaf ears. However, in recent years, Peter Senge, Max DePree, Peter Block, Stephen Covey, and other pioneers of modern managerial and organizational thought have lent significant focus and legitimacy to the idea. And while it is still relatively new to the dialogue of corporate America, this leadership paradigm has been eloquently modeled through the lives of service and enduring accomplishments of some of history's most influential change agents, among them Mohandas Gandhi and Jesus Christ. Both men can be viewed as change agents who brought about transformational change through *radical selflessness* and *radical expressions of love*.

Radical Selflessness

As Greenleaf (1996) himself emphasizes in one of his posthumously published essays, Gandhi was perhaps the greatest leader of the common people the world has ever known. He achieved independence for India and catalyzed an end to the abuses of colonialism. Similarly, Jesus has been referred to as one of the most successful managers and change agents of all time (Briner, 1996). He established 2000 years ago what has since become one of the largest and most successful "organizations" in the world by forcefully challenging the hypocritical religious and oppressive civic forces of his day. Both men ultimately achieved their goals principally through radical selflessness, a willingness to put the needs of their followers above their own, and both eventually made the ultimate sacrifice to that end.

Does this mean that a change agent's success depends on their willingness to submit to execution on behalf of their clients? Yes and no. While servantship in the world of change agency may not entail physical death, it does often require change agents to put their professional necks on the line for their clients—taking unpopular stands, occasionally in direct opposition to the powers that be. More directly, the success of change agents depends on their ability to demonstrate a servant heart towards others, intentionally serving the needs and goals of their clients before their own, making *others* their overriding focus, their purpose for being a change agent in the first place. This is how real trust and commitment are born, and equally important, it's the way a change agent's track record of servantship eventually becomes a source of significant leverage as he or she operates in the core roles of Change Champion and Future Shaper.

Radical Expressions of Love

As a change agent, Jesus was continually looking for ways to communicate to his immediate client project team (the 12 disciples) how valuable they were to him both personally and professionally, how much he appreciated their being a part of the same "engagement"—in short, how much he loved them. Perhaps one of the more compelling examples of this is the familiar story of Jesus humbly kneeling before the disciples and washing their feet, a job normally reserved for the lowliest slaves of Jesus' time.

Once again this does not mean that a change agent's success depends on a willingness to *literally* wash the feet of their project team members, although a current United States senator recently did so upon his successful election and the experience was apparently overwhelmingly moving for both the senator and his project team. Rather, the message is how important it is for change agents to tangibly communicate appreciation to their project team members in meaningful ways and to walk on common ground with them. Such communication can take many forms and can be as simple as change agents rolling up their sleeves and staying late to help photocopy project status reports due out first thing next morning, publicly praising the work of their project team members, or sending one of their project team members an encouraging personal e-mail, just because. Acts such as these demonstrate in concrete ways that change agents and their project team members are all "in the same boat," and can go a long way toward creating a project team that is "radically committed" to the change initiative at hand.

Stewardship

While servantship entails intentionally putting the needs and the success of clients above one's own, stewardship takes it a step further and requires that change agents also be held *accountable* for meeting those needs and ensuring those successes (Block, 1993). Furthermore, change agents must do so without employing a traditional command and control style, lest they slip back from being their clients' steward to being their patriarch. It's one thing to operate as a brilliant yet humble change agent, consistently sharing the glory and giving your clients credit for *your* successes. It's another thing altogether to ensure that *they* have actually achieved the success on their own, and thus have truly earned the praise. Change agents must approach their efforts as a steward—a change agent that *equips* and *empowers* clients.

Equip Clients

Stewardship requires that change agents equip their clients with the knowledge, work skills, and resources necessary for success. Change agents must make significant up-front and ongoing investments in work-skill and behavioral training for their project team members. Successful change agents spend a good portion of every day imparting their personal wisdom, expertise, skills, and experience with at least one of their key clients, always remembering that their goal in doing so is not to impress, but to equip.

Empower Clients

Being a steward means that once their clients have been equipped for a battle, change agents let them fight it without unnecessary intervention. Successful change agents give their project team members the authority and autonomy to make significant project-related decisions. However, this does not mean sending them out to the wolves without any protection. Change agents must legitimize the empowerment of their project team members, formally articulating to the client organization the extent and reason for their autonomy. Change agents must blaze a trail for their empowered project team members. If change agents are unwilling to do this, then they're not ready to empower their clients. Successful change agents always remember that when their clients fail, they fail as well.

Spiritual Accountability

The results of a Gallup poll published in *Business Week* (Conlin, 1999) indicated that 78% of Americans felt the need to experience spiritual growth as part of their everyday lives and that 48% of Americans had spoken of their religious faith in the workplace within the last 24 hours. Another study (Mitroff & Denton, 1999) concluded that organizational spirituality may well be the ultimate competitive advantage. Given the contemporary context it becomes clear that operating in the core role of Servant Leader requires change agents to embrace the spiritual dimension of work and organizational life and to willingly accept accountability for the "spiritual well-being" of their client project team members. Tapping into the spirit of their clients is what enables change agents to holistically—hands, mind, heart, and spirit—engage them in the effort at hand, as illustrated in Figure 4.4.

While spiritual accountability does not involve advocating for organized religion in the workplace, some manifestations of it, such as project team members getting together on company property for yoga sessions, bible study, or meditation, should be expected and embraced. Spiritual accountability involves an overt commitment on the part of change agents to access the spiritually related *terminal values* (Rokeach, 1973) of their clients, to make theirs known to their clients, and to allow those values to be a constant source of personal and corporate meaning and motivation. It is these terminal values that are most influ-

Figure 4.4
Spiritual Accountability and Holistic Client Engagement

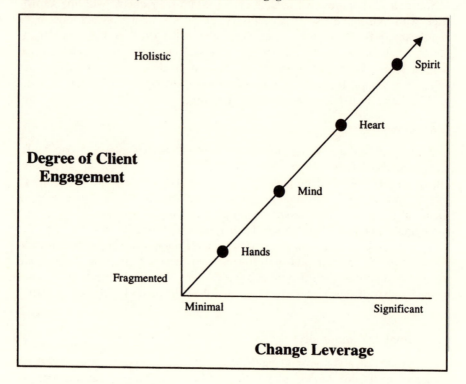

ential and enduring in human beings. The following list provides several steps that change agents must take as they demonstrate and embody spiritual accountability:

1. Eliminate the false dichotomy between the "secular" and the "sacred." For too long now the American corporate world has viewed the topic of spirituality as taboo (Pascale, 1990). Thus, clients are often expected to leave their spiritual values at the door and keep them out of the organizational dialogue. This expectation is narrow-minded, and as spiritual beings, it is a difficult and unnatural thing for clients to do. Change agents must clearly articulate to their clients that they recognize the legitimate place for spirituality in *all* of life, including business organizations and the work conducted within them; that there is a higher purpose for work than simply earning a paycheck, or even becoming a more profitable organization for that matter.

2. Be transparent and uncompromising about *your* spiritual values. In order for clients to feel comfortable with the idea of bringing their spiritual values into the workplace they must see change agents model the principle first. This doesn't mean "attempting to convert" clients to any one specific spiritual perspective. It simply involves change agents openly sharing with their clients what they view as the ultimate purpose for

their work lives. And once they have done so, successful change agents are certain to conduct the activities of their work and personal lives as much as possible in harmony with the spiritual values that they have espoused.

3. Make a concerted effort to know and understand your *clients'* spiritual values. In most cases, clients will naturally and willingly share their spiritual values with change agents in kind. However, there will be cases where change agents will need to make a more concerted effort to know their clients holistically. Successful change agents are creative, persistent, and patient, looking for opportunities to connect with their clients around terminal values. They ask questions like, "Why is that important to you?" and "What have you been doing outside of work lately?" Responses to such questions can give change agents immediate insight into their clients' spiritual values.

4. Make concrete connections between your spiritual values, your clients' spiritual values, and your work together as often as possible. This is really the lynchpin to realizing the direct work-related benefits of being a spiritually transparent change agent. Making these connections is what enables change agents to intentionally leverage holistic understanding of their clients as a source of motivation and effort. Not surprisingly, it is the inability and unwillingness of many change initiative project teams to do exactly this that results in their project vision and mission statements being "soulless" and "empty," as opposed to deeply meaningful, shared, and *leverageable* statements of terminal values.

Jack Welch has commented that he views his main challenge as unleashing the "spirit and potential" of the employees at GE, resulting in a work force that feels rewarded and fulfilled "in both the pocketbook and the soul." Given his track record of success as a change agent and General Electric's corporate success under his watch as chairman and CEO, it is clear that being a spiritually sensitive change agent not only makes good "heart sense," it makes good "business sense" as well. Like Welch, successful change agents are willing to accept spiritual accountability for their clients, ensuring that they are able to holistically engage in the task at hand.

Emotional Empathy

Change agents view organizational life as being all about change—both for them as the initiators of change and for their clients as the recipients of change. They view change as a personal mandate, a challenge, a calling to proactively guide organizations in the right direction. However, successful change agents also understand that change is messy and at times decidedly emotional (Jick, 1993), especially for their clients, who often don't have the same adaptability to change as they do.

Thus the turmoil of organizational change results in a great deal of emotional transparency between change agents and their clients. This transparency needs to be handled with great care and sensitivity—or put simply, with emotional empathy. The following steps are necessary for change agents to employ emotional empathy in working with clients.

1. Change agents must articulate to their clients that it is normal, and even healthy, for them to feel what they are feeling.

2. Change agents must openly share their own feelings and emotions about the change with their clients on a regular basis.

3. Change agents must provide individual or group forums and outlets for their clients to express their emotions and feelings about the change.

4. When their clients do share their feelings and emotions, change agents must actively listen to them, in an open and nonjudgemental, yet discerning, manner.

5. Based on what they learn, change agents must then design and implement additional individual or group interventions as necessary.

Fulfilling the role of Servant Leader requires change agents to be empathically attuned to the emotions and feelings of their clients. Successful change agents remember that these emotions are normal and inevitable, and therefore can't be ignored, and more importantly that practicing emotional empathy allows them to understand and engage their clients more holistically, thereby gaining more change leverage.

Teachability

Successful change agents recognize that they don't always have the right answers and thereby embody a teachable nature, openly embracing situations in which they can learn. In a traditional consulting model the change agent has all the knowledge and viable ideas, and the followers simply soak up what the leader espouses and spit it back as "good" clients are supposed to do. Under such a model the risk of the organization making poor decisions is greatly increased because the livelihood of the group is dependent on the ideas, knowledge, and wisdom of just one person, as opposed to many. The consequences often include severely handicapped organizational performance at minimum, and outright disaster at a maximum. A classic example of the latter is the Challenger Space Shuttle disaster. Lack of teachability on the part of the mission's leadership when confronted with substantiated concerns by two low-level engineers caused the loss of hundreds of millions of taxpayer dollars and the tragic death of seven American astronauts on that fateful day in 1986.

An important connection to make here is that teachability not only results in change agents personally practicing continuous learning, but more importantly, almost always results in their clients following suit. This in turn leads to greater levels of organizational learning, and as Senge and others have so passionately exhorted us to embrace over the last 10 years, it is precisely an organization's ability to learn that dictates its long-term economic success.

John Kotter, perhaps the leading strategic management and leadership consultant in the world today, and Harvard Business School colleague James Heskett conducted a ground-breaking study involving over 175 *Fortune* 500 firms and more than 10 years of operational and financial data (1992). Their goal was to identify what impact, if any, corporate culture has on long-term organizational performance. They concluded that corporate culture is indeed a valid predictor of long-term organizational performance and, more specifically, that those firms that fostered continuous learning and flexibility throughout their ranks consistently performed at higher levels than their inflexible, "non-learning" peers. More importantly, they determined that these higher performing, learning organizations were led and staffed by executives who demonstrated teachability. Walter Wriston, former chairman and CEO of Citibank, once commented that "the person who figures out how to harness the collective genius of the people in his or her organization is going to blow the competition away." Successful change agents demonstrate teachability and do exactly that. They tap into the ideas and expertise—the "genius" of their clients—learn from it, and achieve greater success as a result.

OPERATING IN THE THIRD CORE ROLE: CHANGE CHAMPION

> Garnering the commitment and trust of their client groups through selfless-ness earns change agents the right to demonstrate *courage* and champion change throughout the client organization, proactively addressing organizational dysfunction and managing change efforts to improve organizational performance.

Change agency is not for the weak. It requires change agents to possess the ability to tolerate rejection, even failure. Change agents are inevitably considered "outsiders" even though they are personally invested in the success of the client organization. Further, they are often thrust into the latest organizational "political hot topic," for which they may be conveniently blamed, at some future date, when it fails or has a less than satisfactory impact on the firm. Kotter (1996) has clearly suggested that change agents need a healthy dose of courage as they confront the powerful organizational complacency and inertia around them. The world of change agency is not one for cowards. To fulfill the core role of Change Champion, change agents must develop change alignment, conflict resolution, forthrightness, organizational subordination, and learning facilitation competencies.

Change Alignment

Successful change agents have a thorough understanding of the organizational behavior (OB) dynamics associated with the change process. Far too many change efforts have involved an attempt to design a fail-safe, lock-step change process without adequate focus on the overarching OB elements of the equation. These efforts are futile, and such detailed "recipes for success" must be replaced with a broader set of change imperatives that greatly enhance the probability of success for any change initiative.

Seven Keys to Successful Organizational Change

To operate as a Change Champion with the courage to see the process through to the end, change agents must be equipped with, and be willing to hold themselves and their client organization accountable to, the seven keys to successful organizational change.

1. *Provide Strong, Highly Visible, and Personal Leadership.* Change agents must display an unswerving commitment to the goals of the project at hand. Further, they must claim a personal stake in the success of the project and demonstrate a willingness to be held accountable for achieving that success through teamwork rather than through individual effort alone. Additionally, they must ensure that a clearly dedicated and visible executive sponsor is 100% behind the project and is driving it at all levels of the organization.

2. *Institute Client Involvement Early and Often, at All Levels.* Change agents must ensure that as many employees of the client organization as possible, as early as possible, are actively involved in planning and conducting the change effort in some capacity.

3. *Build a Clearly Articulated, Shared Vision.* Change agents must take the time to develop a shared and formally articulated vision for the change effort at hand, personally endorse it, and build support for it throughout the client organization.

4. *Provide Frequent, Consistent, and Open Communication.* Change agents must ensure that as much information as possible is passed along to all the members of the client organization at the appropriate times, and in the appropriate manner. It's better to err on the side of providing too much rather than too little information, even if the details are still being developed.

5. *Leverage Talented and Trusted Employees as Co-Change Agents.* Change agents must identify those employees who are most enthusiastic about the transition effort and have the highest level of credibility among their peers, and then give them opportunities to lead the charge by exhibiting modeling behavior.

6. *Set Measurable Operational and Behavioral Goals.* Change agents must work with the client organization to develop meaningful individual and organizational goals that are designed to measure operational results and reinforce the development of the work skills, competencies, and behaviors consistent with the desired future state of the organization.

7. *Celebrate Successes and Readdress Shortcomings.* Finally, change agents must hold themselves and the client organization accountable to the stated individual and organizational goals. They must take every opportunity to publicly and positively reinforce successes, while readdressing shortcomings in the spirit of development and opportunity.

Conceptually it may help to connect the seven keys to Lewin's classic change model—the first three with "unfreezing," the next two with "changing," and the last two with "refreezing"—as illustrated in Figure 4.5.

Figure 4.5
Lewin's Model and the Seven Keys to Successful Organizational Change

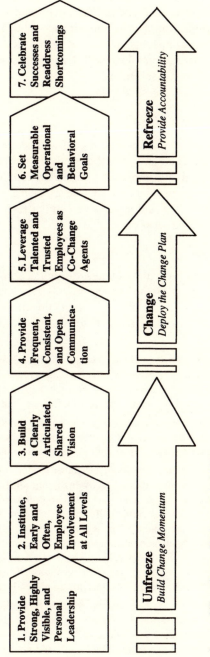

1. Provide Strong, Highly Visible, and Personal Leadership

2. Institute, Early and Often, Employee Involvement at All Levels

3. Build a Clearly Articulated, Shared Vision

4. Provide Frequent, Consistent, and Open Communication

5. Leverage Talented and Trusted Employees as Co-Change Agents

6. Set Measurable Operational and Behavioral Goals

7. Celebrate Successes and Readdress Shortcomings

Unfreeze
Build Change Momentum

Change
Deploy the Change Plan

Refreeze
Provide Accountability

Source: Gilley, Quatro, Hoekstra et al., 2001.

Thus, the overarching strategy for effective change alignment is clear—change agents must employ the seven keys to build momentum for the change effort, deploy the change plan, and provide performance accountability for their clients and the organization as a whole. Change agents must clearly articulate these seven principles as nonnegotiable elements of the change strategy and then remain unswerving as they employ the list and insist on the ongoing commitment of their clients to the seven keys.

Conflict Resolution

Conflict is a common by-product of organizational change initiatives. Change agents must have the courage to work proactively both to prevent unnecessary conflict and to aggressively resolve the inevitable conflicts that do arise. Doing so elevates change agents to the vital role of peacemaker (Goleman, 1998). Moreover, healthy conflict and aggressive conflict resolution can be leveraged to catalyze organizational change.

Leveraging Conflict

Change Champions have the courage to embrace conflict as a natural and often beneficial outcome of the change process and work with their clients to bring those conflicts to a healthy resolution. Leveraging conflict in this way depends on the ability of change agents to implement the following steps:

1. Proactively monitor individual clients and the client organization for sources of conflict. Change agents must always keep their conflict radar in full deployment, recognizing that the sources of conflict may be both human (personality clashes, team dysfunction) and inhuman (business process inefficiency, information system crashes).

2. Once conflict is detected, work aggressively to constructively resolve it. When change agents allow conflict to fester, it simply becomes a cancer to the change effort at hand. As the old saying goes, "deal with the elephant in the room."

3. Bring the parties involved in the conflict together to work through the issue. Attempting to resolve the conflict without directly involving all the parties concerned at the same time may enable change agents to avoid some heated discussions, but the end result is simply a prolonged conflict life cycle and a greater potential for lingering resentment and misunderstanding. Through the 1990s Jack Welch championed a conflict resolution and organizational improvement process at GE called *Workout* that, simply put, involved sitting the people involved in a conflict in a room together until the conflict was brought to a constructive resolution. In short, change agents must have the courage to bring people together to "slay the elephant."

4. Ensure that the proposed resolution is implemented immediately. Nothing will damage a change agent's reputation for leveraging conflict more quickly than lack of follow-through on the resolution. Successful change agents have the courage to decisively implement the solution, even when it will cause individual and organizational pain.

Confronting conflict is messy and even personally and professionally painful at times. However, change agents must remain steadfast in their commitment to proactively and aggressively search out conflict, embrace it as a change catalyst, and constructively bring it to resolution. Those who fail to do so find that the "elephant" eventually sits right on top of them, effectively crushing their efforts as change agents.

Forthrightness

During complex and challenging change initiatives change agents are often required to critically examine the behavior or performance of client project team members. How can this be done and still maintain positive working relationships among the project team members? It certainly cannot be accomplished through overly aggressive, rude, abusive, or sarcastic tactics all too often employed by managers to force changes in behavior. These methods only create resentment and seldom help resolve the problem. Moreover, avoiding problems and pretending they do not exist will only lead to prolonged and exacerbated conflict situations, as previously discussed. Unfortunately, many problems are not addressed until behavior or performance has deteriorated to such a point that drastic action must be taken. Often such action makes the situation even worse.

Successful change agents recognize the critical balance that must be struck between getting project work done and maintaining positive working relationships among the project team members. The only way this is achieved is through forthrightness.

An appropriately assertive and forthright message is nonjudgemental in tone, includes a transparent disclosure of the feelings incited by the behavior, and a clarification of the effects of the team member's behavior on the change initiative at hand (Bolton, 1986). The following are excellent examples of nonjudgemental behavior descriptions, with an accompanying disclosure of feelings and clarification of effects for each.

- When you are frequently late for project team meetings . . . I feel disappointed . . . because it communicates a lack of commitment to the rest of the project team.
- When you overspend your budget . . . I feel annoyed . . . because it means I must make cuts that will affect the overall quality of the project.
- When you don't turn in your project status report on time . . . I feel frustrated . . . because I can't get an accurate picture of our current deliverable progress.

Put simply, successful change agents ensure that they forthrightly address performance and behavior problems among their project team members with clarity and with respect. Doing so greatly enhances members' understanding of the dysfunctional effects of undesirable behavior and leads to smoother and quicker resolution of the problem.

Organizational Subordination

When change agents allow the client organization to get in the way of individual project team member contributions, ideas, and efforts, the message communicated is clear—namely, that the organization at large is more important and valuable than are the individual project team members. This inevitably results in increased disloyalty, mistrust, poor performance and productivity, low morale, and ultimately, increased project team member turnover. These undesirable outcomes are inconsistent with a successful change agent's philosophy and practice.

Organization subordination involves change agents intentionally prioritizing the contributions, involvement, and loyalty of individual members above the ingrained organizational system. Change agents must strive to guarantee organizational subordination to individual client project team members' efforts to improve organizational performance, thereby eliminating the traditional "organization first" approach to change agency. Thus, change agents demonstrate organizational subordination by eliminating policies and procedures that interfere with, prevent, or discourage individual members' growth and development. They must also eliminate organizational structures that inhibit the progress of the change initiative (Gilley, 2000).

Successful change agents create project team cultures in which individual members' growth and development are encouraged and sponsored as actively as is the development of the client organization as a whole. Employing organizational subordination ensures that change agents select project team members based on their readiness to learn, change, grow, and develop and that change agents clearly link individual members' growth and development to the goals and objectives of the project as a whole.

Learning Facilitation

Having committed to the ideal of organizational subordination, change agents must in turn have the courage to facilitate active and meaningful learning for individual members in conjunction with the change effort at hand. Since the publication of his seminal work on organizationl learning, Senge has called change agents to the critical task of learning facilitation. Taking on this responsibility requires change agents to master the art of balancing "advocacy"—*teaching clients*—and "inquiry"—*engaging clients in the learning process* (1990, p. 198).

Teach Clients

Learning facilitation requires that change agents have the courage to teach others throughout the client organization. To that end, change agents must employ the following strategies:

1. Clearly articulate knowledge transfer as a top priority. Far too often, change agents swoop into a client organization, dispense their wisdom and expertise, and leave client

confusion and dependency in their wake. Successful change agents unequivocally commit to transferring knowledge from themselves to their clients and build into their project plans the infrastructures and interventions that enable this to happen.

2. Take advantage of "teachable moments." In the regular course of organizational life, let alone in the middle of a tumultuous change effort, numerous situations arise in which change agents are presented with ideal opportunities to teach. Change agents must have the courage to sieze these moments as opportunties to reinforce knowledge transfer, whether the moments are positive or negative.

3. Hold clients accountable for learning. Successful change agents integrate learning expectations and measurements for their individual clients into the projects' perform-ance management process.

Engage Clients in the Learning Process

In order for change agents to be effective facilitators of learning for their clients, they must draw them out and engage them in critical dialogue. To do so requires change agents to have the courage to employ the following strategies:

1. Ask questions. It is as simple as that. Successful change agents continually ask ques-tions, never falling into the cowardly routine of pretending to know something or understand a situation simply because they don't want to appear ignorant. Equally important, if change agents sense the same dynamic in one of their clients, they ask the question for them, thereby siezing the situation as an ideal teachable moment for the individual client and as an ideal opportunity to reinforce their commitment to knowledge transfer among the project team members.

2. Make connections. As change agents draw out the ideas, knowledge, and expertise of their clients they must take every opportunity to make connections among that col-lective body of critical information.

3. Forgive failure. Some of the greatest learning that change agents and their clients experience happens as a direct result of individual or organizational failure. Successful change agents forgive failures, and embrace them as opportunities to engage their clients in the learning process. For too long now, the traditoinal organizational para-digm has been unforgiving of mistakes and failure. Such an absolute leads to fear of experimentation, and can sound the death knell for a change agent's efforts as a facilitator of learning.

OPERATING IN THE FOURTH CORE ROLE: FUTURE SHAPER

Operating in the fourth and most broadly influential core role of Future Shaper enables a change agent to leverage *vision* and become a major driver of long-term strategic direction for client organizations.

As a Future Shaper, change agents are responsible for identifying the path ahead and making mid-course corrections to avoid dangerous water. To do so, change agents must rely on past experiences as sources of information and wisdom. Moreover, visionary change agents continue to solicit the wisdom of their clients and other change agents, and examine conditions before making commitments. Accordingly, they demonstrate faith in others while dynamically balancing optimism and realism, intuition, and planning.

Although in some rare cases visionary ability seems to be a birthright, for most change agents such talent comes only over a period of time. Just as fine wine needs to age and single malt whiskey needs to mellow, the true development of a change agent as Future Shaper is most typically a developmental process. There is rarely a moment of enlightenment change agents can point to as the moment when they "finally got it." Instead, change agents evolve toward Future Shapers, finding themselves on a journey that can only be described as a process of "becoming" that involves the development of the competencies of reflective learning, comfort with ambiguity, gained wisdom, visualization, and results engineering.

Reflective Learning

What seems to separate truly visionary change agents from the crowd is their inquisitiveness, and their impatience with the status quo—in themselves, in others, and in the organizations they impact. Thus, long-term effectiveness as a change agent is directly correlated with a personal commitment to intentional and reflective lifelong learning.

Many organizations, such as the Center for Creative Leadership, offer leadership development process models with reflective learning built into them that are highly applicable to change agents who desire to become Future Shapers (McCauley, Moxley, & Van Velsor, 1998). Such models must involve assessment (identifying a gap in present and desired states), challenge (experiencing disequilibrium), and support (reflective guidance before, during, and after the experience), thus requiring change agents to begin with an honest critical assessment of where they stand today in relationship to their future goals, expose themselves to new experiences while concurrently requiring them to experiment with different solutions, and through the process metamorphasize themselves into better equipped change agents. Successful change agents understand that true reflective learning only happens when *all three* of the components are present. Assessment itself will not change anything. Experience without assessment and reflection is simply a ride. Reflection without prior assessment and experiences on which to reflect is empty.

Further, truly visionary change agents also recognize that the reflective learning process is not strictly a personal one and that it must also be an organizational process. Such change agents implore their client organizations to employ leadership development programs that encourage assessment, risk taking, and reflection in an effort to improve long-term organizational learning and performance.

Comfort with Ambiguity

Seasoned change agents must develop within themselves a comfort level with ambiguity. Too often change agents struggle with this issue from two different directions. On the one hand, sensate-oriented change agents struggle with *analysis paralysis*, not allowing decisions to be made until *all* the data has been gathered and analyzed and *all* the unknowns have become known. The notion that decisions cannot be made until all the facts are in and all the variables are known simply will not work today with the rapid pace of change in most industries. A second type of struggle is the *back seat driver* approach to change agency. Here, the change agent appears to be comfortable with delegation and decision making but then hovers so closely to ' "inspect" client project team member progress that performance is stifled. Visionary change agents recognize the futility of both of these approaches to change agency.

Future Shapers recognize that decisions must be made with wisdom and intuition based on the known available facts at hand and that they must also be made in "real time" given the numerous opportunities and threats facing their client organizations. They further recognize that moving their client organizations forward to meet their strategic goals and objectives can only happen if the power of individual performance is unleashed through real delegation in a "freedom to fail" environment. Max De Pree, widely regarded as a contemporary sage of leadership and management theory, has commented that "the more comfortable you can make yourself with ambiguity, the better leader you will be" (De Pree, 1992, p. 57). Successful and seasoned change agents heed De Pree's words and develop comfort operating in the "gray" areas of change agency.

Gained Wisdom

> Listen, my sons, to a father's instruction; pay attention and gain understanding. . . . Do not forsake wisdom, and she will protect you; love her, and she will watch over you. Wisdom is supreme; therefore get wisdom. Though it cost you all you have, get understanding.
>
> —Proverbs 4:1, 6–7

Written 3,000 years ago by King Solomon, the "wisest man who ever lived," these words have a timeless applicability to change agency. As change agents evolve into Future Shapers they experience many things and work with many seasoned individuals who afford them opportunities to develop wisdom. Successful change agents embrace those opportunities, enabling them to draw on that wisdom as they map out the future state of their client organizations.

An important reality for change agents to accept right away is that wisdom is most often gained through practical experience and instruction from more experienced colleagues. Many hard-charging change agents of the twenty-first century find this difficult reality hard to swallow, but successful change agents recognize that it is consistent with their makeup as teachable Servant Leaders, as discussed in the previous section on the second core role. To this end, change agents must commit to the following list of absolutes in their quest to develop gained wisdom:

1. Tap into the wisdom of the "elders" in the client organization. Despite the "generation gap" that exists between younger change agents and their older client stakeholders, savvy change agents tap into their clients' wisdom and understanding. Often their insights into the culture, history, and people of the organization prove to be invaluable to the change effort at hand and are available from virtually no other source. Listen to their stories. Observe the artifacts in their offices. In short, honor their wisdom and absorb as much of it as possible.

2. Build a "wisdom war-chest." As change agents' experience bases grows so too do their battle scars. Future Shapers have the hindsight and vision to see those experiences within the broader contexts of both the past and the future, continually asking themselves the following questions: "What can/did I learn from this project/incident/experience?" and "How can I apply the lessons from this project/incident/experience in the future?"

3. Patiently and progressively wield wisdom-based influence on an organizational level. Seasoned change agents must never be in a rush to display their rich wisdom to the rest of the client organization. Remember that wisdom is gained and that change agents must patiently earn the right to influence the direction of the organization when drawing from their wisdom base as the source of that influence. Once they have done so, change agents can then gradually broaden the scope of their wisdom-based influence.

4. Share wisdom with others on an individual level. Once change agents have become established as a true source of gained wisdom at the organizational level, they must then commit to sharing their insights with others throughout the client organization. This must be done in an intentional yet casual way, as a mentor of future change agents who will in turn become future sources of wisdom for the organization.

Understanding and employing this list enables change agents to differentiate themselves as "wise" change agents as opposed to "foolish" ones—change agents who have earned the right to influence and shape the future of their client organizations, as illustrated in Figure 4.6.

Thus, the implications of demonstrating gained wisdom are clear. Seasoned change agents wield a source and breadth of influence that is much more significant than mere intellectual knowledge, extensive practical experience or even seniority.

Visualization

Future Shapers serve a unique role in their client organizations. In a sea of change, choppy water, and uncertainty, Future Shapers are called on to find the

Figure 4.6
Gained Wisdom as a Source of Future Shaper Influence

High **Depth and Breadth of Impact**	**Gained Wisdom**	**Related Experience**
Low	**Seniority**	**"Book" Knowledge**
	Late	**Early**

Relative Stage in Career Life Cycle

Source: Gilley, Quatro, Hoekstra et al., 2001.

horizon for those on board. The definition of what the organization is fundamentally about, what it will and will not do, where it will and will not go, and
where the boundaries are is the work of Future Shapers. Accomplished athletes
often use the technique of visualization in preparation for competition. Michael
Jordan, Jack Nicklaus, Wayne Gretzky, and others could visualize the performance before the moment of truth and then turn that vision into reality during the
heat of competition. So it needs to be for Future Shapers in charting the course
for change in their client organizations.

Such visualization of the future is not always clear, which is a critical reason
that comfort with ambiguity is so important. Often, the first glimpse change
agents have of the future will be fuzzy, unclear, and seem ludicrous. Think of
John F. Kennedy's bold prediction of sending a man to the moon. An inspira-
tional moment to be sure, but at the time he uttered those words, that reality
seemed incredible to most and even for Kennedy must have been a bit of a
stretch. However, his ability to go to the edge of present reality to define a
future state demonstrated the brilliance of his change agency. To become Future
Shapers, change agents must be like Kennedy and break away from certainty.
They must rise above the known to see another, altogether different and higher
plane. They must allow their feet to leave the solid ground of the present.

Results Engineering

Future shaping change agents don't simply have their heads in the clouds
visualizing unrealistic dreams of the future. As bold as his predcition was, Kennedy knew in his gut that he would be able to deliver on his promised deliv-

erable, and he engineered the results of the space program to that end. Thus, the final competency of a seasoned change agent involves an unyielding commitment to results. Once the future reality is defined, effective change agents focus with laser-like precision on the journey to that reality.

The purpose of any change agent is to secure results for the client organization, from increasing market share to improving the healthfulness of the organizational culture. Successful change agents accept the fact that the ultimate accountability surrounding project results is theirs, and theirs alone. However, they are also acutely aware that they will only achieve the desired results in concert with their project team members—in short, that results are ultimately achieved *through other people*. Thus, change agents must employ the following components of results engineering:

1. Clearly articulate the business-driven need for the change. Without legitimate and widely understood business-driven needs, change initiatives are doomed to failure. Seasoned change agents ensure that "felt need" exists within their client organizations.
2. Clearly define the desired deliverables and results. Change agents must outline, as early as possible, the specific deliverables and results for which the project team will be held accountable. They must also ensure that these deliverables and results are concretely related to the business-driven needs for the change initiative at hand.
3. Integrate a performance management process into the project infrastructure. Results engineering requires change agents to abandon the traditional "one-time-annual-event" model of performance evaluation and instead commit to an ongoing *process* of evaluating and managing the performance of their individual client project team members. This includes ensuring that individual members are appropriately rewarded for their results, in terms of both direct (incentive bonuses) and indirect (additional paid time off) compensation.

Future Shapers are obsessed with achieving results. By engineering their project infrastructures in such a way as to create a culture of results orientation among their project team members, they better ensure that the desired individual and client organization results will be achieved.

MOVING FROM THEORY TO PRACTICE

The change management academy exists within the larger academy of management theory. As such, it is interesting to note how organizational and management thought have evolved since the beginning of the American industrial revolution of the twentieth century and what the implications are for contemporary change agents. Maslow's classic hierarchy of needs theory can quite nicely be employed as a metaphor for this purpose.

Taylor, Weber, and Fayol first established management as a true "science" by challenging firms to maximize productivity while minimizing costs, with the focus of most workers of that time clearly on satisfying the lower-order physiological and safety needs. Mayo, Simon, McGregor, Maslow, Follett, and others then began to shift the focus from merely manipulating workers to understanding and motivating them, acknowledging the social and psychological dynamics of organizational life. This clearly corresponded with workers becoming increasingly desirous of satisfying the transitional/middle-order needs of social belonging and self-esteem within a work context. And finally, contemporary theorists such as Senge, Block, Covey, Mitroff and Denton, and Kotter are exhorting us to build organizations that are proactive, values-based, and focused on leveraging and honoring human resources as a true source of competitive advantage. In short, the goal is to build organizations that holistically engage a work force that is increasingly focused on meeting the highest order need of self-actualization.

Thus, it becomes clear that the state of contemporary organizational life dictates that change agents accept responsibility for holistically engaging their clients. No longer can we approach our engagements as solely business analysts, employee advocates, change drivers, or strategic planners. Rather, contemporary change agents must concurrently embody each of these approaches to change agency. Further, we must turn our attention within the change management academy away from the change process itself and focus more time and energy on equipping ourselves as change agents.

The Holistic Model for Change Agent Excellence presents contemporary change agents with four distinct yet critically connected platforms from which to drive successful organizational change initiatives. The competencies required for effectively operating in each of the four roles—Business Partner, Servant Leader, Change Champion, and Future Shaper—have been clearly articulated above. Although it may appear overwhelming and perhaps even impossible for any single change agent to effectively fill all four roles, the contemporary change agency landscape demands nothing less. Successful change agents will begin by critically reflecting on their toolkit in relationship to the model, asessing where the gaps exist, and taking concrete measures to eliminate those gaps. Aspiring holistic change agents recognize that change begins with them.

REFERENCES

Block, P. 1993. *Stewardship*. San Francisco: Berrett-Koehler.

Bolton, R. 1986. *People skills: How to assert yourself, listen to others, and resolve conflicts*. New York: Simon and Schuster.

Briner, B. 1996. *The management methods of Jesus*. Nashville, TN: Thomas Nelson.

Conlin, M. 1999. Religion in the workplace. *Business Week*, November 1, pp. 151–156.

De Pree, M. 1992. *Leadership jazz*. New York: Dell Publishing.

Fuller, J., & Farrington, J. 1999. *From training to performance improvement: Navigating the transition*. San Francisco: Jossey-Bass.

Gilley, J.W. 2000. Taming the organization: Lessons in organizational subordination. *Human Resource Development International*, 3(4), 1–17.

Gilley, J.W., Quatro, S.A., Hoekstra, E., et al. 2001. *The manager as change agent.* Cambridge, MA: Perseus Publishing.

Goleman, D. 1998. *Working with emotional intelligence.* New York: Bantam Books.

Greenleaf, R.K. 1970. *The leader as servant.* Indianapolis, IN: The Robert K. Greenleaf Center for Servant Leadership.

Greenleaf, R.K. 1996. *On becoming a servant leader.* San Francisco: Jossey-Bass.

Jick, T. 1993. *Managing change.* Chicago: Richard Irwin.

Kotter, J.P. 1996. *Leading change.* Boston: Harvard Business School Press.

Kotter, J.P., & Heskett, J.L. 1992. *Corporate culture and performance.* New York: Free Press.

McCauley, C.D., Moxley, R.S., & Van Velsor, E. 1998. *Handbook of leadership development [Center for Creative Leadership].* San Francisco: Jossey-Bass.

Mitroff, I.I., & Denton, E.A. 1999. *A spiritual audit of corporate America.* San Francisco: Jossey-Bass.

Pascale, R.T. 1990. *Managing on the edge.* New York: Simon and Schuster.

Robinson, D.G., & Robinson, J.C. 1996. *Performance consulting: Moving beyond training.* San Francisco: Berrett-Koehler.

Rokeach, M. 1973. *The nature of human values.* New York: Free Press.

Senge, P.M. 1990. *The fifth discipline: The art and practice of the learning organization.* New York: Doubleday.

Chapter 5

The Changing Roles and Responsibilities of Change Agents

Ronald R. Sims

INTRODUCTION

Over the last decade we have witnessed an unprecedented change in the business environment and echoing organizational changes in mission, structure, resource allocation, change intervention strategies, and various human interactions. These changes are not restricted to one industry or one country. They affect all stakeholders in all organizations and industries in all parts of the world. Some of these changes can be understood merely as logical development from the environments of the past, while others are changing the very nature of organizations and the interactions of traditional and new stakeholders. For example, organizations have increasingly faced unprecedented challenges to reduce operating costs and invest in new product development and new market opportunities while growing revenues. Global competition is fierce. Speed of execution is paramount. No longer do organizations have the luxury to take their time setting a strategic direction, nor can they afford not to engage all employees in achieving strategic business goals. As a result, organizations are continuously being challenged to reduce cycle times in many aspects of their operations with innovations designed to foster the mantra of "change, change, change," and to produce products "faster, better, and cheaper" than the obvious and not so obvious competitors from next door and thousands of miles away.

Change agents have the responsibility for designing and implementing change efforts to help organizations respond to the demands of the new economy. Today, people in various positions must take on the role of change agent: internal and external consultants including boards of directors, senior leaders, middle-to upper-level managers, supervisors, frontline personnel, human resource personnel, and so on. All of these people and every other member of the organization has the potential to contribute to organizational change, which means that each must take on the role of change agent in order to change the way we manage change in the new economy. All of these individuals must be able to help their organizations recognize environmental changes, respond on the spot (i.e., sometimes by way of reengineering), and respond with products and services that fit the demands of the new economic marketplace.

This new economic environment puts tremendous demands on those who must help organizations change. A number of today's internal and external change agents have developed solid intuitions, tools, and techniques that help build organizational adaptability and flexibility, and they have found ways to support fast-paced change. For the most part, however, I have found that change agents are increasingly struggling with the demands of the new economy as they are forced to rethink previously relied upon change models, tools, and techniques—models, tools, and techniques that were sufficient in slower and simpler times, but that may be counterproductive when complex adaptation is the only viable survival strategy today or tomorrow.

A basic premise underlying the discussion in this chapter is that everyone in today's organizations must become an intentional change agent. This means that they must become more aware of options to help their organizations adapt to today's new environment. Similarly, external change agents must rethink their roles and responsibilities in working with client organizations if they are going to be able to play active roles in collaboratively working with the organization's internal change agents. This collaborative work is more important than ever before given the increasing influence of the Internet, networking, and partnerships in all organizations and as the landscape of organic systems changes continues to change rapidly. Today's change agents must not only stay abreast of various internal and external organizational developments but in most instances they must even leap ahead of them. These change agents must take the time to understand the old and new patterns that impact creativity, productivity, communications, teamwork, leadership, and many other organization activities that have in the past required different explanatory models. The discussion that follows offers some personal insights on what I believe each group of internal and external change agents must do to improve their efforts toward change.

The chapter looks at the change agent roles and the responsibilities of boards of directors, top management, middle managers, other employees, human resources management personnel, customers, and external customers. The chapter then offers a brief look at the importance of self-knowledge for increasing the effectiveness of change agents. The chapter concludes with some discussion on how organizations can build better change agents.

BOARDS OF DIRECTORS AS CHANGE AGENTS

During the last decade, many organizations have rethought the way they have been filling board seats as they attempt to more effectively include them in the direction-setting or decision-making process involved in change. These boards have more narrowly focused agendas, concentrating extensively on strategic planning and reflecting a growing hunger for members to play more active roles in overseeing organizational decisions as they try to respond to the new challenges of doing business. Thus, board success is more closely tied to the organization's success. The challenge is to ensure that today's organizations change using technological advances and shifts in consumerism in a way that captures market position and financial reward. Meeting this challenge requires not only a new leadership approach at other levels of the organization but increasingly at the board level.

To be successful in the new economy an organization's board must increasingly take on a change agent role. Unfortunately, some organization's boards still live in the past, and their thinking often reflects the realities of days gone by, when what is needed is for them to be thinking in terms of 2005, 2010 and 2015. Part of the problem stems from the perception that board members are expected to show up for board meetings, collect their payments and other perks, and be seen but not heard, possibly having some control over expenses, but little or no control over revenues and the future direction of the organization. In these situations, it often appears that the board members are exempt from being involved in determining how to deal with the competitive forces of today's new economy. In a sense, the attitude may be one of "I don't get paid to worry about it. That's what the CEO or president gets paid to do; to see if customers are going to turn right or left, to come to us or go to the competitor."

The challenge for today's organizations is to ensure that they change, and this means that boards must also change. While this does not mean board members must learn the intricate details of day-to-day operations, they should ask the organization's most senior leadership:

- What are we doing to replace lost business or revenue?
- What new businesses do we need to develop?
- Why are we losing customers, and what will we do about that?
- Why is turnover so high, and what are you going to do about it?

When dealing with things such as declining revenues and loss of customers, for example, board members need to make it clear that the better alternative to cutting expenses is to develop strategies that rapidly grow customers and revenues. Board members must find out if the organization is trying to create more value for the organization and its shareholders. They need to put pressure on the organization to discover, for example, what products and services customers want and how the organization can capture that business by developing the appropriate products and services.

As change agents, board members can provide the most value to their organization by also asking senior leadership questions like:

- Is there an aggressive plan to increase sales in the next two quarters?
- How was our performance last quarter compared with projections?
- Are returns as aggressive as stated?
- Is the organization planning to aggressively thwart a new competitor or market force?

In short, board members must be actively involved in pushing for results-oriented growth. More than a one-time shot, growth is an ongoing use of well thought-out, disciplined strategies designed to increase revenue. Boards must work with senior leaders when the best change solution may be meeting the goals of long-term expense reduction plans. Similarly, with change solutions that, for example, require sustained revenue growth, boards must set an expectation for senior leadership to develop a plan with structure and methodology (i.e., a plan with definitive start date, weekly outcomes, and a concrete date for implementation).

"The devil is in the details" should be the credo for regular board tracking and monitoring and should require that *all* top management incentive compensation programs be focused on results, not merely activity. Some questions boards can ask the organization's senior leaders in order to keep on top of change initiatives such as a growth strategy include:

- Which products and services have increased revenues more than 5% during the past year?
- Which have not?
- What steps, if any, are being taken to grow revenues?
- Is there any structure to develop growth strategies for each key product or service line?
- What has changed about our competitors to concern us? How are we responding?
- What competitive advantages do our competitors have and how will we respond?
- Where are our opportunities for growth? How are we capitalizing on those opportunities?

In fulfilling their role as change agents, boards must become the "pied pipers" of culture. One way they can do this is to see that the organization learns from one of the lessons learned by other organizations in the past—that is, you can't rest on your laurels and wait for the competition to go away. Boards have a responsibility to ensure that their organizations:

1. See the future and anticipate the impact it will have on their business;
2. Have the hunger to get business and to deliver products and services better than their competitors; and
3. Proactively offer what customers want and deliver it in the way customers prefer.

In other words, they have to make sure their organizations have the strong, driving, entrepreneurial spirit necessary to continue to succeed in today's new economy.

Board members must model new behaviors like the rest of today's organizations. First and foremost, from the board level down everyone must show energy, passion, and interest in the development and implementation of new ways of responding to the environment. Boards can also change their culture by offering positive feedback, promotions, and financial compensation based on how well organizational leaders identify opportunities to change, grow and capitalize on innovation, and so forth. To do this, a board must openly acknowledge and address those situations where the organization is not acting much differently from the "thundering herd" when it comes to dealing with meeting the challenges and the demands of a changing economy. They cannot idly sit by and watch the organization's senior leaders spending a lot of their time putting out fires. They must insist that the organization's senior leaders spend time planning how to move the organization forward rather than just minding the store. A board also has a responsibility to make sure that senior leaders realize that the world is not as fixed as it used to be and that the organization must be more fluid to fit in.

So how can a board more effectively fulfill its role as a change agent? They can start by making sure the top management team is looking ahead and not merely putting out fires. Some questions that can help them in this effort are as follows:

- Has the organization's market share eroded because competitors are providing products and services never offered before?
- Has the competition intensified over the past two years?
- Have more resource-rich competitors entered the market?

If the answers are "yes" to these questions, the board may need to think about how to create an environment where people are not afraid to take risks and make mistakes. Today's board members have a responsibility to use their positions and experience to lead organizations out of the comfort zone and into the future of change and more change.

TOP MANAGEMENT AS CHANGE AGENTS

An organization's most senior leaders continue to be key players in any organizational changes. They have traditionally been the sponsors of change and have had the primary responsibility for identifying and championing the new vision that must accompany substantive change in an organization. They have also been expected to assume the responsibility for building an environment in which employees at all levels are free to improve operations, innovate, and make changes. They have also had to relate practical plans for change to strategic plans and organizational problems and issues. But have organizational leaders done enough? Or in reality are they "falling short in their efforts to lead change successfully" (Anderson & Anderson, 2001)?

Many of today's successful organizational leaders recognize that their organizations must be nimble to make it in the new Internet-speed economy. This means they must create change communities within their organizations that are open to new demands and situations and ways of managing change. These organizational leaders are keenly aware of how overwhelming advances in technology, new business practices, and the dizzying rate of mergers and acquisitions can be. They have recognized that the trick isn't just being able to handle (or lead) the necessary organizational changes by themselves. They have religiously tried to make sure that everyone else in the organization is not just brought along for the ride but actively involved in redesigning the ride. This means that they recognize the importance of maximizing employee involvement at every opportunity.

In order to change the way we manage change, organizational leaders must continue to take on more, and more *selective*, responsibility for leading an organization's change initiatives. This still means that they must get in front of change and lead it or be prepared to accept the reality that the new economy will ensure that they'll be a victim of it. They must still take an active role in convincing others of the need for change, setting goals that are achievable, and laying out paths to those goals. But they must also be increasingly open (willing to listen) to the voices of others who are trying to convince them of the need for change, to clarify and set achievable goals, and lay out paths to those goals.

As we think about contributing to the dialogue about changing the way we manage change we must avoid the tendency to "throw the baby out with the bath water." Successful organizational change efforts still need to have strong leadership from the top. Attainable and measurable change goals must still need to be agreed upon by all the key stakeholders. A change blueprint still needs to be agreed upon and organizational members still need to be empowered, which means that among other things multiple change sponsors, agents, and implementers need to be identified, developed, trained, and coordinated to increase the likelihood of successful change.

Given the increased demand for change in the new economy, the need for communication with employees has never been more critical. Senior leaders need to communicate more, and more effectively, to ensure that all employees are regularly communicating with one another and have all the information they need to be proactive rather than reactive. Being proactive rather than reactive means that the senior leaders must help to create an organizational culture in which employees don't sense danger in making changes and automatically build resistance to it. Instead employees must view change as a nonthreatening part of the way the organization does business.

To reinforce such an environment senior leaders must keep communications consistent or they risk derailing the organization's change efforts. Senior leaders (and others) must increasingly use intranets, web sites, e-mail messages, newsletters, and in-person meetings to spread the word about what is or might be happening within and outside the organization. They need to explain why and how from their vantage point as well as from the vantage point of employees, who should all view themselves as change advocates and agents for the organization. While there may always be ingrained resistance to change from top to bottom in an organization, today's leaders must do everything they can to make sure employees develop a new perception when it comes to change. Keeping the message consistent is a good starting place.

Senior leaders must also make sure that they have a personal radar system in place that "captures" what employees are thinking. As in the knowledge management movement where organizations have increasingly recognized the importance of capturing the knowledge within their employees to gain a competitive advantage, having an understanding of what employees think is critical to changing the way we manage change. Senior leaders need to know how and what their employees think because in many instances it is employees' thinking that has to change if we really expect to see behavioral change. Senior leaders must be good listeners and model good listening skills if they want other employees who are helping to lead and manage change to do more than simply resist change.

An organization of good listeners may sound rather simplistic, but being a good listener in today's frenetic marketplace is an important skill because in these times of change all employees must be prepared to express their misgivings about how the process is affecting them and their ability to do their jobs. And just as important, they must hear what senior leaders and others may have to say. In a sense there must be an *open door policy* throughout the organization so that all employees feel they can go to someone else and have someone listen to them.

The information that can be captured in an environment where employees are listening to one another's concerns helps every change effort and ensures success. Ambiguity, which is traditionally inherent in change efforts, can be proactively countered and employee creativity can be freed, resulting in the contribution of valuable insights and fresh ideas to support the change efforts. The ability of an organization's most senior leaders to listen sets the tone for other members of the organization to do likewise, thus allowing the organization to identify and address problems that could derail the fast-paced change that is needed to meet the demands of the new economy.

Changing the way we manage change also means that senior leaders must always be "tellers of truth." Being tellers of truth simply means that senior leaders must be honest. And being honest means not being afraid to admit that they don't always have the answers to questions. This honesty is important at all times, but I think it is even more important today as organizations recognize that there are a lot of unknowns in the business environment. And heading into the unknown is risky. Understandably, we all have times when we may balk or resist because of the unknown. We all want answers to questions that senior leaders may not have yet. But it compounds the situation when senior leaders dismiss our questions or offer guesses about what will occur. Senior leaders must learn that it is all right to tell their employees that they don't know! Again, simply being honest is important to changing the way we manage change.

Finally, in changing the way we manage change, senior leaders have a responsibility to help create a new organizational culture that accepts change as a permanent part of the new landscape, a landscape that is viewed as a change community made up of employees who fully accept the idea of continuous change and see the proactive promotion of change as part of their day-to-day work and responsibility.

MIDDLE MANAGERS AS CHANGE AGENTS

Middle managers (including frontline supervisors) have always been the planners, implementers, and facilitators of change. They have been expected to prepare employees for change, overcome their fears of new systems and processes, and develop in them total commitment to the new way of doing things. They have also had to develop a comprehensive implementation plan for the change. Additionally, they have had to clarify plans, integrate new processes and practices into operations, encourage employees to accept ownership of the change, and provide feedback to their people, the inventors of the change, and top management. And finally they have been expected to develop teamwork within their organizational elements.

Middle managers acting as change agents have been heralds of the daunting tasks of creating, implementing, sustaining, and evaluating change efforts. But initiating and sustaining change today is more daunting than ever before and now making change happen requires middle managers to change the way they think about and manage change and their organizations.

This can be viewed as another step in the ever-evolving role that middle managers have had to play over the years. For example, as recently noted by Tetenbaum (1998), in the industrial era work was usually performed in factories where workers engaged in assembly-line work. Workers engaged in routine tasks and were under close supervision. Management believed that "a good worker was one who was reliable and passive, capable of modest manual dexterity" (p. 26). The organization and its workers were viewed as a machine-like entity. The goal was to predict and control; it was top-down, command and control leadership. "It's all about control: A good machine is one that its operators can control—in the service of the owners' objectives" (Webber, 1999, p. 178). This machine view easily fit the traditional or conventional organization. "You have a broken company, and you need to change it, to fix it. You hire a mechanic, who trades out old parts that are broken and brings in new parts that are going to fix the machine" (ibid.). What was "good" for the industrial era or even the late-twentieth-century era no longer fits the workplace of the new economy. Middle managers must now help their organizations find ways to adapt to new technologies that speed up what and when events occur, to globalization that has created fierce competition, and to continuing change that contributes to the ever-increasing complexity and paradox of "business as usual."

In the new economy work is being conducted at many different locations at all times of the day or night. Information era workers perform their tasks largely without supervision in collaborative efforts as members of self-managed teams. "The prized worker is one who learns quickly and continuously, who works collaboratively, and who is comfortable in an environment of experimentation and risk" (Tetenbaum, 1998, p. 26). Increasingly, middle managers have had to learn to accept and work with employees who operate in an organic "system" made up of interdependent parts that need to be nurtured and grown (Trahant, Burke, & Koonce, 1997).

If organizations want to sustain organizational change in the new economy, they must develop teams of change agents with "everyday" jobs who can act as constructive viruses and "infect" their companies. Successful organizational change and learning in the new economy will not automatically be rolled out from the top. Every change process that succeeds in the new economy must be sustained and spread with the active involvement of middle managers, who are key to getting the support and maximum involvement of all the other employees. Middle managers are key to building networks and carrying change to all employees who are critical to creating the organization's change community.

Today, the middle manager's people skills are more important than ever before. I believe Tetenbaum (1998) recently stated it well when she asserted that twenty-first-century managers must manage transition, build resilience, and create and maintain a learning organization. Thus, one of the most important roles of the new economy manager is to lead employees through the processes people go through to come to terms with change and new situations. We have known for years that it isn't an easy transition for people to move from being told what, when, and where to do things to being in charge of problem solving, making decisions, experimenting, and continuing to learn new skills and behaviors. Middle managers need to make sure people understand what changes are occurring by consistently communicating and reinforcing the attitudinal and behavioral changes that are necessary for sustained organizational change and success.

Just as important as the middle manager's role in managing the transition is his or her role in helping employees increase their resilience, their capacity to "bounce back," no matter the type or extent of the changes. Reaction to change is largely a function of perception and middle managers have a responsibility to help build resilience by helping today's employees adjust their expectations. Middle managers can do this by ensuring that employees have the skills they need so that they feel they are equipped to handle the challenges presented in the new economy.

Middle managers must also prepare themselves to cope with today's accelerating rate of change. This partly means that they must not only be flexible and adaptive in a changing environment but also be able to better diagnose problems and implement needed change initiatives. And they must do all of this in an environment in which there are fewer and fewer employees, increased expectations to do more with less, and constantly changing expectations of them in fulfilling their everyday responsibilities.

So what must middle managers do in their role as change agents? They must help the organization create an environment that elicits, supports, and nurtures creativity and change. This will undoubtedly mean that the status quo is deliberately upset. Thus their role is to create an environment in which everyone is involved in continuous learning and change.

NONMANAGEMENT EMPLOYEES AS CHANGE AGENTS

For today's employees, managing change involves the ability to recognize trends and to have the flexibility to adapt to them. Today's employees need to keep informed about business, social, cultural, and political trends. They also need to understand the implications of these trends for their organizations, and they need to become more skilled at identifying the need for change. The management of change is a highly complex skill that cannot be taught in one training session. Fundamentally, today's employees need to become change agents and learn to roll with the punches.

As organizations refine their strategic management techniques, employees must recognize that the responsibilities are being delegated further down the organizational hierarchy. Thus, each employee must be a strategic manager. Each employee needs to be responsible for continually scanning the internal and external environment and conducting a strengths, weaknesses, opportunities, and threats (SWOT) analysis. Opportunity identification and problem identification are also increasingly employees' responsibilities in their role as change agents.

Although senior leaders have traditionally been seen as the first to notice changes in the environment and then signal the organization to make the necessary changes in strategic directions, in the new economy, those closest to the frontline are now recognized as having key vantage points for seeing changes in the environment and then signaling the organization to make the necessary changes. To be effective change agents these employees must understand the strategic management process from beginning to end. Employees must be open to learning about the strategic (and change) management process and be willing to do their part to increase the partnership between themselves and others at all levels of the organization.

Probably one of the most important things employees can do to fulfill their change agent responsibilities is to better manage their own careers. Managing one's career means actively guiding one's career through taking advantage of training, education, and new learning opportunities. Active career management also involves thinking creatively about one's career in such a way as to be employable by many organizations. Thus, there is the need for self-directed learning and change as discussed in Chapter 2.

Employees must take responsibility for maintaining their capabilities, capacities, and attractiveness given the reality of the new economy and especially the "new" contract between employees and organizations, which clearly shifts the responsibility for career development squarely to the shoulders of the employee. He or she must take the initiative to acquire new skills and capabilities in order to be able to add more value to the enterprise or risk losing continued employment and opportunity. Employees must also push their organizations to understand that they must make these learning, capability-expanding opportunities available or risk losing the value and capability of the employee during these times of change when they may need them the most.

One key aspect of career management is having well-established relationships with people inside and outside your organization. Managing relationships involves the ability to guide and control personal and work relationships effectively. Today's employees must not only be able to manage their relationships with fellow team members and managers, they are also increasingly in constant interaction with their external customers, suppliers, and many other outsiders and as a result must be able to manage more and more external relationships, which often cross all kinds of cultural and geographic boundaries. Employees must also increasingly be able to successfully take active roles in their communities—for example, through charitable organizations—and many are also expected to keep abreast of political developments at home or abroad that may affect their organizations.

In their role as change agents, employees need to recognize and help their organizations respond not only to business developments but also to political developments in the communities in which they work. What will be the short- and long-term impact of political moves on their organization, no matter where it is located? Savvy employees need to think ahead and be able to predict the impact of political events on their business. Maintaining a network of acquaintances across the globe to keep abreast of world events allows employees to become more valuable to their organization.

The active management of relationships requires the continuous development of interpersonal skills required to manage internal and external relationships with others involved in various organizational change initiatives. With a strong focus on cultural and global issues in the new economy, the management of relationships by employees is even more complicated. It is hard enough to manage relationships when people share your values and beliefs. The process becomes considerably more complex when people come from different countries and hold different views of the world and of what is appropriate and what is not.

The functions, roles, and skills of employees are clearly changing. Constant changes, new organizations, the increased call for every employee to be a change agent, rapid technological advances, and the global economy all require constant retraining and education. As all employees are asked increasingly to work with others across the world (i.e., co-workers, suppliers, and customers), handle increasing amounts of information and complicated information systems, do more with less, and be fully competent to provide input for their companies' strategic and change planning, they are under increasing pressure to be versatile and to have numerous skills and considerable knowledge about many very different aspects of business—aspects that have serious implications for organizations that fail to create a change community and maximize employee involvement.

So what must employees do to fulfill their role as change agents? They must recognize that change is the order of the day. As organizations continue to diagnose and respond to the need for change, they need employees who can and will change. Thus, employees must embrace change and even create it if they are to be valued members of the organization. Employees cannot cling to old beliefs and ways of doing things. Employees must look for ways to change both themselves and the organization. In short, to fulfill their roles and responsibilities as change agents they need to be able to roll with the punches and critically assess and manage change.

HUMAN RESOURCES MANAGEMENT PERSONNEL AS CHANGE AGENTS

Extensive technological, social, political, and economic changes that affect what organizations do as well as their employees' expectations have helped increase our recognition that human resources management (HRM) and other procedures used in the past to handle the human side of business are no longer effective. The net result is a tremendous challenge for HRM personnel to rethink their roles and responsibilities in helping their organizations survive and thrive in the new economy. HRM personnel have seen a dramatic increase in their change agent responsibilities with the development of a strategic human resources management (SHRM) perspective within organizations.

One prominent figure in the development of the SHRM perspective argues that changes like those we are seeing in the new economy present a number of competitive challenges that are quite different from those faced by organizations in the past (Ulrich, 1997). All of the challenges place additional pressure on organizations to be innovative and create new ways of doing business with new technologies, new products, and new services to meet an increasingly diverse and demanding group of employees and customers. The enhanced value of innovation in determining competitive advantage requires organizations to attract, train and develop, and retain employees of the highest quality. Over time and throughout rapidly changing circumstances, organizations must be able to sustain the competitive advantage that the knowledge and skills of these employees provide. In the past, competitive advantage could be gained through finding better, cheaper access to financial capital, marketing a new product, or inventing some new technological gizmos. While cheap and ready access to capital, high quality products, and new technology remain important components of any organization's competitive advantage, today's new business environment requires a greater focus on the human resources element in business. Out of this realization has come SHRM and the increased change agent role of HRM personnel.

As change agents in the new economy, today's HRM personnel must increasingly share responsibility with senior executives, managers, and other employees for creating and maintaining a climate in which change can be accepted rather than resisted. In their own area of responsibility, and with respect for the HRM function in other elements of the organization, they are responsible for introducing and evaluating change; they must actively participate in developing plans for making change happen. In addition, HRM personnel have another significant responsibility: they must help other members of the organization effect changes of their own. They can best do this through formulating and implementing HRM strategies (i.e., specific HRM courses of action the organization uses to achieve its aims) at three key organizational levels—corporate, competitive, and functional—that are designed to achieve desirable end results, such as high-quality products and services and socially responsible behavior. In other words, sound strategies are intended to result in growth, profits, and survival.

To successfully fulfill their change agent roles HRM personnel must plan HRM activities that expand awareness of possibilities, identify strengths and weaknesses, reveal opportunities, and point to the need to evaluate the probable impact of internal and external forces. Helping their host organizations develop well-designed organizational strategic plans permits HRM personnel to develop HRM plans and be better prepared to cope with changes in both the internal and external environments.

It is quite evident that today's organizations require more than a traditional personnel model of HRM activities. The traditional model simply involved putting out small fires, ensuring that people were paid on the right day, making sure the job advertisement met the newspaper deadline, finding a suitable supervisor for the night shift, and making certain a manager remembers to observe due process before sacking a new employee who didn't work out. As a result of the new change agent and strategic view of HRM in organizations, today's HRM personnel play a significant role in helping their organizations change, reaching strategic objectives, and interacting fully with other functional areas within the organization. For example, HRM personnel must help select employees who are able to innovate, train them to provide top-class customer service, and measure and reward entrepreneurial behavior.

HRM personnel must help other members of the organization (especially middle managers and senior leaders) learn as much as possible about HRM best practices and then design a practice that's consistent with what their organization wants to achieve. The reality is that today's organizational success is increasingly dependent upon flexibility in HRM practices (such as the organization's reward system) and the ability of HRM personnel to change as competitive conditions pressure their organizations to continually change their strategy and ways of doing business.

In today's new economy it is important to recognize that the viability (and strategic future) of the role of HRM personnel in organizations means that HRM needs to focus more and more of their efforts on activities that clearly add value to the organization's success or bottom line—activities such as strategic planning, change management, corporate culture transitions, and developing human capital. Ulrich (1998) has noted that HRM can help deliver organizational excellence in four main ways. First, if strategy implementation requires, say, a team-based organizational structure, HRM would be responsible for bringing state-of-the-art approaches for creating this structure to senior management's attention. Second, HRM should become an expert in the way work is organized and executed, delivering administrative efficiency to ensure that costs are reduced while quality is maintained. Third, with employee behavior increasingly becoming the key to competitive advantage, HRM should become a champion for employees, vigorously representing their concerns to senior management and at the same time working to increase employees' commitment to the organization and their ability to deliver results. Fourth, HRM needs to ensure the organization has the capacity to embrace and capitalize on change, for instance by making sure that "broad vision statements get transformed into specific behaviors" (Ulrich, 1998). As the tasks they face grow more complex, HRM personnel have an important change agent role to play in their organizations.

CUSTOMERS AS CHANGE AGENTS

In today's new economy, an organization's ability to win, maintain, and look after customers is fundamentally a precarious business. Customers are increasingly fickle. Why should they bother being your customer unless you have a tremendously good proposition to offer them? Nor can today's organizations assume that just because they have been brilliant at meeting customer needs in the past, they will automatically continue to do so in the future. Sometimes, of course, an organization puts a change into effect that is actually harmful to its market share. For example, years ago Coca-Cola changed its formula and launched "New Coke." Once the public had expressed its distaste (literally) for the new beverage, Coca-Cola "reintroduced" its original drink and even gave it the name "Classic." No one has seen or tasted "New Coke" in years.

The mistake Coca-Cola made was a classic example of how *not* to manage change. Change, whether in the past, or (especially) in the new economy, must not derive from the personal whim of a company chairman or from someone on the board having read something in a favorite magazine and brooded on it until Monday morning, nor even from the organization responding to what is clearly a mere passing fad. Change in today's new economy must come from one thing only: customer needs. Today's customers are all too aware of their power and their importance to organizations that try to sell them products and services.

This feeling of power expresses itself in many ways. For one thing, more than ever before, customers want a better deal and will take their business elsewhere to get it. This is why so many organizations strive to offer new products and services even when they already have many successful ones out in the marketplace. This is why today's organizations increasingly try to add enhancements to already popular products and services even if the underlying product or service remains fundamentally unchanged. A popular brand of car, for example, might be sold with a better engine or a wider choice of custom features. A popular shampoo might be offered at the same price with 10% extra shampoo in the bottle. True, there will always be some situations in which customers are famously conservative. Well-established and well-loved drink and food brands, for example, are notoriously dangerous areas: people get used to a particular taste, like it, and feel betrayed if it changes. But this is very much an exception. There are few other areas where customers are innately conservative.

Faced with fickle customers, who are able to exercise their power to obtain products and services from a wider range of delivery channels (the Web being an increasingly important example), as well as from rival sources, today's organizations must confront the reality that customers can demand change, and organizations must constantly find ways to energize customers. Perhaps the most obvious way in which customers are serving as change agents for organizations is in speed to market. Successfully responding to pressures from customers to change in this area is not so much about being first off the base (the number of dot com start-up failures, for example, shows that rushing in can be lethal) but about getting the right balance of information. Today's customers require organizations to be prepared to go into areas that don't have absolute answers and to be ready to confront the unknown. Waiting for 100% certainty may slow down the initiative to the extent that it risks ceasing to offer a significant competitive advantage. It's all a question of balance: balancing the need to respond to the changing needs of customers with the need for some caution and enough knowledge of what the organization is doing to be reasonably confident of making the necessary changes important to organizational success.

Inevitably, responding to the changes driven by the needs of customers involves changing many aspects of how today's organizations work, think, and behave. Ultimately, too, as has historically been the case, new customer demands and needs require changes in the behaviors of employees in organizations. Change and reorientation around new organizational goals means that organizations must be able to manage the movement toward a new status quo. The status quo moves away from focusing on customer satisfaction to focusing on customer enthusiasm. Customer enthusiasm means excitement and loyalty on the part of customers, fueled by service and products that exceed expectations (Chowdhury, 2000). The way to survive and thrive in the new economy is not just to find customers but to keep them. As suggested thus far in our discussion the means of creating and keeping customers must change every day. Customers will continue to force today's organizations to improve their interactions with them. They will demand more and more attention as they continue to exercise their power to put pressure on organizations and their employees.

Clearly customers are smarter than they used to be, partly thanks to the revolution in information technology. They do not care about management structures, strategic planning, the financial perspectives, problems an organization is having with its employees, or the leaders of the organization. What they do care about are products and services available to them. Customers value quick and easy access to products, and they demand a lot of information before making a decision on whether to buy.

In the end, as change agents, customers will expect organizations to inspire employees to meet their ever-changing needs and retain an organizational focus on the overall objective of managing change to keeps customers' needs at the forefront of any decisions to change. One way that some organizations have started to respond to customers is through customer appraisals. These organizations believe it is important to obtain performance input from this critical source. These organizations use this approach because it demonstrates a commitment to the customer, holds employees accountable, fosters change, and identifies more specific goals for the organization's employees. Customer-related goals for senior leaders generally are of a broad, strategic nature, while targets for lower-level employees tend to be more specific. For example, an objective might be to improve the rating for accurate delivery or reduce the number of dissatisfied customers by half. Ultimately, the objective must be to sustain the organization's reputation for superior, understated customer service, replete with stories of employees who go out of their way for customers.

There should be no doubt that the change agent role of customers will continue to grow. Smart organizations will do everything possible to enhance customer monitoring and input to influence product-related decisions. They will do everything they can to define customer expectations and design operations to meet those expectations. Customers will continue to force organizations to value this orientation as the primary path to repeat business. And those who don't value such an orientation (i.e., that the customer is the boss) face decreased customer satisfaction, profitability, return on sales, and return on equity.

EXTERNAL CHANGE AGENTS (CONSULTANTS)

Managing change, especially in the private sector, is big business, and hiring external change agents to assist in efforts to change is a major factor in this ever-growing business. As a result, external change agents must rethink their roles, changing the ways they help organizations manage change in the new economy.

Perhaps one of the most important things external change agents need to be able to do today is help client organizations transform themselves when necessary to meet the demands of the new economy. This means that consultants need to help organizations institutionalize ways to nurture a culture characterized by far greater individual and organizational entrepreneurship. Given the long-standing traditions and methods of some organizations (or the lack thereof in others), however, there is no doubt that this could prove to be a painful process unless mitigated by a well-conceived, well-executed change plan that delivers sequential and cumulative benefits within reasonable time frames—time frames that are expected to be shorter and shorter by client organizations.

It is evident that because of the large size of many of today's organizations, one cannot expect to turn them around on a dime. However, the use of outside resources often brings the fresh perspective needed to create and manage a transformation process. Indeed, as organizations turn to external change agents who have helped other organizations and industries better serve customers and better position themselves to meet new challenges, they may experience fewer mistakes, a smoother and speedier transition, and better overall investment value.

How can external change agents help client organizations bring about cultural change that stimulates entrepreneurship? First they have to recognize what this new culture is—and what it is not. For example, it is not only about working with client organizations to cut costs. Rather, it is increasingly about helping them to develop the confidence to make tough choices about where to commit resources and where to cut back and then having the courage to see plans through to fruition. It is also often about trying to help client organizations make the needed investments to change their culture to one that is characterized by a spirit of entrepreneurship. Or it may involve using technology to automate and integrate processes and information. It's also about helping clients find innovative ways to increase customer satisfaction and loyalty through, for example:

- Improving response times
- Enhancing operational methods
- Improving service to customers through integrating information and processes to create a single, consolidated view of the customer

So what do external change agents need to do to in their consultancy role to help organizations move from their current modus operandi to one that can succeed in the new economy? They need to help client organizations understand the gap between the new marketplace with its new needs and expectations and the organizations' current products, services, processes, and policies. Once that is understood, the next step is to help them clarify and direct carefully managed resources to close the gap by implementing new policies, products, services, and processes. Rather than a zealous but uncoordinated change campaign, a change climate that encourages coordination and exploitation must be fostered. Success in these steps still depends on good diagnosis, development, implementation, and evaluation of a change plan.

Many organizations have been confronted with technology, information, and change gaps in the new economy that have limited their ability to consolidate employee views and get a consolidated view of their customers. A silo mentality often exists without a lot of cross-team, cross-functional, or cross-divisional communication and cooperation. The result is a fragmented view of employees, customers, and the new marketplace.

In some cases, cross-functional and cross-divisional communication and co-operation are the mantras of the day, but little behavioral change is actually occurring. Employees and management alike are still highly focused on their part of the organization and what they must do to succeed. In short, today's organizations have been thrown into a fiercely competitive environment, in some cases without adequate planning, preparation, or tools to navigate. I believe that there are a number of immediate critical success factors that external change agents must help organizations focus on if the organizations are to survive and thrive in the new economy.

First, not only must external change agents increase their own facilitative skills, but they must also help increase the facilitative skills of their client organization's employees. The reality of today's highly complex and rapidly changing environment is that there are few, if any, individuals who have the required information to act without consulting co-workers, other stakeholders, or experts. It has been my experience that a more facilitative style will help organizations succeed in the highly competitive marketplace. This requires increased education and training of leaders, managers, and other employees so that they can act as coaches, helping others in the organization develop an understanding of how factors may influence and create opportunities or risks for the organization. External change agents must work with senior leaders and others to articulate an organizational vision that motivates employees and serves as a guiding light to direct the organization's future decision making.

External change agents need to work with clients to identify, communicate, and challenge their assumptions and mental models and create an organizational culture that encourages all employees to do the same. Helping clients develop the process of unlearning may be one of the most important roles that consultants can assume, since the existing organizational culture may need to give way to the realities of the new economy, which requires that input from every part of the organization is encouraged and valued. External change agents must help clients develop perspectives, ideas, and alternative approaches that are in keeping with the demands of the new economy.

Second, they must work with clients to develop new processes and plans that become the filters for aligning everything that happens in the organization. For example, many have already embraced what is commonly referred to as a market-driven strategy, where the basic premise guiding the strategy formulation and decision making is based on a clear understanding of the market and most important, of the customers and competitors that make up the market. In effect, the strategy must tell an organization who its customers are, what they need, and how they want it delivered. To be an active and welcomed member of the strategic planning process, external change agents must develop a better understanding (and some even say expertise) of business performance, environmental assessment, and customer opportunities that are harvested from disciplined research. Additionally, to be welcomed into senior management business planning initiatives, external change agents must be able to help these leaders and other members of the organization in their efforts to carefully integrate business and marketing planning to ensure alignment of objectives with marketplace realities and opportunities.

I believe there is merit in the criticism that many consultants have overly relied on humanistic approaches to working with clients and lack a "systems" approach to change or a bottom-line understanding of the reality of business. Whether we believe this to be the case or not we must remember that perception may be reality for many of critics. An external change agent's value as a member at the senior leadership table, or any other table in the organization, means, for example, that the change agent must be able to help business units develop their own business reviews and roll them up into an organizationwide view of the business, the risks, and the opportunities. This may also mean that consultants need to be able to assist organizations in developing repeatable processes that are effective and efficient. These processes must increase the organization's speed and ability to plan and manage the business. They must provide end-to-end solutions that begin with the analysis and formulation processes and then support implementation, management tracking, and control measurements.

Many of today's organizations need the assistance of external change agents to help them take a more fact-based approach to decision making and problem solving. This means that consultants must understand that while there may be opportunities to help client organizations refine this with some intuition and tacit knowledge, these decisions ideally need to be driven by accurate, consistent, and current information that is crucial for organizational success in the new economy.

Third, external change agents must be better able to help today's organizations improve their ability to understand the metrics required for measuring customer value as well as for establishing accountability for increasing customer value, both of which are critical for success. This means, for example, that they must be able to work collaboratively with clients to assess customer or segment value measured in total contributions as opposed to a fragmented view based on a silo approach. In other words, consultants must help client organizations develop sound measurement strategies that can be predicated on a balanced scorecard approach (in order to develop the measurements from a customer and competitive standpoint). As noted in Chapter 11, the balanced scorecard approach is a sound methodology that captures the key measurement elements of an organization's strategy and ties these measurements to the strategic progress.

Fourth, working with clients to improve the gathering and understanding of internal and external market research data is another area in which external change agents can demonstrate their value to clients. Solid internal and market research that delivers rich, quantifiable results is required to ensure a thorough understanding of employees, customers, and opportunities. Given their expertise and background in developing surveys and other data collection tools, consultants have an excellent foundation to provide assistance to their clients in this area.

More and more organizations must find ways to better understand employees and customers, and external change agents should be able to help client organizations achieve this objective. Because of this organizational need, it is important for consultants to be able to help clients validate the feelings and beliefs expressed by employees and customers. Are these feelings and beliefs generally held by a target group of employees or customers who may participate in a focus group, or are they unique to the focus group participants? To answer that question, many consultants may need to advise clients to use broader quantitative surveys as research tools that can be statistically analyzed to provide an in-depth understanding of employees and customers.

In working with client organizations to conduct internal and external market research, consultants must continue to use multiple methods to acquire information and insights and avoid relying on a single method that may inappropriately skew results. Ensuring statistical validity before taking action on high-risk decisions will put them in a position to help their clients significantly decrease the cost and impact of misreading internal and external markets.

I believe it is necessary for external change agents to become better at helping client organizations use market research to develop employee and customer relationship management (ECRM) strategies. They must therefore help clients see the value of developing an ECRM mind-set. An ECRM mind-set is invaluable for today's organizations as they wrestle with changing employee and customer expectations compounded by the new economy. By working with client organizations to develop an ECRM strategy, consultants in effect help to encourage organizations to regularly gather, analyze, and disseminate information about employees that is important to meeting customers' needs.

It also encourages common "touchpoint" environments so that if, for example, a current customer contacts any department within an organization for any reason, the relevant employees have access to the customer's pertinent data or profile, history, previous correspondence (telephone or e-mails), and so forth. An obvious advantage to this is that customer interactions across the organization can be made more sensitive and responsive.

A critical factor for success in working with client organizations in the new economy is to help them undertake significant organizational change that balances what is being changed with how it is being changed. Working collaboratively with clients in coordinated changes ensures that individual pieces do not conflict with, or detract from, the overall quality of change in a process or product. This means that at times the change must be done in a sequential and supportive manner so that it is not out of sync with the rest of the operation.

In addition, external change agents must work with client organizations to help them recognize that becoming customer-centric is a dramatic cultural shift for any organization that may have a history of being run from a product or silo perspective. Therefore, consultants must assist organizations in staying the course when the goal is to have a very rigorous culture change management program in place. This could include, but may not be limited to, initiatives in areas such as communications, education, training, skills, and responsibilities.

External change agents must also help organizations recognize that becoming customer-centric is a journey that generally takes longer than a single year, but they may not have a year to make the transition given the challenges and demands of the new economy. To help an organization change its orientation and to assure an appropriate return requires open and facilitated dialogue in which consultants can play an important role. To ensure success of client's change initiatives consultants must seek observable employee buy-in and support, consistency in messages delivered over time, and leadership that portrays the new culture.

External change agents will also need to help client organizations develop and build bulletproof business cases for change through proper understanding of the business case and its meaning. For example, it may be very difficult to justify ECRM with a short-term view. ECRM is a cultural process and a change that process has major implications for how people do their jobs over the long-term. Since it is long-term, a good business case will identify the organizational development that must take place to support the effort, create appropriate expectations, show an identifiable return, and help defend it over time. It is important for consultants to avoid a common mistake in a business case of portraying technology as the solution when in fact technology is merely an enabler to support organizational change. And, as we know, organizational change takes time.

Doing a better job of building the business case for change can also help overcome potential resistance to change as the hopes, fears, and dreams of those affected by the change are identified. Conducting present state analyses through focus group meetings, for example, helps client organizations get a clear indication of what is going on in the organization and what employees think about a variety of issues important to building a bulletproof business case.

External change agents have an obligation to help clients avoid the tendency to look in the rearview mirror rather than looking ahead. A captain of a ship may continually alter course to adjust for various weather or current conditions but must always look far enough ahead to land at the right destination. Similarly, consultants must work with client organizations to continually scan far enough ahead to ensure that short-term tactics (which deliver more immediate benefits) flow through to support a long-term strategy. Any short-term initiatives must ultimately support the long-term strategy to avoid mixed messages and creating a "flavor of the month" approach.

Although there is a dramatic need for change in the new economy, transformation, or any other type of change, will only be supported if identifiable business benefits are shown. An immediate primary benefit is that transformation can often result in an organization's becoming more strategically focused and concentrating its resources where they will do the most good. The organization focuses on its strengths and core competencies and sees the inherent value of potentially outsourcing other functions that lie beyond its core competencies. Other benefits include: (1) increased return on investment for shareholders and employees, (2) improved competitive positioning in the market, (3) enhanced customer satisfaction, and (4) ability to retain and expand skills through satisfied, involved employees. External change agents must do their part by asking themselves how they can help to better articulate these and other benefits of change, whether it is incremental or transformational.

The new economy has created exciting new opportunities for organizations, employees, and other stakeholders. These opportunities include expanded markets, increased self-awareness, increased access to capital, and the ability to create greater value for shareholders and employees. Along with the exciting new opportunities posed by the new economy, there will increasingly be a significant need for external change agents to help their client organizations develop new leadership styles, processes, philosophies, approaches, and actions and a cadre of internal change agents.

Clearly, there is a role for external change agents to play in helping organizations change the way they manage change. However, these consultants must first be willing to recognize the importance of being able to demonstrate to clients that they understand their business and the challenges the new economy presents for them. This means they must be able to speak the language of business and do so fluently. They must also be willing to rethink the models they have relied on for years. And in those instances where the theories and models and favorite interventions cannot be shown to really make a contribution to the success of change initiatives, then they must abandon them. Finally, they must remember that despite the need to become more proficient in the language of their clients and the dynamics of the new environment, they must still be facilitators of change who never forget how important people are to any change.

In the end, external change agents need to be able to help client organizations inspire what may be a handful, hundreds, or thousands of internal and external people while retaining the organization's focus on the overall objectives. They also need to understand that they must be better prepared to work with all managers and level leaders to help them realize that the short-term results being achieved in a particular part of the organization may be less relevant to the overall objective than the head of the department or higher leaders might believe. For the experienced external change agent this may not sound extremely complex and difficult, however, its complexity and difficulty are compounded by the challenges and demands placed on today's organizations. Change management is becoming more and more demanding, which means that external change agents must recognize that they cannot avoid questioning and changing where appropriate the interventions and models they rely on when working with clients. In short, they must take the lead in looking for ways to change the way they manage change. They cannot bury their heads in the sand and pretend that they will be able to continue to fulfill clients needs without seriously rethinking what works, what doesn't work, and how to better measure their contribution to organizational success.

KNOW THYSELF

Before bringing this chapter to a conclusion, I think it is important to spend some time focusing on the importance of self-knowledge in increasing one's effectiveness as a change agent. The last section of this chapter provides some insights on how organizations can build better change agents.

In my view, self-knowledge is a minimum requirement for being an effective change agent. Good change agents recognize their shortcomings and continue to seek feedback, love to learn, and are always open to learning new ideas, regardless of the source. As a result they continue to change, improve, build their skills, and become more effective. The best change agents are open both to their gifts and to their underdeveloped qualities. The worst change agents don't have an accurate picture of themselves. For example, they may see themselves as great with people when they're not at all. The worst change agents may be technically brilliant or business smart but they are also rigid, close-minded, and not open to feedback. Because they don't recognize their shortcomings, they see no need for improvement. As a result, they aren't committed to ongoing or continuous change and learning necessary to match the changes that take place in the external environment.

To become an effective change agent, I believe you must recognize the importance of increased self-knowledge, and the best way to do that is by studying yourself intimately, learning how you behave, and the effects you have on others. Then you must actively develop behavior skills (i.e., effective listening, trust-building, collaboration, etc.) to cultivate feedback. I think it is similar to learning just about anything in life (e.g., golf or music). Feedback is essential, practice is essential, and so is the willingness to realize that you don't know it all when it comes to change management, even if you're the CEO.

BUILDING BETTER CHANGE AGENTS

A keystone to building better change agents in today's business world involves working with people to improve their ability to manage change. In my experience this means improving their communication skills. It only makes sense that a person cannot possibly be a truly effective change agent unless he or she is able to articulate the views, the vision, the story of how and where the change efforts ought to or should be going. In addition, change agents must be able to energize people by what they say and don't say and how they say it. They must also learn what motivates people by probing and listening carefully.

Building change agents means improving such skills as communicating, motivating, resolving conflict, and sharing responsibility. Building change agents also means developing employees' team building skills and their effectiveness in operating in a team environment. Building change agents is about teaching and helping employees learn how to communicate vision, mission, values, strategic goals, how to get there, and how every single person on the team contributes to the big picture by helping the organization reach its strategic or other change goals. Through building change efforts employees learn not only how to manage change but how to lead.

Growing Leaders

If there is indeed a dearth of effective change agents today, smart organizations recognize that the solution is to grow change agents at every level of the organization. Being a change agent today is not about the individual skills you look for in any one person at the moment of selection but about what an organization has to think about in terms of creating a cadre of change agents from the moment they enter the organization. To bring people up through an organization to be effective change agents, organizations have to rotate employees through multiple job assignments that expose them to the challenges of change. They have to be exposed to cultural norms that reinforce the importance of change to their own and the organization's success. The attention given to developing change agents has to be as strategically approached as the attention given to the development of the new business unit.

Drafting Change Agents

Change agents are made—or developed—not born. But hiring the right people can help jump-start the change agent development process. What should you look for in the hiring process? You want to hire people who demonstrate the capacity to learn and change as opposed to those who demonstrate a particular narrow skill or competency. You're not hiring for the job anymore, you're hiring for core capabilities that can be leveraged across the organization (i.e., in multiple assignments and internal and external relationships).

There are three broad generative skills: a demonstration of interpersonal competence, credibility and trust, and the capacity to think systemically and in an integrated way about how work systems and people need to collaborate. If these skills are present at hiring, they can be leveraged into all kinds of professional competencies for managing change in the organization. Organizations would do well to hire people who have good self-knowledge, who are open to increasing their self-knowledge, who actively listen and seek and give feedback, and who are open to learning. Today's organizations should attempt to answer these questions when hiring and assessing new employees' skills to find out who can fulfill change agent roles and responsibilities:

1. Do they take extensive initiative on their own?
2. Are they committed to self-directed learning and change?
3. Are they extraordinarily trustworthy, have excellent credibility?
4. Do they feel comfortable in taking charge of situations and producing results?
5. Do they have resiliency (i.e., the ability to recover well from setbacks or failures)?
6. Are they risk takers?
7. Do they enjoy people and have great people skills?
8. Do they love ambiguity, uncertainty, flexibility, and innovation? Are they highly creative, and do they enjoying trying to do things they are not good at?

CONCLUSION

Our receptiveness as agents of change will be enhanced by acknowledging the need for changing the way we manage change; understanding the change needed by organizations, the new metrics, and the plans that support organizational shifts; and working with clients to help them move rapidly to better understand employees, customers, and the competition. Failing to be able to rethink the way we work with our clients may pose severe limitations on our growth and prosperity.

The time to start changing is now. Like time and tides, today's organizations and the demands of the new economy have little patience to wait. As the world in which organizations must survive and thrive becomes even more volatile and less predictable, all change agents need to keep alert so that their organizations don't calcify by staying too long with an obsolete strategy or by missing new requirements demanded by a changing environment. There is no room for complacency. As internal and external change agents, we either survive together or we will surely experience a merciless death at the hands of the new economy.

REFERENCES

Anderson, D., & Anderson, L.S.A. 2001. *Beyond change management: Advanced strategies for today's transformational leaders.* San Francisco: Jossey-Bass/Pfeiffer.

Chowhurdy, S. 2000. *Management 21C.* Upper Saddle River, NJ: Financial Times/Prentice Hall.

Tetenbaum, T. 1998. Shifting paradigms: From Newton to chaos. *Organizational Dynamics* (April): 26.

Trahant, B., Burke, W., & Koonce, R. 1997. 12 principles of organizational transformation. *Management Review* (September): 17–21.

Truss, C., & Gratton, L. 1994. Strategic human resource management: A conceptual approach. *The International Journal of Human Resource Management*, 5(3): 663.

Ulrich, D. 1997. *Human resource champions*. Cambridge, MA: Harvard Business School Press.

Ulrich, D. 1998. A new mandate for human resources. *Harvard Business Review* (January–February): 124–134.

Webber, A.M. 1999. Learning for a change. *Fast Company* (May): 178–180.

Wright, P., & McMahan, G. 1992. Theoretical perspectives for strategic human resource management. *Journal of Management*, 18(2): 292.

Part II

Global Views and Experiences
of Change

Chapter 6

Why The Bridge Hasn't Been Built and Other Profound Questions in Multicultural Organizational Development

Terry R. Armstrong

INTRODUCTION

It is a truism that people really "believe what they believe," and there are sound reasons for their behavior based on the cumulative historical experience of their culture. I cannot possibly make you an expert in cultural anthropology, but I can provide you with some concepts and tools for cross-cultural analysis of human behavior. I can also share some of my experience and insight, which can serve as a shock absorber for those of you who are anxious to get on with the business of doing multicultural organizational development (OD) for the foreign branch of your organization, implementing quality improvement, or trying to design training and OD programs for a diverse work force.

NAIVE BEGINNINGS

Like many who find themselves engaged in cross-cultural OD, I was extremely naive when I began. Armed with a baccalaureate degree, the puritan work ethic, and three months of intensive Peace Corps training, I charged into Colombia, South America, like the Yankee into King Arthur's Court. I was convinced that all Colombia and other underdeveloped countries needed to make the great ascent was a pragmatic technological assistance program supported by a good training program. As I look back on that naive American pragmatism from my now more-tempered perspective, I can see that the only thing that saved me from destroying U.S.-Colombian relations was my capacity for *aguardiente* (hard liquor) and love of bullfights. It was my luck that a true aficionado of the bullring can do no wrong.

As a baccalaureate degree holder trained in the tradition of American social science and Western philosophy and reared in a small midwestern town, I rode a mule into the Colombian jungle, carrying a belief system about human nature and American technological know-how. Of course I had read about ethnocentrism and cultural imperialism and had heard numerous war stories from returning Peace Corps volunteers. I knew the most modern views on learning theory, community development, technological assimilation, comparative linguistics, and cultural anthropology. Six years of studying Spanish, three months on an archaeological expedition in Spain, three months of sensitivity training, and a one-month living experience with a rural Mexican family should have certainly provided me with enough intellectual and experiential knowledge to start an educational revolution in those coffee-growing mountains. Like most of my colleagues I was an amateur cultural relativist intellectually, but most importantly I believed in the progress of humankind and that technology and know-how could easily be transferred to any cultural environment.

Anyone who has had an undergraduate course in sociology or anthropology must certainly recognize the contradictory position I found myself in. I even recognized the contradictions as I rode my mule into the small Colombian hamlets and talked with peasants about the virtue of hybrid seeds, boiled water, and literacy. However, I can assure you that logical contradiction and selective perception is as much a part of the American way as the Boy Scouts and apple pie. I like apple pie and am a legitimate Eagle Scout, so in spite of cognitive dissonance theory and formal logic, I accepted my paradoxical position like I did the draft—with bitterness but loyalty.

PEASANT WISDOM

I had been a Peace Corps volunteer working in rural community development for about 18 months before discovering the limits of my pragmatic perspective. Working cooperatively with local and state government officials, the community action groups I had been advising had completed over 20 schools, two health centers, a couple of bridges, and had organized a transportation cooperative. I was confident that progress had come to these mountain people. Then leaders of a community action group I had helped form in my first few months in Colombia asked me to come to their village to discuss the possibility of building a swinging bridge over a narrow river gorge. The bridge would shorten their journey to the market by three hours during the dry season. It seemed like a good project, so I arranged to go to their community action meeting the following Sunday. I had forgotten the rainy season was about to commence, but the next Sunday I had my mule saddled and took off in a tropical downpour to carry out my promise. Seven hours later I arrived at the small bamboo village; ate a meal of rice, eggs, and brown sugar water, and chatted with the peasants about their coffee, corn, and village affairs until late afternoon. When the rain finally stopped they took me to the gorge where they planned on building the swinging bridge. The gorge was only about 30 feet wide, and my Yankee ingenuity went to work immediately devising a way to construct the bridge. It seemed simple enough. North American pioneers must have built bridges across more dangerous ravines, I thought, and so this small band of peasants should be able to do likewise.

"It should be no problem," I said with confidence. "I'll talk with the departmental engineer and have him come out here if necessary. Of course, you will have to build it yourselves," I added in the tradition of community development projects.

An old barefooted man standing on the outer edge of the small band of villagers spoke. "Señor," he said, "before you go about planning how to build the bridge, why don't you ask why it hasn't yet been built?"

There was a long silence. I felt foolish for not having asked the question myself. Indeed if the bridge would save the peasants so much time, why hadn't it been built long ago?

A few weeks later, after asking numerous people why there wasn't a bridge over the River Tenerife, I learned just what problems the bridge would bring. If the bridge were built, conservatives would have to travel through liberal territory before they could reach the market. As an outsider I hadn't realized that the pangs of La Violencia still burned deep in the hearts of the mountain people. The old peasant taught me to ask why things are the way they are. If that question can be adequately answered, then begin the planning, but not before.

UNINTENDED CONSEQUENCES

We North Americans take progress so much for granted that we often do things without thinking about their consequences. We build freeways and giant skyscrapers and start change programs without thinking about unintended results. We develop miracle drugs and seeds before asking what they will do to our way of life. If humans have lived so long upon this planet, why is the technological revolution such a recent phenomenon? I do not wish to sound like a reactionary, but I cannot help but marvel at the wisdom of that poor old Colombian peasant. Managers and OD consultants can profit much from asking the same question that was asked of me in Colombia by the old illiterate peasant.

In order to hammer home my thesis that people really believe what they believe and that there are sound reasons for their behavior, I will recapitulate the classical analysis of why cow worship in India is a necessity. Marvin Harris, in his now well-known and controversial book *Cows, Pigs, Wars and Witches: The Riddles of Culture*, provides an exhilarating account of how cow worship in India is essential for the peasants' survival even though it seems absurd to our agribusiness view of the situation. To our way of thinking cow worship plays a significant role in India's survival. According to Harris (1974):

Some Western-trained agronomists say that the taboo against cow slaughter is keeping one hundred million "useless" animals alive. They claim that cow worship lowers the efficiency of agriculture because the useless animals contribute neither milk nor meat while competing for crop lands and food stuff with useful animals and hungry human beings. A study sponsored by the Ford Foundation in 1959 concluded that possibly half of India's cattle could be regarded as surplus in relation to feed supply. And an economist from the University of Pennsylvania stated in 1971 that India has thirty million unproductive cows. (p. 12)

However, Harris and others have shown how the cow is a vital element in India's ecosystem. Most India farmers cannot afford tractors, petrochemical fertilizers, and cooking fuel. Harris (1974) argues:

To convert from animals and manure to tractors and petrochemicals would require the investment of incredible amounts of capital. Moreover, the inevitable effect of substituting costly machines for cheap animals is to reduce the number of people who can earn their living from agriculture and to force a corresponding increase in the size of the average farm. . . . If agribusiness were to develop along similar lines in India, jobs and housing would soon have to be found for a quarter of a billion displaced peasants. (pp. 17, 18)

I am well aware at what happens to individuals caught in such a situation. I have seen them by the thousands living in paper shanties on muddy river banks in despair and alienation. We often forget how the one-room schoolhouse made it possible for us to make the transition from a rural to an urban society and the enormous amount of foreign capital that made American industrialization possible.

THE NACIREMA

To bring my thesis closer to home I will sketch an account by Miner (1960) of the now famous Nacirema, a North American group living

between the Cree, the Yaqui and Tarahumare of Mexico, and the Carib and Anawak of the Antilles. Little is known of their origin, although tradition states that they came from the east. According to Nacirema mythology, their nation was originated by a culture hero, Notgnihsaw, who is otherwise known for two great feats of strength—the throwing of a piece of wampum across the river Pa-To-Mac and the chopping down of a cherry tree in which the Spirit of Truth resided. (p. 521)

According to Professor Horace Miner,

the Nacirema culture is characterized by a highly developed market economy. . . . While much of the people's time is devoted to economic pursuits, a large part of the fruits of their labors and a considerable portion of the day are spent in ritual activity. The focus of this activity is the human body, the appearance and health of which loom as a dominant concern in the ethos of the people. While such a concern is certainly not unusual, its ceremonial aspects and associated philosophy are unique. (p. 521)

The households of the Nacirema have one or more shrines devoted to the body with the more powerful members in the society having several shrines.

The focal point of the shrine is a box or chest which is built into the wall. In this chest are kept the many charms and magical potions without which no native believes he could live. These preparations are secured from a variety of specialized practitioners. The most powerful of these are the medicine men, whose assistance must be rewarded with substantial gifts. However, the medicine men do not provide the curative potions for their clients, but decide what the ingredients should be and then write them down in an ancient and secret language. This writing is understood only by the medicine men and by the herbalists who for another gift, provide the required charm. (p. 522)

Professor Miner did not recognize the interdependency of ritual and market economy in the Nacirema culture. However, it has since been observed that the success of the economy is due in large part to their metaphysical beliefs about the body.

It is easy to laugh away Professor Miner's rather humorous analysis of North American culture. Surely we are more sophisticated than other peoples; however, if we are to understand why OD programs that are used in cross-cultural situations seldom work it is necessary to step beyond our ethnocentric bias. This is extremely important today because the other cultures are not only across the seas but in our factories, and we are beginning to import ideas about management and training from abroad. Also, most of us work with employees and co-workers who have different values, belief systems, and norms than ours, and we do not necessarily see the world the same way they do.

A WORLD OF DIFFERENT COLORS

Because people of different cultures and subcultures see the world differently, cross-cultural conflict often arises. This point was driven home to me by a very personal experience. While I was a teenager, I use to get in heated arguments with my mother about the color combinations of my clothes, and I was harassed continuously by the police for running red lights. It was not until I took my army physical and discovered that I was color blind that I realized that both my mother and the police saw the world differently than I. It was a humbling discovery that taught me an unforgettable lesson. If I saw the physical world differently than others then how was I ever to be certain that others interpreted social behavior the same way I did? I had argued with my mother and the police knowing that I was right and they were wrong, and I interpreted their behavior as hostile and reacted in anger. My anger met theirs and conflict was born because genetics had provided me with a world of different colors. The accident of birth, environment, and cultural heritage provides an individual with a worldview that is modified through experience. Differing worldviews often lead to cross-cultural misunderstanding and human conflict.

It is indeed difficult to be certain that we see the world as others do, but an understanding of the other's view is of utmost importance when involved in cross-cultural situations.

In her article "Training Needs of Overseas America's as Seen by Their National Co-Workers in Asia," Mary Boppell-Johnston (1974) stated that Asians ranked human relation skills, understanding of the other culture, and adaptability as the three most important training needs. What is even more impressive is that the Americans in the study arrived at the same rankings. This study should not be the last word on the subject, but I must say that my experience coincides with her findings.

I feel that any training or OD program designed to cross subcultures or cultural lines must help all involved develop an awareness of self and others and a sense of compassion. I admit that there is an increasing awareness on the part of consultants and administrators to deal with what McGregor termed the "human side of enterprise," but regrettably the American pragmatic tradition tends to look for fast answers. This tendency of trying to find "how" answers before asking "who" questions has led to the development of numerous gimmicks that only deal with symptoms. Human beings, no matter their culture, are significant to themselves and others and they finally have come to recognize that they have been tricked. There are no quick, "how-to" solutions for solving human misunderstanding—cross-cultural or otherwise. I cannot emphasize enough the danger of taking our pragmatic perspective too seriously.

"WHY" QUESTIONS

"Why don't you ask why the bridge hasn't been built?" the peasant asked me. Thirty years later I still ponder the depth of his question. It was a simple question about a simple problem in the Colombian jungle, but it is a question upon which I have built my consulting practice. How many organizations have been changed because of the peasant's question he'll never know, but his wisdom has endured long beyond that moment.

Another question that has had a profound effect upon my practice is St. Benedict's question, "Why are you here?"

I have modified these two questions often. Have tailored them to the client's situation. Many times I don't even ask the questions directly. Often they are simply the template behind my diagnosis.

I always ask myself, and often ask the client, a version of St. Benedict's question. "Why has this particular client called me? What does this particular client want or need from me?" I am never called unless there is a need. What is the need? This is true whether the call is from Alabama or South Africa. If someone calls me, there is a reason. I need to find out what it is.

"Why hasn't the bridge already been built?" is also a very powerful question that I modify in practice to such questions as:

- Why hasn't the system already been installed?
- Why doesn't the client already have a strategic plan?
- Why hasn't the planned changed already been implemented?
- Why hasn't _____ already taken place?

In the case of the peasant's question, the bridge had not been built because if it had been, hundreds of peasants would have been killed. It hadn't been built for sociological reasons—not technological or engineering ones. I find the same to be true in most organizations. Blank hasn't been done because of human reasons—not technological ones. Yet, so often I find client organizations encountering human problems when they think they have technological ones. Or they are trying to solve a physics problem with chemistry. In other words they are just looking in the wrong place because they haven't asked the right question.

St. Benedict's question also brings many insights, whether it is asked of a new recruit or a seasoned executive. His question, "Why are you here?" has to be modified slightly, but not much:

- Why are you in this market?
- Why are you implementing this system?
- Why do you want to promote her to vice president?

In other words, why does the client want anything?

I am often amazed to find that clients don't know what they want or why they want it. In fact clients seldom know what they want. Often my first task is to figure out why a client has come to me. I have to ask myself and sometimes the client:

- What is it that the client wants?
- How does the client think I can help?
- Why has the client come to me?

Clients, of course, come in all shapes, types, and sizes, and when one is involved in multicultural OD, the clients are definitely multidimensional. Often I don't even know the language they speak. This can also be true in the United States, where my clients speak a version of English such as chemistry, engineering, corrections, medicine, or pharmacology. I don't have to become fluent in their language, but I have to learn enough of it to get along—enough to be accepted.

In all cases they believe I have something to offer, or they wouldn't be seeking me out. They have heard or read about me. They have some beliefs about me that I must determine if I am to be of any help whatsoever.

I must listen to what they have to say: fact or fiction, real or mythical, but most of all I must be attentive. No matter the culture, I learn more from their presence than their words.

BEING CALLED

Over the years I've found that I am generally called for one of two reasons: (1) clients don't know what they want—they can't answer St. Benedict's question without a lot of help or (2) they don't have the slightest idea why something they are trying to do can't be done or isn't working. Poor or inadequate problem identification is often the problem. They haven't asked the peasant's question, "Why hasn't it already been done?"

My job as a consultant is first to identify which of the two questions clients are struggling with and then to help them frame the problem so that either they or I have a chance of discovering or creating a solution.

Profound questions often lead to new insights and creative solutions. They help us reframe the situation—at least they knock us out of our cognitive trap. Try using the Columbian peasant's and St. Benedict's questions or create your own versions of them with your clients and watch what happens.

When involved in multicultural or cross-cultural OD situations, I find these two questions are most profound. Having worked as an OD consultant in over 20 different cultures in settings as diverse as Ethiopia, Poland, Spain, Finland, Saudi Arabia, and South Africa, I have come to appreciate the power of basic questions. First and foremost in multicultural settings, OD is about questions rather than solutions, techniques, or theories.

Good questions lead to reflection and self-directed learning in all cultures. Since OD is primarily a change strategy based on education rather than authority, power, or expertise, the Socratic focus on process as opposed to content or correct answers is hardly new to the field. A growing number of OD practitioners believe OD is ethnocentric, but I contend that OD is geocentric or multicentric. In a recent conversation with Noble Kumawa, a multicultural OD consultant, we got into a lengthy discussion about the need for OD practitioners to be culturally sensitive even when working in their "own" or "home" culture. Granted, a lot of the theory OD practitioners use is Western; however, this does not mean that theory necessarily is culturally blinding, though it can be.

UNDERSTANDING

My first job, when doing OD in a new or different culture, is to understand. Before I can diagnose I must understand the culture. Sometimes this takes a long time. Once when working in South Africa, I traveled the country for three weeks just to gain an overview of the culture. I met with many people and each day I changed my interpretation of what I saw (Armstrong, 1989).

Once when consulting in a large meatpacking house, I took two months familiarizing myself with the operation before I ever attempted an intervention. It paid off because I took the time to listen nonjudgementally before offering any suggestions or ideas. By then I had learned that things are not always as they seem.

When engaged in multicultural OD, it is especially important to be aware of one's own culture. This does not mean that one should be hypersensitive but simply attuned to how one's culture influences what is seen and heard. It also can be a great help to have a cultural informant or guide. This person need not understand OD. However, I try to work with a local OD person when I work in other cultures. This has not always been possible and I have worked with only a translator. In such cases I have worked very slowly and found that my impact was marginal.

Consultants must be more than tourists or they will cause more problems than they solve. It is always best to take time to learn not only about the culture but also the language (Armstrong, Barber, & Najafabagy, 1986).

Even though it is true that many people around the globe speak English, it is very difficult to understand another people thoroughly if you don't speak their language. We tend to forget the power of language upon thought and action, and we do so at our own peril. Certainly, being multilingual helps OD consultants even when working in their home country. It helps because multilingual individuals understand that there are at least two ways to view any situation. Grasping the same situation from several perspectives leads to creative and innovative solutions. It is this ability to see a situation from multiple perspectives that is the main value that OD consultants have to offer even on their own turf. When I ask clients how I have helped them, I am generally told that I helped them see their situation differently. I have brought a new angle of vision to the problem. This has been true no matter where I have practiced OD.

Dawn Mulcahy, an internal consultant at Fidelity Investments, reflecting on what she learned in one of my consulting workshops, neatly capsulated the essence of multicultural consulting (Mulcahy, 2001):

With your guidance, Terry, I discovered that all I ever needed to know about consulting, I learned in kindergarten.

- Be nice. You can't help a client if you offend him. Clients are living with their current people, processes, and procedures. They may realize that something needs to change, but by knocking down the old, you close clients off to the new. Instead, to consult effectively, and have a chance at change, you need to validate what is working well, and not just focus on what is not.

- Make friends. Establish a relationship with your client. Sometimes, you are not welcomed into an environment with open arms. You need to earn trust and respect before you can expect any change to be considered.

- Play. Clients are more likely to buy into a change if they are a part of it. Let the client experience, brainstorm, role-play . . . anything that is needed to help them to discover the solutions for themselves. The consultant is there as a guide, not as an expert.

- Draw pictures. It's said that pictures speak louder than words. A model is often the best way to help clients understand the current situation and the need for change. Models can often show connections between factors better than the spoken word. Don't lecture your clients—let them see it for themselves.

- Too many cookies can make you sick. The consultant who can do everything is probably the consultant that can't do anything extremely well. Focus your efforts on your core skills. Don't take on assignments where you can't add value. With the clients you do take on, focus on the biggest impact solutions—don't overwhelm them with too many models and ideas. Choose one or two and focus on those. Overwhelming a client with too much information is the best way to ensure that nothing will change. If the solutions are not manageable, the client will not manage them.

- The world looks different through a kaleidoscope. Nobody in the organization has the right answer. Nobody in the organization knows what the problem is. Only by exploring various viewpoints can you hope to understand the situation. Managers, employees, customers—everyone together will help you to understand the big picture. If you hope to create change for the better, work with all of them.

TEAM BUILDING IN SOUTH AFRICA

Case studies are often helpful in clarifying essential theoretical elements. For my purposes here I will review a rather complicated case that Joanne Preston and I published (Preston & Armstrong, 1991).

This case is about cultural synergy and breaking through ethnic barriers. It involves work carried out in 1986 through the Community Development and Management Association of Africa (CDMAA). We worked with a group of business and community leaders whose common goal was to establish a non-violent atmosphere for dramatic paradigm shifts in their country. We used a cultural synergy paradigm model that focused on the emergence of a new culture using the best of both cultures (white and black) while appreciating the importance of each. It was our goal to create an atmosphere in which cultural synergy could occur. The idea of cultural synergy as we understood it assumes an understanding of the following elements: culture, synergy, systems, and creative problem solving. We knew that we had to create conditions of trust, effective communication, rapid feedback, creativity, and creative conflict. This synergy occurred in the form of building common ground among the participants. To build a team based upon a common ground was the first hurdle.

Our first task was to permeate the various cultural boundaries so that dialogues among the participants could ensue. I provided a short keynote address to more than 300 participants on the concept of cultural synergy. A vital function of my presentation was to frame the issue beginning with the broader concept and then slowly move closer to the underlying issues. It was important to put boundaries around the issues because of the complexity of the problems facing South Africa at the height of apartheid.

The next step was to create a "cohesive work unit" (i.e., breaking up into small units) to brainstorm how the concept introduced in the keynote address could be projected into the situation at hand. These groups were comprised of strangers and acquaintances from many different racial and ethnic groups. We used the term "cross-cultural teambuilding" to create positive atmosphere through the use of positive terminology. It was important that the group start at ground zero (i.e., as a new team looking to a hopeful future rather than at the painful past). As the group divided into small teams we noticed an increase in energy, and the noise in the room increased as the conversation became animated. Each small discussion group then summarized its findings with much applause from the other groups. By breaking into "teams" to brainstorm together, a common ground was created: a team with a theme emerged.

The third step was to create strategies from outlined themes and commonalties. About 50 of the participants then met for several days to create strategies and to draft a report to be reviewed by the total group. Essentially this group of 50 used brainstorming techniques to address the question, "What are the helping factors or existing resources that would create peaceful change?" By framing this exercise as essentially an exploration of positive elements, there was neither blaming nor name-calling. Instead, here was an exercise focused on how individual strategies can have an impact on the whole. The participants felt a sense of empowerment instead of the usual disempowerment.

The last task was to work out the issues and draft a report. The major outcome of the two-day session was the willingness to emphasize the common issues and differences locally. We learned later that some of the participants implemented some of the strategies in their townships and communities.

Though I was one of the major participants, I was still impressed with how easy it was to create a "common ground" with such a diverse group. I think that there were five critical factors in this intervention:

1. We understood the importance of our task and the urgency of the situation.
2. The co-facilitators knew each other well, though we had not worked together previously.
3. We created a theory, which had emerged from our experience, and were using that theory—a good example of "praxis."
4. We kept the intervention simple.
5. We were flexible and went with the flow of the group, trusting that the participants intuitively knew what they had to do.

Now there is a more public case that gets at the complexity of multicultural change—the famous case of the Ford/Firestone "fiasco." To put the case in perspective, Karen Shoneman (2001) created the following timeline. She simply found published articles about the case and established a timeline of events.

Ford/Firestone "Fiasco" Timeline—Selected Events

Mid-1997: "Ford and Firestone begin to receive concerns from Saudi Arabia" (Audi/ Dixon 10/6/00).

January 28, 1999: "Head of Ford's Dubai, UAE division expresses concern to Detroit Ford headquarters" (Audi/Dixon 10/6/00).

May 10, 1999: "Ford sends task force to the Middle East" (Audi/Dixon 10/6/00).

August 1999: "Ford recall of tires begins in Middle East" (Skertic 8/31/00); "Ford says these are their first reports of tire failures; Replaces Firestone tires on 6,800 Explorers and Mercury Mountaineers in Saudi Arabia" (AP 9/29/00); "Email sent from a Ford engineer in Venezuela to Detroit headquarters asking whether similar tire problems were occurring in U.S." (Chardy 10/9/00); "Response one week later: Replace Firestone tires with Goodyears" (Chardy 10/9/00).

Fall 1999: "Ford has begun replacing tires in 10 Middle East countries" (Audi/Dixon 10/6/00).

September 15, 1999: "Memo to Ford CEO Nasser regarding accidents in the Middle East and South America; no accidents noted in U.S." (Audi/Dixon 10/6/00).

November 1999: "Ford initiates Firestone tire study in southwestern U.S."

May 2000: "Replacement/recall begins in Venezuela, Colombia and Ecuador" (Skertic 8/31/00); "Eventually Firestone tires are replaced on about 60% of 30,000 Explorers" (Eldridge & Kiley 9/1/00); "46 deaths in Venezuela linked Bridgestone/Firestone tires (primarily on Explorers)" (AP 9/29/00).

May 2, 2000: "NHTSA investigation begins into U.S. Ford Explorer accidents involving Firestone tires" (Skertic 8/31/00); "4 U.S. deaths reported at time investigation begins" (Skertic 8/31/00);

Late May 2000: "Investigators learn about recalls in other countries" (Skertic 8/31/00); Later, "101 U.S. deaths linked to Bridgestone/Firestone tires (primarily on Explorers)" (AP 9/29/00).

First week of August 2000: "Ford provides documents including recall notices from other countries" (Skertic 8/31/00).

August 9, 2000: "Bridgestone announces recall of 6.5 million tires in U.S. used primarily on Ford SUVs" (ATX, ATX II and Wilderness AT tires); by this time, Ford had replaced or recalled tires in 16 foreign countries (AP 9/29/00).

September 2000: "Bridgestone/Firestone recalls 62,000 Wilderness AT tires in Venezuela" (Reuters 10/5/00); "NHSTA alerts public of potential defective tires in addition to those recalled" (Consumer Advisory 9/1/00).

October 5, 2000: "U.S. House Commerce Committee passes bill imposing new reporting requirements on auto manufacturers" (Johnson/Skrzycki 10/6/00).

What was the cause of Firestone's and Ford's slow response? I am certain that the Firestone/Ford case will be analyzed and reanalyzed indefinitely from numerous perspectives, including corporate responsibility, business ethics, and public relations. Though all of these may have had a role to play, it is my contention that a major difference had to do with cross-cultural issues and differing values. Had Firestone been a U.S. company, would it have responded differently? Given the global emphasis of modern business, will we see similar fiascoes? I suspect we will. Societies and the decision makers in those societies make decisions based on a multitude of values and value hierarchies. As the world becomes more global because of communication technology and growing global markets, decision makers and their consultants will have to be increasingly attuned to the value kaleidoscope of the modern world. As a consultant working with business and organizations around the globe I find that I must not only be aware of the value diversity and its implications, I must help my clients understand and appreciate that others see the world differently than they do. This is not easy.

The South African case I briefly described earlier was much easier to deal with than the Firestone/Ford situation. Though there were a number of cultures involved with numerous values, it was still possible to get most of the groups represented in one room. It was also possible to describe the concept of cultural synergy and to find common concern, the "survival of their children." It appears that Firestone and Ford didn't even realize they had a problem. Certainly not a joint problem. It also appears from the timeline that they must not have been communicating with one another effectively. Theoretically, one could have identified all the stakeholding interests and put them in a room somewhere. With a super facilitator it is possible that this fiasco could have been avoided. But in actuality this would have been very difficult to achieve.

SEVEN LESSONS LEARNED FROM THE CASES

From the South African case and the Firestone/Ford case I've learned seven critical lessons about consulting in a multicultural situation:

1. Understand your personal motivations and concerns.
2. Listen to everyone—especially the disenfranchised.
3. Identify the informal leaders and work with them.
4. Help legitimize unspoken issues.
5. Use models, theories, and questions to help bring understanding to the situation.
6. Build communication linkages across cultural barriers.
7. Constantly look for new ways to get parties in conflict to communicate.

With increased globalization I can foresee numerous cases of global corporations coming into conflict with various world constituencies. As OD and other consultants work in multicultural settings they must learn to confront their clients and world leaders with profound questions that will make them think and reexamine what they are doing. I suggest they start with St. Benedict's question, "Why are you here?" and the peasant's question, "Why hasn't the bridge already been built?"

REFERENCES

Armstrong, T.R. 1989. Experiencing large systems change in South Africa. *Organization Development Journal*, 7(3): 42–51.

Armstrong, T.R., Barber, I., & Najafabagy, R. 1986. Creating cultural synergy. *Organization Development Journal*, 4(4): 35–40.

Boppell-Johnston, M. 1974. Training needs of overseas Americans. *Focus*, 4: 21–25.

Harris, M. 1974. *Cows, pigs, wars and witches: The riddles of culture*. New York: Vintage Books, pp. 12, 17–18.

Miner, H. 1960. Magical practices among the Nacirema. In W. Godschmidt (ed.), *Exploring the ways of mankind*. New York: Holt, Rinehart & Winston, pp. 520–526.

Mulcahy, D. 2001. All I ever needed to know about consulting, I learned in kindergarten. Unpublished paper.

Preston, J.C., & Armstrong, T.R. 1991. Team building in South Africa: Cross-cultural synergy in action. *Public Administration Quarterly* 15(1): 65–82.

Shoneman, K. 2001. Ford/Firestone "fiasco" timeline—Selected events. Unpublished paper.

Chapter 7

Reconciling the Dynamic of Symbols and Symptoms in Bringing about International Change

Edgar J. Ridley

INTRODUCTION

Change, as we all know, is easier said than done. Unfortunately, traditional change management methodologies have proven impotent in our present economy. A major impediment to change implementation involves risks that few are willing to accept. Because few people have the necessary courage to follow through on programs that would produce qualitative change, the situation leads to concepts that are circular. This is known as business as usual. In short, the new economy is really the old economy with new names. Accordingly, it is a misnomer to suggest that we need new concepts for a new economy. This so-called new economy still has the same ambitions, trends, and goals as the so-called old economy. It does not usher in a qualitatively new world or qualitatively new concepts.

The engines currently in use for qualitative change are hoped to be quick fixes for our economy. One of those engines is the trend toward globalization. Globalization is a sophisticated method for keeping developing countries in a mode of permanent underdevelopment with no possibility for competitive growth. One author recently noted that "the impact of globalization is extremely uneven. It implies rising inequalities within countries. It leads to greater polarization across countries; and has resulted in greater vulnerability to macro-economic shocks that lower growth and employment rates resulting in widening the gap with developed countries" (Mbeki, 2001b). Today's change consultants must bring new tools to the table in order to challenge the status quo.

THE NEED FOR CONSULTANTS TO UNDERSTAND CHANGE

Management consultants are called upon to solve some of the most crucial problems facing the world today. Twenty-first-century consulting firms will have tremendous influence on not only the companies they serve but also on the world as a whole. With emerging economies and technological advancement, complicated symbol systems have surfaced that have produced an abundance of myths and metaphors that regulate every phase of our daily life. To be sure, consulting firms use symbol systems to produce new metaphors. (In fact, consultants have been coined "symbolic analysts" by Robert Reich [1995], former U.S. labor secretary.) Over the past several years, these new metaphors, also known as mythological symbols, have been presented as new business slogans such as *reengineering, process engineering*, or even *best practices*. However, nothing ever changes. As stated earlier, it is business as usual. This is why we agree with Professor Max Müller, who wrote many years ago, "Mythology is a disease of language, and the ancient symbolism was a result of something like a primitive mental aberration" (cited in Massey, 1998, p. 165).

We call this mental aberration the "neurological misadventure of primordial man" (Ridley, 1982). That neurological misadventure caused brain activities that produced mythological thinking, which resulted in symbolic behavior. With that state of being in place, superstition and ritualistic behavior become the norm. Sound decisions cannot be made, and there is little or no chance for productivity or cultural harmony.

Productivity improvement has not taken place on a global scale consistent with our technological advancement. This is because business leaders continue to make decisions from a mythological framework that renders technological advances impotent. Until we realize the necessity of living in a world without myth, our global economy will never be stable. Symbol systems produce metaphors that are totally inadequate for addressing the changing trends in the global work force. A new concept must be applied and that new concept is the *symptomatic thought process* (STP).

It is important to understand what a symptom is. A symptom is a natural sign.

A natural sign is immeasurably more valuable than a symbol. Where it has been held in the past that signs were inferior to symbols, that is totally incorrect. A sign indicates the existence—past, present and future—of a thing, event, or condition. Wet streets are a sign that it has rained; a smell of smoke signifies the presence of fire. All examples here produced are natural signs. A natural sign is a part of a greater event or a complex condition, and to an expert observer, it signifies the rest of that situation, of which it is a notable feature. It is a symptom of a state of affairs. (Susanne K. Langer, as cited in Ridley, 1992, p. 27)

"Thinking symptomatically is seeing things as they really are, in their ultimate state." There is no going behind the actual entities to find anything more real. The sign, then, is the concrete form, the symptom, of an invisible and inner reality, and at the same time, the means by which the mind is reminded of that reality. "It has been traditionally held that when the brain crystallizes stimuli, it creates a symbol. That is a misadventure. When the brain crystallizes outside stimuli, the correct process is that it creates a natural sign" (Ridley, 1992, p. 27).

The STP replaces the symbolic thought process, which has been a standard since time immemorial (see Figures 7.1 and 7.2 for illustration). The reader should understand that the symbolic thought process is one that produces mythology, rituals, and superstitions. This symbolic thought process can be called a neurological misadventure. The neurological misadventure can be described as an event in human history that occurred when symbols and symbol systems evolved in a symptomatic environment. In other words, when man began to symbolize and mythologize out of his symptomatic environment, a neurological misadventure took place at that moment. Out of that scenario, all the events that we know as history began to take place—through the industrial revolution all the way to the information revolution that produced the digital economic system and the Internet.

I maintain that as long as consultants insist on creating metaphors, they will continue to be bogged down in a global mythological abyss. The only way for consultants to serve their client base effectively is to cease creating new metaphors. These mythological metaphors that become superstitious rituals inhibit true productivity. To completely eliminate metaphors, the STP should be implemented.

THE FRICTION BETWEEN SYMBOLS AND SYMPTOMS

What has to be understood is a step-by-step method in which the STP is implemented. The STP makes it possible for individuals to interact with each other in a way that is sincere, without phoniness. It opens up relationships as never before. The dynamic of an STP on the brain is the most important experience one could ever have in one's lifetime.

Figure 7.3 depicts matter, or stimuli, being funneled into the human brain. These matter are natural signs, not symbols. They have not yet been processed neurologically. Only the human brain can create a symbol. There is no such thing as symbols existing before they are processed within the human brain. All entities that exist before being processed within the human brain are natural signs. What does that mean for us as we go about our daily lives? This means that whenever we see anything, we look at it without the mythological symbols that produce connotations. We do not think in connotations. We see things as they really are in their ultimate state as they are presented to us. This is ex-

Figure 7.1
Symbolic Thought Process Leading to Symbolic Behavior

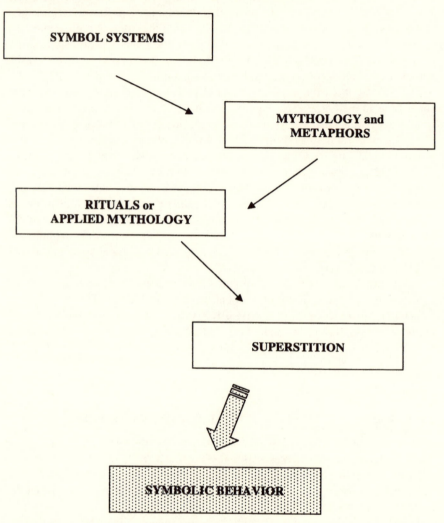

tremely important. When we see things in their ultimate state as they are presented to us, we do not mythologize about these entities.

The human brain processes energy and entities continually, and that processing is the key to individual decision making. As stated before, that process is what we have called the neurological misadventure of primordial man. The correct and effective behavior process is the STP. The stimuli that the brain processes become symptoms of a state of affairs. These symptoms are always qualitatively ultimate, not only in their character but in the matter that makes

Figure 7.2
Symptomatic Thought Process

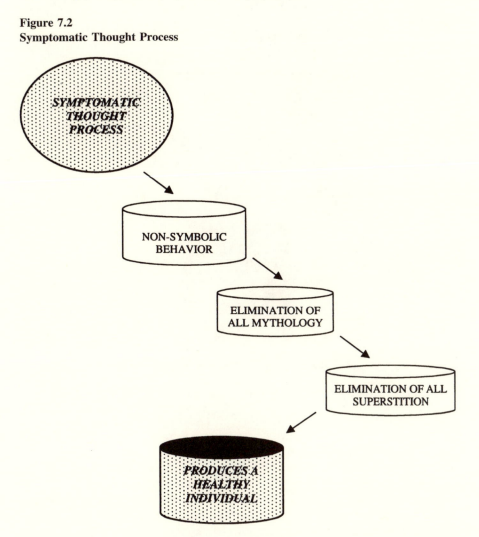

up the entities. The correct neurological adventure that takes place is that the brain crystallizes natural signs from our experiences. These natural signs, or symptoms, create reality, or bits of reality, from ultimate reality, which are those experiences that are originally part of one's core truth.

We know that countries that are oriented toward symbol systems produce mythological cults that destroy productivity. What we maintain here is that the area of crisis is the dynamic that occurs between symbols and symptoms. As we look around the world, we see the results of those clashes between symbols and symptoms. That is why Marjorie Garber, in her book *Symptoms of Culture* states that "One of the most striking symptoms of culture in our time has been

Figure 7.3
Dynamics of the Symptomatic Thought Process on the Brain

Source: Drawing courtesy of A. Curtis Alexander, Ph.D.

the phenomenon of the so-called 'cultural wars,' a conflict that might be located precisely in the clash between symbols and symptoms" (Garber, 1998, p. 7). Garber goes on to state, "We should look for a theory of the symptom" (p. 9). That theory is the STP, which replaces the symbolic thought process.

United Nations Secretary General Kofi Annan has expressed bewilderment and puzzlement at the viciousness of acts around the globe. These acts are due to mythological symbols played out as rituals, and the countries who participate in these acts on a large scale are usually the poorest countries who depend on the World Bank and International Monetary Fund for handouts. These countries have not yet realized the potential of their own human resources to solve their economic plight.

One might ask, what does this have to do with the economy, or economic growth, or even productivity? To the degree that a country is able to resolve that friction between symbols and symptoms, is the degree to which its economy will be stable and productive. Symptomatic thinking—in other words seeing things as they really are—can liberate developing countries from an over-dependence on the West for problem solving. For example, it was noted by South African President Thabo Mbeki during his briefing at the recent World

Economic Forum that it is now time for Africans to step to the forefront to solve their own problems (Mbeki, 2001a). African leadership is slowly discarding the model of total disregard for African resources and sweat equity. African leadership is coming together to plan growth initiatives via a partnership that includes the best African minds in concert with world business leaders—this is symptomatic behavior at its best.

OPPORTUNITIES FOR QUALITATIVE CHANGE IN A NEW ECONOMY

The U.S. work force has suffered negative labeling, not the least of which has been characterizations of sexism and racism among corporate managements. This is due to the obvious—that 95% of America's top corporate positions are populated by white males. Interestingly, the nation is about to undergo a demographic sea change. A recent U.S. census report revealed that the states of California and New Jersey are now predominantly nonwhite. The report predicted a white minority throughout the United States by the year 2050. This changing work force is the engine causing apprehension and paranoia among whites who have traditionally been thought of as the majority. There has been a rush to solidify white empowerment and entrenchment in the upper echelons of corporate and political life. This is due to an unreasonable fear that the work force will become saturated with people of color from top management on down. This fear is understandable, in light of the manner in which blacks and other people of color have been treated by the white majority. The sheer number of lawsuits that corporate America has faced and/or is settling currently is an illustration of the roadblocks that have been placed to bar achievement by people of color. These roadblocks are erected by individuals who oppose change. That opposition can be overt or subtle, but it is equally harmful. Of no small consequence is the collateral damage heaped upon the corporate landscape by the litigation experienced by such giants as Coca-Cola, R.R. Donnelly, Texaco, American Airlines, Eastman Kodak, and Denny's Restaurants. The lucrative settlements only serve to shrink corporate profits.

In 2000, Coca-Cola settled a racial bias lawsuit for $192.5 million in which eight current and former African-American employees accused Coca-Cola of discrimination against black employees in pay, promotions, performance evaluations, and terminations. If that weren't enough, the company still faces a $1.5 billion lawsuit filed by a separate group of four former workers, who allege that Coca-Cola maintained racially biased hiring practices and a hostile work environment for blacks.

Reaching even further back into the corporate landscape, we can't forget the infamous Texaco crisis, in which senior executives were audiotaped making cruel comments about black employees as well as discussing the destruction of documents that were linked to an ongoing discrimination lawsuit. Texaco settled this lawsuit for $115 million in cash plus salary adjustments for the 1,400 employees involved.

Change consultants should recognize that the symbolic behavior that generates workplace bias can reach proportions that exceed egregious. American Airlines was confronted with a $10.5 million racial harassment lawsuit in which a black airline mechanic endured hanging rope nooses, having his photo placed on a dart board, and racist scribbles in the men's room (Sappenfield, 1999). This worker, like many before and after him, lived within this environment with no assistance from his superiors, who were reluctant to handle the problem and allowed it to worsen.

A similar atmosphere existed at R.R. Donnelly & Sons. At this commercial printing firm, systematic bigotry existed: "Black workers [were] prohibited from training for senior-level jobs and routinely denied promotions that went to less qualified whites; white co-workers dressed as Ku Klux Klansmen for laughs; and joke fliers were distributed that described 'hunting season' on black people. . . . however, the firm denies any wrongdoing" (Miller, 2000, p. 1).

The previous examples were just the surface of what black workers experienced at R.R. Donnelly. Needless to say, a change consultant entering this environment would be severely challenged, given the firm's denials. The irony is that R.R. Donnelly's corporate diversity program was highlighted in 1999 as a national best practices case study by Watson Wyatt Worldwide Consulting (Miller, 2000). This is a perfect illustration of a business-as-usual stamp placed on a firm by consultants who are ignorant of the dynamics of symptoms and symbols.

Often, bias in the workplace is so subtle that it can easily be argued that it doesn't exist. Nonwhite executives are dismissed, disrespected, and embarrassed in myriad small ways. A 1999 court shed light on the damage caused by "unthinking stereotypes or bias" in a lawsuit against Eastman Kodak. Judge Sandra Lynch of the U.S. Court of Appeals, First Circuit, said: "Racial discrimination can occur whether the employer consciously intended to base the evaluations on race or did so because of unthinking stereotypes or bias. . . . skewed perceptions may have come into play. . . . discrimination may arise from stereotyping, which is unconscious" (Blanton, 1999, p. B1).

This so-called unconscious behavior is an excellent illustration of symbolic behavior—instead of viewing nonwhite executives symptomatically through a prism that only sees skills and performance, a mythology of inferiority is introduced. This happens repeatedly. True change is difficult if not impossible to implement in corporate environments like this. Change management consultants must fully understand this dynamic if they wish to be effective in advising corporate management.

A symptomatic approach was the course of last resort for Denny's Restaurants. Denny's "became a national punch line and a symbol of the resilience of racism in America" (Segal, 1999, p. A2). However, after a stinging lawsuit that resulted in a $54 million settlement, Denny's initiated a complete culture change within the corporation: "As this country grows in the next 15 years the racial composition of the country will change dramatically. . . . If you're not in touch with the tastes of minorities or in a position to reach them through ads, you're going to miss an incredible opportunity" (John Romandetti, Denny's CEO, as quoted in Segal, 1999, p. E1).

Denny's recognition of the changing demographics is a symptomatic response. Denny's reaction to its crisis was to proceed symptomatically rather than symbolically. Denny's understands that it must cultivate its core client base (nonwhite customers), as opposed to allowing negative behavior by its employees against those customers. Prior to the lawsuit, Denny's employees nationwide were free to discriminate against nonwhite customers by refusing or delaying service as well as providing substandard service in general. It was common for people of color to be asked to show identification when ordering food, pay for their food in advance, wait until all other diners were served, or not to be served at all. Denny's management, in typical symbolic behavior, maintained a posture of denial, until the lawsuit generated reams of negative publicity as well as lost sales. Cynics may infer that Denny's had no choice other than to change course. However, Denny's response can only be described as symptomatic, when, instead of remaining in denial about its racist practices, new management looked reality in the face and didn't flinch.

Denny's management recognized that a cultural overhaul was necessary in order to win back its nonwhite customers, since its very livelihood depended on them. Denny's new management launched a multimillion-dollar public relations campaign targeted toward people of color. They initiated a corporate diversity program that tied executive compensation to diversity goals. Managers were given diversity training, and waitstaff were given communications training. The company increased the diversity of its work force as well as increased its partnerships with minority suppliers from 0% to 18% of all business. Additionally, prior to the lawsuit, less than 1% of Denny's restaurants were owned by people of color; new management expanded that ownership to 36%. This is clear evidence of management's willingness to disregard the mythologies surrounding people of color (i.e., thinking symbolically) and instead capitalize on the contributions offered by such diversity. This is symptomatic behavior.

HOW MYTHOLOGY PREVENTS CHANGE

The corporate world perpetuates myths to enforce practices that are destructive to the overwhelming masses employed in the global work force. Subliminally, such myths are documented and entrenched in the corporate lexicon by books such as *The Bell Curve* (Herrnstein & Murray, 1994) and *Not Out of Africa* (Lefkowitz, 1996). The change consultant must be clear: the philosophy espoused by a book such as *Not Out of Africa* attacks the revamping of African history to reflect an honest view of the African contribution to civilization. This philosophy supports a global philosophical viewpoint of whites that intellectually justifies their superiority and dominant position in the global arena.

Racism is easily the number one impediment to qualitative change and productivity in the corporate arena. In *The Bell Curve*, the authors emphasize that no matter what level of academics or profession that blacks achieve, they will always be subordinate due to their genetic inferiority. The authors allege that this inferiority is due to a lower IQ score than Asians or whites. "What IQ tests actually gauge is the ability to reason with information presented through the medium of systems of symbols. . . . The ability to reason is in terms of a symbol system, which is essentially the same as 'general intelligence' " (Dixon, 1990, p. 3). In other words, IQ tests are symbol systems that have no relevance in measuring either intelligence or performance. IQ tests perpetuate myths. The philosophies of *The Bell Curve* and *Not Out of Africa* simply reinforce the notion of racial superiority in the white population. This philosophy provides academic justification to those industrial psychologists consulting with corporate management—it allows whites to continue to think of blacks as inferior no matter what degree of success they attain. David Olson notes: "IQ has been used to exclude people from educational opportunities from which they would benefit and from jobs that they are entirely capable of handling" (Sternberg & Wagner, 1990, p. 32).

It is imperative that change consultants understand this philosophy when servicing corporate clients. Indeed, a philosophical approach is critical. (One only has to read George Soros' approach to the global economic picture to understand the importance of philosophical orientation [Soros, 2000].) Corporations are simply a microcosm of the larger society. The climate within an organization is fostered by the attitudes and beliefs of management, and it trickles down to the common employee. Americans, and American management, are in severe denial regarding the issue of race. However, due to systemic racism, blacks in the corporate world live in a totally different world than their white peers.

A familiar example is Joseph Jett, a top bond trader at the former Kidder Peabody & Company. Jett was charged with masterminding one of the largest securities scams in Wall Street history. He was eventually exonerated but only after going through the experience of living while black. Jett's impeccable credentials from MIT and Harvard Business School, as well as a golden resume from General Electric, Morgan Stanley, and First Boston, mattered little. The fact remained that Jett was a black man, and, according to *The Bell Curve*, he would always be genetically inferior to his white counterparts. Stated Jett: "If my white counterparts said one and one is two, it would be fine; if I said one and one is two, they'd say, I'll get back to you on that. . . . I was wrongly accused and made the scapegoat for a culture in which racism remains rampant" (Jett & Chartrand, 1999, p. ix).

The specter of racism within corporations is an unpleasant subject at best. However, change consultants must focus on so-called diversity issues when advising corporate management. These consultants must be sophisticated and learned enough to recognize that typical corporate diversity programs rarely reach beneath the surface to thoroughly remove the symbolic behavior effectuating itself as institutional racism. "The corner office remains an exclusively white preserve. . . . Explicit racial bias impedes progress. . . . In most industries, blacks remain invisible. That's business lost" (Hammonds, 1998, p. 26). This is very important. The backlash behavior of whites within corporations does not emerge from a vacuum. Inappropriate stereotyping and unfortunate belief systems (also known as symbolic behavior) come to work with white employees. According to J. Bolig, "Whites feel more and more powerless. They have less and less control and influence. Whites feel like they're losing their grip. It's provoking a kind of racial angst" (Kaufman, 2001, p. A1). Of course, corporate managers are not going to broadcast their personal biases for public consumption. Instead, those biases are integrated within the corporate culture in subtle, insidious ways. It is critical for change consultants to put a name to this behavior if they wish to provide advice to their corporate clients that is noncircular.

General Electric is held out as the nation's leader when it comes to innovative management systems. American firms routinely imitate GE's management training initiatives. Yet this industry leader is stymied when it comes to locating talented executives that vary from the white male norm. This is consistent with the typical symbolic thinking—that white men are more skilled at running companies and manufacturing earnings for their shareholders. Lloyd G. Trotter, president and CEO, GE Industrial Systems, recently stated, "If I managed my business the way I had managed diversity, I think I'd have gotten fired" (Walsh, 2000, p. 3-13). "General Electric requires every business unit to be first or second in its market, or risk sale or closure. There is no such requirement for diversity" (Walsh, 2000, p. 3-1).

The fear of a nonwhite majority work force causes absurd and ridiculous concepts such as *The Bell Curve*, which, as we know, states that no matter what the level of education and achievement of black people, blacks will always be inferior to whites due to a symbolic IQ score.

The theories of Herrnstein and Murray derive from a deeply held mythological view in which racism and hysteria rule the thought patterns of the authors. It is important to understand that the origins of such unhealthy feelings are in the myths that serve as a vehicle for those feelings to be transported to all levels of human activity. The danger of these myths is that they serve to undermine and inhibit the productivity essential for qualitative change in the global work force. Unfortunately, consultants and academia have acted in concert to not only reinforce these unhealthy concepts but to use them as a justification to impose a sense of unworthiness and inferiority in the work force. Again, it is important for the reader to be clear that behavior does not present itself in a vacuum but instead emanates from a culture that reinforces white superiority over the input and contribution of nonwhites.

We point to an academic example: Gunter Dreyer, head of the German archaeological institute, discovered clay tablets in southern Egypt from the tomb of King Scorpion, representing the earliest known writings by humankind. When Dreyer's find was published, academia noted that the discovery would rank among the greatest ever in the search for the origins of the written word, since carbon dating placed the tablets between 3300 B.C. and 3200 B.C. The problem with this announcement was the unchallenged suggestion and inference that no scholarship preceded Dreyer's as suggested by Dr. Molefi Asante: "The idea that language originated in Egypt rather than Mesopotamia is not a new one," (Glover, 1998, pp. C1–C2). "Asante cited the works of Cheikh Anta Diop, a Senegalese professor, who wrote a book in the 60's that claimed that the Egyptian language is older than Sumer, which was an ancient country in the area known as Iraq. 'African and African-American scholars made this argument many years ago', Asante said. It has only received press attention because it was a German scholar who was now saying it" (Glover, 1998, pp. C1–C2). In short, the archaeological discovery would have had no merit were it not endorsed by the German scholar, as opposed to volumes published by African scholars many years prior. Academic examples provide valuable fodder for the explanation of symbolic thinking, and change consultants must be educated and clear about this type of symbolic behavior. It is ingrained in American, indeed, Western, corporate culture that contributions of significance do not emanate from nonwhites. This allows the traditional mode of doing business to remain in place. There is no change in the way business is done or in who runs the businesses.

There is strong resistance to change, especially when dealing with racial issues. Change agents must be courageous; they have a daunting task. Fear of repercussion, such as demotion or dismissal, is pervasive in the minds of not only change agents but also of anyone who would seek to break the myths that inhibit qualitative change. In corporate America, people have significant fear of retaliation if they were to step out of their box and change their behavior to one of advocacy for a just and nonracist work force. We can, however, take certain steps to solve this problem when we understand how symbol systems produce the mythologies that produce an unhealthy work force. These symbol systems that produce these mythologies call for superstitious, ritualistic behavior. This disrupts harmony and prohibits a just environment. Marc Bendik, a labor economist, stated that "The effect of unchecked workplace discrimination can be deep, and corporate culture is partly to blame . . . because the tone for tolerance is set at the top. A company's personality is a living and 'enduring thing' . . . Employees who are sought and promoted often are compatible with the existing culture and therefore perpetuate it" (Poe, 2000, p. A2). Those of us who are charged with instituting change within corporations have to exhibit the courage required to break the circle.

My consulting firm, Edgar J. Ridley & Associates, was approached by a Southern African company for assistance with an infrastructure project. The emphasis of the consulting assignment was to secure funding; on-the-ground management of the project was less of a concern. Unfortunately, many African projects deemphasize management and behavioral procedures that affect critical business decisions. Symbolic thinking leads Africans to feel that currency alone will solve their problems. This has often not been addressed in Africa, which has led to chaos and nonproductive behavior. A serious problem in Africa has been its dependence on symbol systems to provide relief. Africans don't realize, as stated by Aleksandr N. Solzhenitsyn, the Nobel Prize-winning writer, that "Symbols, for all their apparent power, do not bestow greatness. You cannot save a dying country with symbols" ("O say can you see," 2000, p. B11).

Conversely, an ASEAN (Association of Southeast Asian Nations) country in the Pacific Rim expressed an interest in implementing the STP in their management arena with an emphasis on management and productivity. This Asian country makes prolific use of its natural resources, and management decision making is nonsymbolic. Accordingly, management decisions enhance efficiency and create a scenario of independence and information sharing.

Additionally, Edgar J. Ridley & Associates was called to China to provide advice on management concepts for increased productivity based on the unique methods of productivity improvement that are part of the STP. Because of its emphasis on proper behavior patterns and effective business decisions, China is growing at an extremely rapid rate, achieving an excellent measure of economic independence.

These consultations emphasize the need to evaluate the damage caused by symbols in the creation of mythology and superstition. By exploring the necessity to eradicate decisions based on myth, managers can go to the core of cultural beliefs. This core is often difficult to weed out. The change consultant must remember that assumptions are based on long-held beliefs. The objective in change management should be to convince managers to think symptomatically—which means seeing things as they really are—and encourage people to make decisions void of superstition or mythological assumptions. This would lead to smoother business transactions and the elimination of damaging behavior.

There is no getting around it: behavior patterns and increased productivity are not just closely related but synonymous. An encouraging example of symptomatic thinking is shown by the attempts by many countries in Africa to remove the obstacles to trade within African countries. It is well known that much of African productivity has been hindered by the lack of a common market among African nations. Nine members of COMESA (the Common Market for Eastern and Southern Africa) are making a fast-track attempt to remove trade barriers preventing intraregional trade. Six more countries will probably join this effort within a year if five of those countries can get beyond their differences. These five countries are on opposing sides in the war in the Democratic Republic of the Congo. In addition, two of those five countries are Eritrea and Ethiopia, recent enemies in a border war.

Many African economies suffer from numerous ills, not the least of which are considerable bureaucracy, inadequate infrastructure, skills in short supply, and a high cost of transporting goods from one region to another. These challenges need to be met by African leadership, and the removal of trade barriers between countries is certainly a giant step in the right direction. It is well known that Africa has minimal to no manufacturing relative to the global economy. Intraregional trade between African countries would go a long way toward enhancing the view that Africans can solve their own problems rather than depend on entities outside their regions, such as the West. Although economists differ on whether intraregional trade would accelerate, rather than reverse, deindustrialization, an important component of this process is the degree to which African countries cease their symbolic decision making. It is symbolism that drives African managers to only consider business expertise if it is delivered from the mouths of Western policy makers. The belief that Africans cannot solve their own problems is driven by symbolism. The extent to which the various countries are liberating themselves from this mind-set is the degree to which an STP is taking place.

A paradigm for symbolism versus a symptomatic thought process is most evident in the dynamics surrounding events in Zimbabwe during a July 4, 1986, U.S. Embassy reception. This is one clear-cut case where Africans acted in a symptomatic way as opposed to symbolic overtures. Former President Jimmy Carter walked out of this July 4 reception because of criticism of the U.S. administration for rejecting severe economic sanctions against South Africa while imposing them on Nicaragua because Carter felt that those statements were improper at a celebration. This is very interesting, since Jimmy Carter, during his presidency, was known as a president of symbolism because of his symbolic overtures while in office. This is a case where a Western leader wanted to remain in the realm of symbolic activity and criticize the African official for expressing concrete and true statements about the Ronald Reagan administration. In fact, the timing of those remarks by the Zimbabwean official was entirely appropriate. The July 4 celebration has severe connotations of freedom for all people. However, that freedom is a myth in terms of the U.S. commitment toward nonwhite people (in this case, South Africans). It is inarguable that the Reagan administration had no real rationale for not supporting sanctions against South Africa due to U.S. relations with other countries such as Nicaragua and Poland. President Carter was wrong by walking out and admonishing the Zimbabwean official (Ridley, 1992).

It is critical for change consultants to understand the ramifications of symbolism in neurological thought that affects judgement and decision making. That ultimately always translates and transfers to the business and corporate arena.

The following is another perfect illustration of the STP being used in place of a symbolic one. A *Wall Street Journal* article described a black MIT graduate, Omar Green, and his relationship with his boss, the CEO of Xionics Document Technology, Inc. This symptomatic behavior ultimately raised the productivity of the company and made it possible for new ideas to form and take shape. Note the following: "Mr. Gilkes, who was hired as a change agent for Xionics, did not look at Omar Green symbolically, but symptomatically: For Mr. Gilkes, Mr. Green represents technical and entrepreneurial thinking critical to his company's future, a chance to shake up resistant middle managers who have bucked many of his efforts to change Xionics. 'He can tell me things I am not seeing as a 58-year-old white man,' Mr. Gilkes says" (Kaufman, 1997, p. A7).

The article goes on to say: "All things did not go smoothly, as there was some discomfort: One day, he [Omar Green] startled a roomful of senior engineers by questioning the power capacity of a Xionics computer chip. 'Who the hell is this loudmouth, smart-aleck kid?' Mr. Morris, his fellow engineer, recalls thinking at the time. Mr. Green was later put in charge of testing the new chip, overseeing eight engineers, most of them at least ten years older.' "

What is key here is that Gilkes looked at Green and saw a black man but did not mythologize Green's existence as a black man. Instead, by making him a member of an important team, Gilkes saw the contribution that Green could make to the company. The article goes on:

Mr. Gilkes says he sees Mr. Green as crucial in his drive to turn around Xionics. In his 2½ years as CEO, Mr. Gilkes has taken Xionics public, doubled the number of employees to more than 200 and boosted sales to an estimated $40 million this year from $9 million in 1994. Mr. Gilkes has assigned Mr. Green to an elite team to develop an easy-to-use box that would give users access to their televisions, stereos, VCRs and computers, enabling customers to send and receive everything from music to computer files. (Kaufman, 1997, p. A7)

This is a clear-cut example of productivity derived from using an STP.

There was no mythologizing, no connotations, but seeing things as they really are in their ultimate state. This is extremely important. Gilkes saw things as they really are— he saw reality—he did not add to it—he did not mythologize the facts. This importance cannot be over-emphasized. If this situation were approached from a symbolizing point of view, things would have turned out much differently. (Ridley, 2001, p. 91)

The so-called new global economy can never prosper as long as symbols affect the neurological process of the human brain, which causes people to act out in totally irrational and unreasonable ways.

A CHARGE TO CONSULTANTS

Consultants must understand the dynamics between symbols and symptoms if they are to be effective in solving the immense diversity of problems they face in the world today. Remembering that symbols and myths are synonymous, it is easy to see the havoc caused by myths in civilization today. Again, we use academia to illustrate our point. David Mac Ritchie in his book *Ancient and Modern Britons* quotes Andrew Lang in his statement on mythology: "Max Müller observes that most of the ancient myths are absurd and irrational, savage and senseless. Was there a period of temporary insanity through which the human mind had to pass? Indeed, wherever we look, in every part of the world,

142   *Global Views and Experiences of Change*

we find the same kinds of stories, the same traditions, the same myths" (Ritchie, 1884, p. 90). Ritchie goes on to state, "The future student of mythology will ask, is there any contemporary stage of thought and of society in which the wildest marvels of mythology are looked on as the ordinary facts of experience?" (Ritchie, 1884, reprinted 1991, p. 91).

Despite all the literature, the one example that we try to avoid is racism. Racism must be weeded out if corporate productivity is to be realized. Racism is the "one absurd myth" that we experience in our corporate lives all over this world. Racism is the myth that answers the question posed by Ritchie. As long as mythologies exist, racism will exist. In order to eradicate racism in all its forms, we have to eliminate mythology. This includes eliminating the symbol systems that create mythology. Any other starting point for the eradication of racism will prove to be futile unless we deal with the symbol systems that produce the behavior that makes racism a global practice.

The statements by Ritchie leave no doubt of the importance of the study of symbolism and its resulting mythology to the human condition. Consultants may not realize that they are symbolic analysts. As such, they must study the dynamics of mythology; indeed, they must be students of mythology. Unfortunately, our traditional educational system is inadequate in providing the tools to solve problems in this highly technological environment. As stated several times in this chapter, we live out our lives in a mythological mode that we deem to be the norm, no matter how ridiculous, absurd, and vicious that mythology is. That mythology is malignant, and as Max Müller states, it can be found from one end of the globe to the other. This is what makes the job of consultants so critical—they must work in that environment and recognize the trend toward symbolizing every area of activity and mythologizing to justify that symbolization. Unless we understand those dynamics, change consultants will be ineffective.

CONCLUSION

The STP concept is used as the key mechanism in my consulting efforts to provide management and productivity services worldwide. When asked, we offer preliminary suggestions on what is needed to solve a corporation's or country's particular problem. Not unlike W.E. Deming, we require total support from the highest echelons of management to implement our concepts. With that understanding, we provide education on the dynamics of symbolism and the use of the STP in place of symbolism. This education is offered in the form of workshops, seminars, and training sessions. Our consultations last as long as the company feels necessary; sometimes our client relationship is long-term. What we provide that other consulting firms do not is the creation and implementation of a concept that radically rearranges the behavior of people as never before. Because it advances a way in which people are able to make better decisions, both business and personal, and because it has such a direct effect on people's behavior patterns, our STP rearranges the structure of the world in a way that has never been experienced before.

Consultants who hope to render change must be clear: The operative business mode that has been in existence since time immemorial has shown the results of a symbolic and mythological thought process. This is totally unacceptable, for it has wreaked havoc in every area of human activity. Unless that is changed, nothing will take place that can be deemed to be sane. By changing that mind-set through the symptomatic thought process, we can change those long-held assumptions that have castrated every area of business from one end of the globe to the other. Changing our mind-set is a most difficult task, but there is no doubt we cannot continue as we are now, which is business as usual.

REFERENCES

Blanton, K. 1999. Massachusetts cases raise questions of subtle forms of workplace bias. *Boston Globe*, October 15, p. B-1.
Dixon, M. 1990. The missing measures of practical promise. *Financial Times*, December 7, p. 3.
Garber, M. 1998. *Symptoms of culture*. New York: Routledge.
Glover, C. 1998. Ancient tablets bolster idea Egypt was first civilization. *Philadelphia Tribune*, December 17, pp. C1–C2.
Hammonds, K.H. 1998. Invisible in the executive suite. *Business Week*, December 21, pp. 22–28.
Herrnstein, R.J., & Murray, C. 1994. *The bell curve: Intelligence and class structure in American life*. New York: Free Press.
Jett, J., & Chartrand, S. 1999. *Black and white on Wall Street*. New York: William Morrow & Co.
Kaufman, J. 1997. Odd couple: How Omar Green, 27, became the point man and protégé for a CEO. *Wall Street Journal*, July 22, p. A7.
Kaufman, J. 2001. Trading places: Where blacks have more than whites, racial tension erupts. *Wall Street Journal*, February 8, p. A1.
Lefkowitz, M. 1996. *Not out of Africa: How Afrocentrism became an excuse to teach myth as history*. New York: Basic Books.
Massey, G. 1998. *Gerald Massey's lectures*. Brooklyn, NY: A&B Book Publishers.
Mbeki, T. 2001a. Briefing: Millennium Africa renaissance program: Implementation issues. Paper presented at the World Economic Forum, Davos, Switzerland, January 28.
Mbeki, T. 2001b. Addressing the backlash against globalisation: A southern perspective of the problem. Paper presented at the World Economic Forum, Davos, Switzerland, January 28.
Miller, J.P. 2000. Bias complaint put in new light. *Chicago Tribune*, September 10, p. 1.
O say can you see what that flag means? That anthem? 2000. *New York Times*, December 16, p. B11.
Poe, J. 2000. African-American plaintiffs seek full rewards of corporate workplace. *Atlanta Journal and Constitution*, October 15, p. A2.
Reich, R. 1995. Are consultants worth their weight? *Financial Times*, February 24, pp. 1–2.

Ridley, E.J. 1982. The neurological misadventure of primordial man. *Journal of Black Male/Female Relationships* (Autumn): 59.

Ridley, E.J. 1992. *An African answer: The key to global productivity*. Lawrenceville, NJ: Africa World Press.

Ridley, E.J. 2001. *Symbolism revisited: Notes on the symptomatic thought process*. Lawrenceville, NJ: Pine Hill Press.

Ritchie, D. 1884. *Ancient and modern Britons*. Reprint, Freeman, SD: Pine Hill Press, 1991.

Sappenfield, M. 1999. Harassment: New race-bias issue: The workplace climate. *Christian Science Monitor*, August 17, p. 1.

Segal, D. 1999. Denny's serves up a sensitive image. *Washington Post*, April 7, pp. A2, E1.

Soros, G. 2000. *Open society: Reforming global capitalism*. New York: Public Affairs.

Sternberg, R., & Wagner, R. (eds.). 1990. *Practical intelligence*. London: Cambridge University Press.

Walsh, M.W. 2000. Where G.E. falls short: Diversity at the top. *New York Times*, September 3, pp. 3-1, 3-13.

Part III

Change Cases

Chapter 8

Change Management Methods in an Exciting New World of Business-to-Business Commerce

Ronald R. Sims and William J. Mea

INTRODUCTION

Traditionally, change management is associated with helping people in well-established large organizations adapt to new realities of business due to a new software application, reengineering, reorganization, or merger-acquisition. Most practitioners in consulting firms and academics have focused on the adaptive mechanisms that help resolve organizational issues during such transformations. The lessons learned from the study of change management and organizational behavior have exciting new possibilities for organizations that are now emerging in the business-to-business marketplace. Although in its infancy as an area of study, change management when applied to business-to-business (B2B) and business-to-portal (B2P) commerce represents dynamic new business models at the core of major changes in industry.

Imagine that you are a change consultant given an opportunity to shape the future of business models in B2B and B2P. What would you do and how would you make your decisions on what the most effective activities are in this exciting area? Practitioners from organizational development (OD) and similar backgrounds are being offered exactly that opportunity in developing new B2Bs. Few, if any, practitioners in OD or other areas of management have prior experience building these new models. The classics of OD literature (such as Dyer, 1987; French & Bell, 1978; Hurst, 1995; Lippitt & Lippitt, 1986; Schein, 1987, 1988, 1992), which could normally serve as a guide, have more limited relevance. This chapter offers some insights on the background and context of change management as well as suggestions for specialists who wish to consult effectively in B2B/B2P. It relies on the experience of the authors and their colleagues in working with these new organizations. Throughout the discussion

Figure 8.1
Illustration of Value Model for Business-to-Portal Commerce

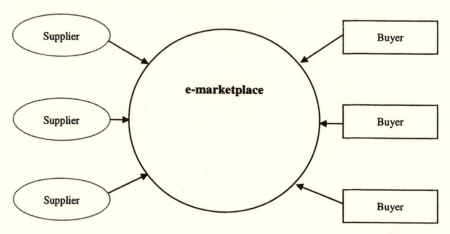

we will refer to new organizations, B2B, e-marketplaces, and B2P. E-business
is understood to mean the more generic form of new business purposefully built
on an Internet platform. B2Bs are businesses founded primarily for commerce
between companies. E-marketplaces are a specific type of e-commerce in which
suppliers are brought together with buyers to expedite sales of products and
services, much as Wall Street is a trading post in New York where potential
buyers and sellers congregate for exchange.

EMERGENCE OF THE NEW B2B AND B2P MODELS

The core objectives and practices of B2B have been in existence for some
time. Businesses have been exchanging data through electronic data interchange
(EDI) for many years. Since most major companies have already automated
their key functions, the remaining major challenge has been to automate processes which would connect companies to one another. What makes the new
B2B unique is the addition of the Internet as a platform (with the adoption of
common standards) that makes it possible for companies without huge information technology budgets and preestablished partnerships to enter this business
space. The addition of B2P adds yet another dimension to the options available
for businesses. E-marketplaces answer a key business challenge by bringing
together sellers and buyers to exchange products and services in one location
without concern for location, prior existing relationship, or time. This is illustrated in Figure 8.1.

There are two types of e-marketplaces that develop either vertically or hori-
zontally. Vertical marketplaces focus on a specific industry and work to resolve
their supply-chain inefficiencies. Horizontal marketplaces, on the other hand, cut
across industries and automate functional processes from end to end. In our

Figure 8.2
Illustration of Vertical vs. Horizontal Marketplaces

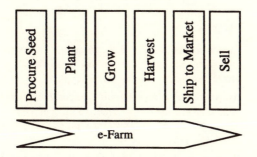

fictitious e-farm example (see Figure 8.2), there could be an e-marketplace that brings together buyers and sellers focused in each of the markets to increase and automate efficiencies. The type of market, horizontal or vertical, depends on the type of inefficiencies that are currently operating in the market, the solution offered, the model for transactions, and how revenues are going to be generated ("Shaping the B2B universe," 2000). The benefits that the new e-marketplaces bring to the market include (Means & Schnieder, 2000):

- Aggregated purchasing power;
- New process efficiency;
- Supply chain integration;
- Aggregation of content and communities of interest; and
- New market efficiency.

In the future, all businesses will be forced by this new business model to examine their own efficiencies. Rapid disintermediation of non-value-added participants out of the supply chain and reintermediation of other value-added or customizing agents forces swiftness to become features of all successful organizations. In a Darwinian sense, those organizations that can adapt quickly, change to meet customer desires, and do so effectively while partnering with others will shape the future of successful businesses.

KEY TERMS AND DEFINITIONS

With the introduction of Internet terms into the language of business, we find that much of the nontechnology public feels lost in a jumble of acronyms. For example, one day while we were preparing the new CEO of a dot com to sell B2P services to his former vertical industry colleagues, he quipped, "Hey, I've just started to drink this fancy coffee and you're telling me I have to tell people java beans have something to do with our software?" For those who have similar needs, we provide some of the key terms and definitions (see Table 8.1) to enable you to quickly adapt to the language of B2B commerce.

Table 8.1
Key Internet-Related Terms

Term	Meaning
Aggregate spend	In an e-marketplace or B2B situation, to combine the dispersed requirements for buying of commodities into one grouping in order to create purchasing leverage with suppliers.
Auction	Allows multiple buyers to bid competitively for products from individual buyers and is well suited to sales of hard-to-move goods such as surplus and excess inventory; types include English, Dutch, Reverse, and Japanese, among others.
B2B	Business-to-Business—describes the transactions between one organization and another. This differs from business-to-customer.
B2P	Business-to-Portal—describes business for trading, buying, and selling which takes place over a third-party electronic intermediary who acts as a hub to bring together buyers and sellers.
Catalog Aggregator	Normalizing product catalogs for several vendors to enable speedy comparisons; Catalog Aggregators make sense of purchase options from multiple vendors.
Channel	Means of distribution for goods and services.
COIN	Community of Interest—a location on an e-marketplace where individual participants can gain vertical content knowledge and share information with each other.
Critical Mass	When a critical number of buyers and sellers participate in an Internet marketplace, a point is reached where the exchange of goods and services becomes more efficient than traditional channels.
Disintermediation	Removing non-value-added intermediary companies or functions from a supply chain in an effort to seek competitive advantage. Was thought of as the primary benefit of e-marketplaces.
E-commerce	Commerce conducted over the Internet or electronic data interchange (EDI); may be to consumers or companies.
EDI	Electronic data interchange—an older and more expensive form of data transfer between companies.
E-marketplace	Also known as Net Market, MetaMediaries, e-portals, e-hubs, or exchanges—electronic gathering places where buyers and suppliers gather to trade and sell goods and services.
ERP	Enterprise resource planning—complex software applications used to manage inventory and integrate business processes (e.g., SAP, Oracle, and Baan).
Fragmentation	A market situation in which there is no dominant group of buyers or suppliers; it is inefficient for many buyers to be chasing after many suppliers.

(continued)

Table 8.1 (continued)

Term	Meaning
Liquidity	As an e-marketplace adds suppliers in response to the needs of initial buyers, it increases the potential benefits of being a member and also increases the benefit to buyers. As the number of buyers increases and the cost of transactions decreases, the purchasing power of buyers increases. In addition, buyers who have materials or services for sale can also benefit by becoming suppliers to others.
MRO	Maintenance, repair, and operating equipment are routine purchases that are required to run a business but do not go directly into the product developed by a company.
Onboarding	The process steps involved in the legal and technical integration of new businesses as they join an e-marketplace.
Reintermediation	Following disintermediation and evaluation of a new value chain business model, reconfiguring to add intermediary companies who bring value to the customer supply chain.
RFP	Request for Proposal—an invitation to suppliers to bid on supplying products or services that are difficult to describe.
RFQ	Request for Quote—an invitation to suppliers to bid on easily described products or services needed by a company.
Reverse Auction	Where buyers post their need and suppliers bid to fulfill the need.
Sticky	Ability to retain participants on a web site or e-business.
XML	eXtensible markup language—the standard for Internet e-marketplaces which provides a flexible way to describe product specifications or business terms.

Why Does B2B Matter for Change Management?

The challenge of any new business solution is not the technology. Technology solutions generally have been developed, tested, and adapted to meet specific process challenges. Moreover, technology solutions are replaced as new technologies are rapidly developed and supercede older ones. Where new business solutions fall potentially short is on the people side. Because B2B and B2P are focused on the process of communication and exchange between companies, a new level of partnership is required between businesses so that they can effectively carry out new operations that will benefit them. The major challenges, talent notwithstanding, are the people issues. When these efforts are not well managed, it can result in "brutal infighting, backstabbing, and blind panic" (Kirkpatrick, 2000, p. 87). Much of what has been learned in change management in recent years has been learned through enterprise resource planning (ERP), which focuses on automating and integrating internal business functions.

The advent of e-marketplaces (also known as value-added communities or trading communities) carries the boundary of change beyond the walls of the current organization and into relationships with other companies as they learn to navigate new rules of business solutions. As one can see from Figure 8.2, the number of relationships to be managed increases exponentially, which begs for the skills provided by change consultants.

CONTRASTING OLD AND NEW CHANGE MODELS

In the old model, a change consultant's role is to facilitate the people process in an organization that must accept changes that come with reengineering, information systems implementation, or organizational restructuring. The role for change consultants in the new model, especially the founding and developing of B2Bs, is still facilitation, but it is a facilitation in which change is already accepted as a way of doing business, in which leaders have drive, and in which transformation is part of everyone's desire.

The work of change management practitioners has an entirely different focus in the new B2B/B2P organization. Whereas consultants in more traditional organizations concentrate their energies on building acceptance and working through issues of resistance to help manage change, consultants operating in this new space concentrate their efforts on managing the project energies. That is, there is typically so much activity in a new Internet business as it forms that the challenge of change consultants is to use their skills in managing the people side of business to help the project maintain consistent focus. Table 8.2 summarizes the differences of operating in the two different models.

Leadership

When working with leaders in organizations undergoing change, the frequent focus for change practitioners is to get enough attention from the executive group to communicate with their organization about the "burning platform" reason why the change is being initiated, how this relates to the vision of the company's strategic future, and how the plan will be implemented. Change consultants frequently become trusted business advisors and counselors, assisting management to get stakeholders to accept change. In the new model/situation of change, leadership is focused on being points of reference with whom staff meet frequently and who must reiterate the objectives while simultaneously playing a tactical role in the development of the new organization.

Human Resources

Much of what change consultants do on standard projects in organizations in the old model focuses on adapting traditional human resource processes to meet the needs of the projected changes, including getting them the right training. In the new model/situation one cannot do without application of traditional human

Table 8.2
Old and New Change Models

Area	Old Model	New Model
Leadership	• Focus on getting leaders visible to support projects	• Focus on employing the leader's capabilities as a convergence point for the key goals that must be accomplished quickly
Human Resources	• Focus on a review of systems in place and redefining the objectives of the organization	• Focus on developing a process that supports the organization through its infancy but is not too rigid to adapt
Communications	• Focus on helping the organization be clear about key project "messages" that support a project	• Focus on the broad spectrum of communications techniques that reflect the new identity of the organization and organize even as the organization is moving quickly
Involvement	• Focus on getting stakeholders engaged in supporting the project	• Focus on coordination of stakeholders who are already engaged but managing their sense of ownership

resource processes for recruiting, hiring, benefits, and rewards. However, there is a different focus in such organizations on the rewards being more at risk, hiring creative people, and putting together teams of people who can adapt quickly to situations that can transform almost overnight. Recruiting people with industry expertise, comfort with information technology, and who are constitutionally built to adapt quickly is a challenging prospect. Moreover, the challenge of organizational design in B2Bs, where changes may be rapid, is also demanding.

Communications

The framework of typical change projects involves using communications vehicles already in place to reach out to stakeholders and help them understand why a major change is underway and how it will enhance the business. To some degree in the case of Internet businesses there needs to be a focus on communicating core messages as well. However, the options for communications vehicles can expand quickly, and the focus of communications needs to switch to external stakeholders so that they can develop confidence in the value of the new relationship they are forming with, for example, an e-marketplace that will be an intermediary for their products.

Involvement

Within the context of standard projects, some change consultants try to avert resistance issues by getting stakeholders to participate at some level in the requirements gathering and by encouraging their design input. In the new situation in B2B organizations it is taken for granted that the work force is mobilized to be involved in designing the future and to be involved at every step of the organization's development. The challenge in this case is to get staff, many of whom are drawn to B2B by an aggressive constitution, to cooperate and pull together enough to drive toward goals that achieve future objectives. The facilitation expertise which most change consultants possess can play a major role in helping these new organizations quickly build the momentum they need to compete effectively.

THE NEW CHALLENGE FACING CHANGE

In the face of exciting new models for business coming out of B2B and B2P, in which change consultants have an opportunity to play a role in shaping the future of industry, we find it surprising that many practitioners are themselves resistant to change. While some change consultants borrow freely from other areas, most tend to define their specialty more narrowly in terms of traditional organizational development techniques and human resource practices. For instance, we have often heard of change consultants in the Big Five consulting firms who say, "It came on so suddenly that we haven't figured out what we can do on these B2B engagements." In some cases there are others who tell us: "That's just not the kind of work we do." In taking this approach, they write themselves out of the chance to influence the foundation of the future of business.

Much of the new Internet marketplace consulting is dominated by developers. These talented colleagues understand the technical challenges but often do not have the specific business or relationship understanding that is required to meet the challenges of B2B. While working on a B2B engagement, one of the authors found himself explaining the nature of change management to an associate who was a developer. A telling response to this was, "Oh, you have to deal with those squirrelly end users." Because B2B is not just about changing technology, project leaders need change management specialists to create success in their B2B projects.

NEW FOCUS AREAS IN CHANGE MANAGEMENT

Given the importance of B2B in shaping the future of commerce and given the needs that change management consultants can fulfill, it stands to reason that practitioners should be quickly gathering whatever skills they can. In order to meet this challenge, we reference a number of concept areas that can supplement traditional approaches to change consulting for use in B2B situations. Our experience shows that borrowing from these concepts and translating them into change management activities leads to better delivery and new opportunities for B2B projects. From a change practitioner perspective, they add new skills, and from a project perspective, they add value. These additional foci, along with translations of traditional focus areas, are summarized in Table 8.3 and expanded upon in the text that follows. This does not, of course, exhaust the possibilities, but rather it sketches the areas where we have found initial successes in B2B change.

Speed

It is often said that one of the key areas of difference between operating in more traditional companies and the organizations involved in Internet business is speed. To some degree this is true, but we would qualify that statement by saying that the true difference is not the absolute speed of change but the speed at which decisions are made and the comfort level with making potential mistakes. Let us illustrate. In Figure 8.3, the center of the oval is used to represent the starting point for making a decision. Given that there is little prior experience in B2B/B2P, no player in the organization can rely on consultations with peers or leaders. He or she must make a decision quickly. Movement in any direction, based on whatever information is available (from point A to point B) will provide some feedback on the value of the decision. As it crosses the threshold of becoming a decision that cannot be changed, the decision maker will have learned something and can make directional changes that will ultimately lead to a different decision (from point B to point C). In a more traditional organization one would normally want to get information from many sources before making a risky decision. The point here is that in the process of working in B2Bs it is more valuable to make a speedy decision and modify it with incoming data than to analyze what data is available to make a decision. Failing to make movement in any direction is more likely to lead to failure than a fast decision based on solid but scant information. Just as the imperatives of speed and improvising during wartime yield better surgical procedures, the decision speed for B2B will generate improved business solutions.

Leadership

One of the major issues faced in B2B situations, not unlike more traditional projects, is to get the chief executive officer (CEO) focused on delivering consistent and understandable core messages that link to the company vision. Where a vision has yet to be developed, as is the case at the beginning of many B2Bs, this is all the more critical, since many CEOs are drawn away in external sales

Table 8.3
B2B/B2P Change Focus Features

B2B/B2P Change Focus	Focus Features
Speed	• Focus on quick decision making to avoid paralysis of analysis
Leadership	• Focus on helping CEO communicate a solid message about the value of the business to suppliers and key potential partners, and keeping executives focused in a dynamic environment
Technology	• Understanding core technology basics as well as applying concepts to control the dynamic atmosphere; thus preventing surprise delays, overelaboration of detail, and increasing conflict
Human Resources	• Employing time-tested processes for building the infrastructure, but with the realization that new B2B staff have different needs than in traditional companies
Communications	• The new focus is for keeping internal staff from being overwhelmed, and at the same time keeping them up to date on the most critical information
Involvement	• Ensuring that people are not working at cross purposes
External Relationships	• Working across functions to get an effective relationship developed with potential market peers and participants
Strategy and Metrics	• Recognizing the limitations of decision making that is based too much on impulse and not enough in terms of time-tested financial outcomes
Project Management	• A focus on generic project requirements, simplicity in scope, and a focus on the fundamental process and products that must be delivered
Conflict Management	• Focus on resolving issues quickly as opposed to resolving them to everyone's satisfaction
Process-Quality Improvement	• Using simple tools developed in a new setting to get teams "off the dime" and moving for speedy solutions

efforts. Because time for reflection is rare in these circumstances, the change consultant rarely has an opportunity to become a trusted business advisor at the very beginning. On the other hand, because the initial start-up of a B2B involves sorting out style issues among the other executives, there are opportunities to become an advisor by helping the executive leadership team focus less on stylistic differences and personal agendas and more on the action imperatives of the new B2B. Because few executives have been through the experience of a B2B start-up, a change consultant is the ideal candidate to provide feedback and

Figure 8.3
Illustration of Speed of Decision Making

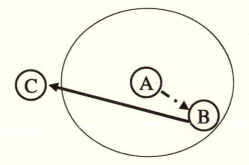

case examples about what leadership behaviors are effective, and the consultant can exert tremendous influence at the outset of building the organization's foundation. Another area of influence in which change consultants can make a difference is in helping clarify the leadership's rules about how decisions are made. Clarifying the foundational understanding about who makes what decisions and under what circumstances helps the leaders quickly establish a pattern of action with one another and with subordinates in B2B. It also frees up energies that can be devoted to work as opposed to managing conflicts and unclear communications about decisions.

Yet another area in leadership in which change consultants can play a role is in the process of developing the vision and mission statement. Because change consultants bring solid listening skills, capacity for personal understanding, and capabilities in helping people reach decisions together, they are good candidates for this type of activity. In one B2B case, we observed "hard-baked" executives, who were initially even opposed to a vision statement, find that it became an effective external marketing tool to help potential partners understand the value proposition as well as a tool for common dialogue with one another when conflicts arose.

Technology

While change consultants are not called upon to be coders, it pays for them to be aware of the main features and capabilities of the systems with which they are working. Software forms the structure upon which modern business and government is run. A basic understanding of Enterprise Resource Programs (ERPs), such as SAP and Oracle, Customer Resource Management (CRM), such as Siebel, and Web-based procurement systems, such as Ariba or Commerce One, can be indispensable if one is going to quickly adopt the language required for B2B situations.

Because software and those who work with it has "helped us create, access,

Figure 8.4
Rational Unified Process

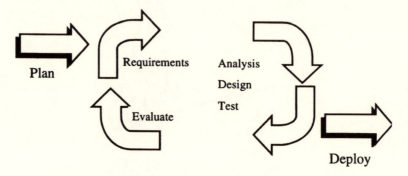

and visualize information in previously inconceivable ways," (Krutchen, 2000, p. 3), it also pays to be aware of some of the ideas shaping its development. One of the more interesting approaches shaping technology development is Rational Unified Process (RUP). While it is a software engineering development methodology, its concepts lend themselves well to the practical aspects of managing the change aspects of B2B projects. For example, it notes that a number of change challenges are typically faced on B2B projects. These include inaccurate understanding of what end users need, team members who get in each other's way, imprecise communications, subjective understanding of the project, and propagation of changes. Figure 8.4 illustrates that managing software development—or in the case of B2B, organizational development—requires iteratively forcing the team to drive closure at each new step for incremental process in short time frames. This contrasts the standard approach to the traditional development project that uses a waterfall approach in longer time frames. In this case, development is planned in small steps, beginning with planning, making collaborative decisions on design, testing, and evaluating before moving on to planning the next step. Using this process specifies creating no more detail than is necessary so as to avoid needless energy that may require backtracking. This methodology has much to offer as a guide. Development in RUP employs constant evaluation of repeated steps, to make firm decisions based on real user/customer need case examples, to help people understand the practical challenges at hand. In essence, it helps guide a team to avoid heroic efforts and too much unnecessary detail, to drive agreements to avoid late conflicts, and to focus on user requirements. In terms of managing requirements, this means having a clear strategy with a clear understanding of the stakeholder needs and translating this into clear and easily understood requirements before unnecessary steps are taken.

Human Resources

Building a B2B from the ground up, as most are being developed these days, requires change consultants to employ well-established human resource processes. In the context of B2B, some additional considerations are worth high-lighting. Compensation systems need to motivate behavior that is more team focused. These organizations tend to attract people who are less risk averse but also aggressive. In these circumstances compensation can be used as a means to guide more cooperative behavior than might ordinarily be the case for such individuals. It also argues for putting a higher level of potential reward at risk with incentives for creative yet practical results that can be brought to market quickly. We have observed that leaders in B2Bs tend to be overconfident in people's ability to operate in a matrix type structure. Unless an organization is extremely small, we would advise against this because people quickly become overwhelmed with uncontrolled levels of incoming data and conflicting demands.

Communications

As previously noted, much of what constitutes effective communications in a B2B situation is an extension of the communications one would normally employ in a traditional situation. However, because the options and the media expand so dramatically and occur in such a rapid fashion, there needs to be an even greater effort at communicating the core message well. Executives need to be very clear and very consistent. Because the interface with external partners and customers is so swift, and because the business situation can change very rapidly, it is critical that each communication have value and add something new. At the same time communications must maintain a signature theme or else they risk getting washed out in a sea of other communications. B2Bs must attract and maintain relationships (for example, with supplies), which means that building trust and confidence is a central theme in effective business where change consultants can assist. A unique example of communications venues in B2B is the development of communities of interest, more commonly referred to as COINs. B2Bs, in an effort to attract potential customers, provide an electronic venue where vertical industry knowledge is captured and where individual participants can gather to deposit, share, and access knowledge from a repository or from each other. Structuring the COIN correctly can lead to the development of a preference for a site, and as positive experiences build, individuals may influence their companies to become new partners or at least increase their participation. All of this leads to greater liquidity of a marketplace, increases the human dimension, and represents another area where change consultants can have influence.

Involvement

As previously noted, change consultants in B2B organizations can play a critical role in assisting the facilitation of the people process of newly emerging organizations. In the midst of building the solution they bring to the marketplace, organizations will have a number of teams "heads down" and focused on their own deliverables without an appreciation of the needs of other teams without whom they cannot develop an overall solution. In these cases we have found it useful to employ change consultants to act as liaisons between teams. These consultants can quickly identify issues that could undermine teams and can project where cooperation across teams is needed to develop joint solutions. In this way change consultants can help teams understand what steps will lead to the success of the entire system. In one case, we developed a global process view of an organization's processes in relationship to the typical customer and product development life cycle. This helped new members of the organization quickly understand how their activities influenced the entire system, and it helped current employees understand where areas of cooperation were required across team boundaries to enable development of solutions that provide value to customers.

External Relationships

Another key area where change consultants can add value in B2B/B2P is in developing new relationships with suppliers to buyers. Typically a new e-marketplace is launched under the sponsorship of a large buyer or set of buyers with the hope of leveraging buying power through aggregating spending across internal and external organizations. Suppliers who have never had to negotiate under these conditions fear for the viability of their companies. Threats to suppliers include decreasing margins, elimination of smaller suppliers, and being cut out of business in a world that has been relationship based. Anyone with experience in the auto industry can recall periods in history where automobile manufacturers placed their suppliers in threatening positions with hard negotiations on suppliers' margins. In many cases, managing suppliers' relationships is left to sales and marketing people alone, without integration across the many internal functions that must interact with suppliers to make a win-win relationship.

Change consultants can be critical in identifying the specific business issues faced by suppliers and can build these concerns into solutions that are developed by the e-marketplace. Within the e-marktplace, change consultants can play a critical role in integrating the work with marketing, sales, customer resource management (CRM), technology, and legal functions, which all bring a different interest to the onboarding of a supplier into an e-marketplace. The primary benefits in joining an e-marketplace for suppliers include expanding the number of buyers who may be purchasers and developing new products in partnership with large buyers as the product requirements and niche offerings can be developed. The challenge for change management consultants is to play an effective role in working with suppliers on their concerns and weaving these back into integrated win-win decisions and solutions across the e-marketplace functions that must develop the solutions.

Strategy and Metrics

Another related set of concepts developed for strategy uses a "balanced score-card." This approach, first developed by Kaplan and Norton (1996), helps leaders define the mission, vision, goals, and metrics for a company in key areas such as financial, customer, learning, and business process. In terms of change management, the balanced scorecard provides a sequential approach to developing and implementing company strategies so that stakeholders understand what the company is trying to achieve and how it will be measured. By developing targets at the leadership level, involving managers in the metrics, communicating the scorecard through team and individual performance management, and using the resulting feedback, an organization develops cohesive direction that provides competitive advantage.

Project Management Techniques

While change management skills are part of every consultant's and project manager's "bag of tricks," the drive toward speed in B2B organizations requires a blending of the best methodologies into one seamless effort with new twists. Change specialists often ignore the literature on project management as if it were only a semi-technical specialty worthwhile only in very large projects. Because the literature assumes that one can bring a rational method to managing the chaos often a part of projects, it offers some of the most fertile ideas for incorporation into B2B projects.

We find that during initial stages of B2B projects when the team must determine what must be accomplished, there is a flurry of activity with few tangible results. Often the team's thinking is constrained by project management software tools, by a focus on details, and by what that team wants to produce from its prior experience. Less coordinated thought is given to the true needs of the B2B organization and more to what the consultants have done before that is similar. Instead of planning with a joint end in mind, they focus on what they want out of the project. Since B2B projects are all new and unique, there is little awareness of the constraints imposed by other teams' needs, by what the likely issues are, and by the issues that could thwart the success of the project. Fortunately there are "tools" that change consultants can quickly adapt for these B2B situations to prevent project teams from going down a track that leads to a joint wreck.

One of the best methodologies we have found for helping a project stay focused, and which lends itself well to B2B projects, is the SMART methodology developed by Hartman (2000). This methodology specifies defining project priorities, understanding what stakeholders need in terms of tangible outcomes from the beginning, defining the key results, and developing a schedule around realistic time frames with time built in for managing risks and conflict. Change consultants can use the methodology to help guide B2B project teams more successfully. This methodology also catalogs a number of simple, yet practical, tools that can be used at each stage of B2B development. For example, a tool called the "priority triangle" can be employed at the beginning of the project to ask organizational leaders whether time, quality, or cost is the highest priority of the project. When the responses are compared in a group setting, the leadership team can come to a clear and shared definition of what the project priority will be. Without this, issues and conflicts can be built into the project from the outset.

Conflict Management Techniques

While conflict management plays an important role in traditional change management situations in which parties may argue over limited resources, in B2B situations it plays a role in quickly gaining required agreement in decision-making situations in which differences in approach need to be quickly resolved. Negotiation techniques play a central role in traditional literature (for example, Fisher & Ury, 1981). We feel that approaches that are based on a brief process that focuses on developing minimum required agreement to move forward is more productive than one in which all parties to a conflict feel they have won something. Once again, the speed with which one comes to conclusion often has greater value than a negotiated settlement. If a change consultant in a B2B situation can assist the speed of a decision in a problem area, all parties are eventual winners (for example, when the company succeeds and options packages yield financial rewards). Although compromise is often not the best result in B2B situations, an interesting approach to conflict management is provided by Al-Tabtabai, Alex, and Abou-alfotough (2001). Their approach provides a systematic methodology for resolving differences by using cognitive feedback to focus on the process, as opposed to focusing on the end result.

Quality and Process Improvement Techniques

While quality and process improvement does not draw the attention, and the literature about it focuses on improving systems in place, the principles and tools associated with this movement still provide excellent resources for consultants on B2B and B2P projects. For example, one organization, Goal/QPC, provides an excellent set of reference tools for process (Brassard & Ritter, 1994), team management (Joiner, 1995; Scholtes, 1988), creativity (Ritter & Brassard, 1998), facilitation (Benz, 1999), and problem solving (Goal/QPC, 2000). On B2B projects there is rarely enough time for full consideration of a "seven-step process" when issues arise. However, there are frequent issues in building B2Bs because the experience is unique and there are few well-worn paths that consultants can follow. In these circumstances workstream teams get mired in their own objectives without taking other considerations into view. In such circumstances tools such as the Ishikawa ("fishbone") diagram can help teams work out the root causes of issues. Similarly, when teams find that their work is slowing down, it is useful to use Pareto charts to get them to focus on speeding up the project by not letting the 20% of minor source issues hold up the project. For example, if a change consultant can get teams to focus on achieving the major gains and not allow minor details that have little affect slow them down, momentum can be gained on a B2B project.

As evidenced by the new focus areas in change management described above, there are a number of skills or techniques that must be considered to enhance organizational success and ensure that organizations avoid becoming "e-culture" challenged. The introduction of B2Bs is having a profound impact on today's organizations as new models, techniques, and approaches to doing business are constantly being developed and old techniques discarded. Like many of their clients, change management practitioners are also facing future shock as they wrestle with redefining their role and change management approaches to fit the rapid changes and ever-growing challenges posed by new business models and new corporate cultures for the e-business economy.

An awareness of the complex environment in which today's organizations operate is evidenced by the new business models and their efforts to address the challenges imposed by the need to traverse such uncharted waters. As shapers of change, change management practitioners can play a critical role in helping organizations adjust to the changing focus and trends that affect them. However, to play such a role means that they must develop the skills necessary to be proactive agents of change. Proactive agents who help their clients win in the e-business environment do so by (1) developing corporate cultures that are not mired in the old economy, (2) building e-business strategies that provide a competitive advantage, and (3) responding to a constantly changing environment.

TRENDS AND FUTURE CONSIDERATIONS FOR RESEARCH

As we look to the future of changing the way we manage change, those change management specialists who wish to consult effectively in B2B/B2P must begin to recognize the limitations of the older change management models. For example, there are limitations to rational models of change produced by the strategic management theorists. Their view, that change is a series of strategic episodes in which each element of change has a specific beginning and a finite end, is insufficient when working with these new organizations. Another limitation to this view is the problem historically found in the change management literature—to limit the diagnosis of change processes to a relationship between the change management consultant and singular client. Both of these limitations share a common "limited frame of reference" which views organizational change as purely concerned with the mechanics of change in an organization. Thus, it ignores the absence of historical, processual, and contextual issues that inform the underlying dynamics of new organizations like B2Bs, e-marketplaces, and B2Ps. This is clearly an echo of Burns and Stalker's (1961) research from a contingency perspective, which suggests that organic structures (i.e., B2B, e-marketplace, and B2P) require the management of more dynamic processes. This is the foundational reality of the new organizations found in the new e-business environment as they struggle to survive and thrive in a dynamic global marketplace. As a result, the traditional planned change approach will continue to come under increased scrutiny when change management specialists try to apply it to organizations in the quick-paced and turbulent e-business environment.

Movement toward Process

Change management consulting with new e-business-oriented organizations is becoming more process focused rather than task focused. Change management within these organizations must operate at varying depths, ranging from the surface (task) level to the deeper behavioral (psychological and sociological) level. However, operating at varying depths must occur in a more rapid fashion than that to which change management specialists are typically accustomed. In short, time is of the essence, since these organizations have little patience for long, drawn out change diagnoses and interventions that in their view may slow them down. Increasingly, change management will be conceptualized as a dynamic process of modifying behavior by way of dramatically speeding up Kurt Lewin's (1951) "unfreezing, changing/moving, and refreezing" process. Alternative approaches to change management will increasingly emerge, founded on a different set of basic assumptions to those of the older planned change models.

New Consulting Roles

There is also every indication that the change management specialist's role will continue to expand. Change management specialists, therefore, need to be aware of their limits. They must realize that they will be constrained by their knowledge and skills. Change management specialists will need to improve their process consultation skills, since working with the new e-business-oriented organizations requires, in our view, an interpretive ability that relies on the knowledge and experiences of the organization's members in order to jointly anticipate, identify, and solve problems. Because change management specialists come from various backgrounds, more than ever before they need to know when to involve themselves or others in diagnostic evaluation or in the implementation phases. These organizations take on more generic forms, and their businesses are

• Purposefully built on an Internet platform;
• Founded primarily for commerce between companies; and

• Based in an environment in which suppliers are brought together with buyers to expedite sales of products and services.

Therefore, change management consultants must be prepared to work with multiple clients who may have different incentives or lack of incentives for participating in change management initiatives. Edgar Schein's (1997) work can be particularly useful to change management consultants working with e-businessss-oriented organizations, since his approach attempts to identify who the multiple clients are in a much more sophisticated way than previous approaches. Process consultancy is diagnostic precisely because it is based on a body of knowledge and depends on the skills necessary for working with these new organizations.

There is every indication that the business creations and transformation funneled by information technology, e-commerce, and e-business-oriented organizations will increasingly be the focus of change management specialists in the future. These organizations shift organization structure, labor skill sets, work design, and work processes in a move from traditional ways of doing business to B2B and B2P commerce. This represents the kind of change that many other organizations will face and the challenges change management consultants must meet.

New Models

B2B and B2P commerce represent dynamic new business models at the core of major changes in industry. This means that issues in these environments will be even more complex. Estimates suggest that the B2B form of business will grow to over $2.7 trillion by 2004 (Cummings & Worley, 2001; Dunn & O'Dell, 2000). Change management consultants will need to be there with the appropriate interventions to help both old and new organizations become more streamlined and flexible. Additionally, they must become more capable of improving themselves continuously in response to trends in the economy, the work force, and the technology. There is, however, every indication that many organizations are not aware of these practices; still others will resist the help that change management consultants can offer them. For example, despite the attention given to the growth of e-commerce in an economy that knows no boundaries, many organizations have not begun to prepare themselves to be active players in e-commece and are not prepared to organize into networks or to successfully manage strategic alliances. But these are the organizations of the future, and they will, with the assistance of change management specialists, invent entirely new entrepreneurial structures capable of exploiting new ideas and technologies quickly.

Impact of Technology and Users

As the economic and technical demands facing organizations require faster, more flexible organizations, the ability to help organizations manage change continuously will increasingly become a key role that change management specialists can play when working with B2Bs and B2Ps. Increasingly, change management consultants will also have to recognize that many interventions they jointly try to introduce into the lives of these new organizations will have to be planned and implemented in ways that encourage contributions from a variety of stakeholders at times that are convenient or at times when creative ideas emerge. New information technology (e.g., e-mail, newsgroups, and bulletin boards) now allows organization members to make these contributions at any time they are ready. Consider also the fact that groupware technologies allow members to discuss issues in chat rooms, in Web and videoconferences, and in more traditional telephone conferences.

As a result, the process of change management will continue to change. As technologies are used for the exchange of ideas, discussion of policies, decisions about changes to implement, and so forth, group dynamics will differ from those found in face-to-face meetings. Cummings and Worley (2001) note that not only will change management specialists need to be comfortable with this technology, they will also need to develop virtual facilitation skills that recognize these dynamics, which are so prevalent in the world of B2Bs and B2Ps. Our experience suggests that change management specialists will need to be able to use these more structured and assertive approaches to ensure that all organizational members have an opportunity to share their ideas—ideas which are key to organizational success in the e-business marketplace.

Finally, the world of the B2Bs and B2Ps means that organizations and their employees must deal with much more information with a greater number of participants in a shorter period of time. We have found that change management processes need to be adapted to recognize that members have more information at their fingertips. For example, organization intranets provide employees with an information channel that is richer, more efficient, more interactive, and more dynamic than are such traditional channels as newsletters and memos. Thus, intranets can provide a timely method for change management specialists to collect data on emerging issues, to provide performance feedback on key operational measures, and to involve members in key decisions, such as those involved in different phases of B2B projects.

Becoming Participants in Change

In order to be relevant in the years to come, change management specialists and the change management field as a whole must act together to be prepared to help meet the change needs of new organizations, B2Bs, e-marketplaces, and B2Ps. If we are to help influence or shape the future of e-business-oriented organizations, we must be prepared to adapt and change ourselves. We must equip ourselves with the knowledge, skills, and values necessary to help shape the future business models of these organizations. Our hope is that this chapter was able to inform readers enough to get them to prepare for a world of work dominated by immediacy, speed, instant solutions, and just-in-time approaches to change and change management.

CONCLUSION

Today's and tomorrow's companies will not have a guarantee of success if they fail to adapt to the new economy—an economy in which the harnessing of new business models like B2Bs and B2Ps is a key success requirement. Change management consultants must both understand themselves and help their clients to understand, emotionally and psychologically, that today's business environment is something different from anything that came before.

Since the emergence of the Web as the defining medium of business communication, many of the basics of business life have been reshaped: where businesses get their news, how they search for information, and what it takes to communicate with clients, employees, and partners. In a world that will continue to change so rapidly, there's an ever-growing amount to learn about new business models and new corporate cultures for the e-commerce economy.

The successful companies of tomorrow should be able to rely on change management specialists who are comfortable working in environments of uncertainty. These change management specialists must be able to provide high-quality, responsive, and continuous change management assistance for organizations that must create short-cycle innovation aimed at creating new markets for both new and mature products and services. To successfully serve their clients, change management specialists must continue to move beyond traditional approaches to change management and incorporate a wider range of interventions to meet the challenges of the new economy. Change management specialists must continue to change along with their clients. Such continuous improvement will undoubtedly lead to a new vitality, potency, and creativity, which is needed if change management specialists are to continue to add value to their clients and contribute to their own growth and evolution.

The following best practices or lessons learned are offered as a point of departure and dialogue for our colleagues as we all wrestle with the challenges and promises of working within organizations and with clients in the exciting new world of B2B commerce.

Practice 1. Recognize and be prepared to help these "new" organizational clients identify and manage multiple internal and external relationships.

Practice 2. Make sure that you are not "e-culture" challenged by ensuring that you understand, emotionally and psychologically, that the e-business marketplace and B2B and B2P environments are different from anything that came before. Increase your comfort level with "process," both the speed at which it must move and your ability to facilitate it.

Practice 3. Be prepared to expand your competencies or skills portfolio to include your speed at conducting organizational diagnoses, introducing change interventions, conducting evaluations, and undertaking rediagnoses in order to keep pace with the speed of the e-commerce environment.

Practice 4. Change management consultants, while not needing to become developers, need to become familiar and conversant in the language of Internet technology and new B2B models in order to effectively operate in this environment and provide value for the future.

Practice 5. Expand your change management "frame of reference" to incorporate, to be open to, and to appreciate the underlying dynamics of the new e-commerce.

Practice 6. Supplement traditional approaches to consulting in B2B situations with new focuses in change management (i.e., quick decision making, quick conflict resolution, project management skills, etc.).

REFERENCES

Al-Tabtabai, H., Alex, A.P., & Abou-alfotough, A. 2001. Conflict resolution using cognitive analysis approach. *Project Management Journal*, 32(2), 4–16.

Benz, I. 1999. *Facilitation at a glance.* Methuen, MA: Goal/QPC.

Brassard, M., & Ritter, D. 1994. *The memory jogger II: A pocket guide for continuous improvement and effective planning.* Methuen, MA: Goal/QPC.

Burns, T., & Stalker, G.M. 1961. *The management of innovation.* London: Tavistock.

Cummings, T.G., & Worley, C.G. 2001. *Organization development and change*, 7th ed. Cincinnati, OH: South-Western College Publishing.

Dunn, A., & O'Dell, J. 2000. Auto makers plan behemoth e-business. *Los Angeles Times*, February 6, p. A-1.

Dyer, W. 1987. *Team building: Issues and alternatives.* Reading, MA: Addison-Wesley.

Fisher, R., & Ury, W. 1981. *Getting to yes: Negotiating agreement without giving in.* New York: Penguin Books.

French, W.L., & Bell, C.H. 1978. *Organizational development: Behavioral science interventions for organizational improvement.* Englewood Cliffs, NJ: Prentice Hall.

Goal/QPC. 2000. *Problem solving: Seven steps to improved processes.* Methuen, MA: Goal/QPC.

Hanson, W. 2000. *Principles of Internet marketing.* Cincinnati, OH: South-Western College Publishing.

Hartman, F.T. 2000. *Don't park your brain outside: A practical guide to improving shareholder value with SMART management.* Sylva, NC: Project Management Institute.

Hurst, D.K. 1995. *Crisis and renewal: Meeting the challenge of organizational change.* Boston: Harvard Business School Press.

Joiner, B.L. 1995. *The team handbook.* Madison, WI: Joiner & Associates.

Kaplan, R.S., & Norton, D.P. 1996. *The balanced scorecard.* Boston: Harvard Business School Press.

Kirkpatrick, D. 2000. ePocalypse now. *eCompany Now*, 1(4): 87–94.

Krutchen, P. 2000. *The rational unified process: An introduction.* Boston: Addison-Wesley.

Lewin, K. 1951. *Field theory in social science.* New York: Harper & Row.

Lippitt, G., & Lippitt, R. 1986. *The consulting process in action.* San Francisco: Jossey-Bass.

Means, G., & Schnieder, D.S. 2000. *Meta-capitalism: The e-business revolution and the design of 21st century companies and markets.* New York: John Wiley & Sons.

Ritter, D., & Brassard, M. 1998. *The creativity tools memory jogger: A pocket guide for creative thinking.* Methuen, MA: Goal/QPC.

Schein, E.H. 1987. *Process consultation: Lessons for managers.* Reading, MA: Addison-Wesley.

Schein, E.H. 1988. *Process consultation: Its role in organizational development.* Reading, MA: Addison-Wesley.

Schein, E.H. 1992. *Organizational culture and leadership.* San Francisco: Jossey-Bass.

Schein, E.H. 1997. Process consultation principles in respect of clients. *Journal of Organizational Change Management,* 10(3): 206–210.

Scholtes, R.R. 1988. *The team handbook: How to use teams to improve quality.* Madison, WI: Joiner & Associates.

Shaping the B2B universe. 2000. *www.upside.com* (August): 139.

Chapter 9

Privatization of Public Utilities
Drives Change in Consulting Firms

Kathi Mestayer

INTRODUCTION

The trend toward privatization of public services has engendered a series of changes in public utility (water and wastewater) organizations. This chapter describes how those organizations have been impacted, how their consultants have attempted to meet their changing needs, and how those attempts are, in turn, requiring the consulting firms to manage their own change processes.

BACKGROUND AND HISTORY

For most of the twentieth (and twenty-first) centuries, the majority of water and wastewater utilities in the United States have been publicly owned and operated. But that was not always the case. The gradual conversion to public from historically private ownership took place during the first quarter of the twentieth century in the United States, but began in London in the mid-nineteenth century, where the Metropolitan Sanitary Association was created in response to a "particularly ghastly season for typhus and cholera" (Donahue, 1989, p. 74). Similarly, conversion to public ownership of water treatment facilities in the United States resulted from a combination of poor water quality or service (which motivated governments to take over), the need for major facility upgrades, and low rates of return on private invested capital (which motivated private water companies to sell their aging assets) (AWWA, 1996, p. 4).

However, England (and France) eventually re-privatized water and wastewater facilities; by 1990, England had privatized its entire water and sewer system, and 75% of France's population was served by private water companies (Neal et al., 1996, p. 1). Once again, the trend was exported; in 1996, the Reason

Foundation observed that French and British companies "dominate the world market in the development of new water and sewer systems" (ibid., p. 16). In 1997, *Public Works Financing* magazine reported on growth of private-sector activity in operations and maintenance of water and wastewater facilities in the United States: "The number of private operating and maintenance contracts has increased from 100 to 200 in the late 1980s to nearly 1,000 in 1997" (Miller et al., 1995, p. 4). And the Reason Public Policy Institute wrote that "the really big news of 1998 came when privatization burst into the big-city market with long-term contracts to operate the sewer system in Milwaukee and the water system in Atlanta. Each was in turn the largest such contract ever let in the United States, and each highlighted the way privatization contracts have adapted to the political realities of local governments" (Reason Public Policy Institute, 1999, p. 34).

PUBLIC UTILITY ORGANIZATIONS

It did not take long for public utilities to recognize the threat posed by the aggressive marketing of foreign firms in the United States. However, the ability of public utilities to respond was determined in part by the fact that they are fundamentally different from their private counterparts. They are, for the most part, located geographically in one contiguous service area (a city, county, or region), and therefore limited in their ability to expand, take over new systems, and gain the kind of scale economies that large multinational firms bank on. Like other regulated utilities, they own the means of service delivery (water and sewer pipes embedded in the ground), making it difficult for competitors to develop parallel delivery systems.

Because public utilities are overseen by elected and/or appointed boards and commissions, public policy objectives often take precedence over "bottom line" goals. It is not uncommon for a public utility to have a strict "100% regulatory compliance, no matter what the cost" policy, which is stricter than the regulatory compliance standards in most cases.

In addition to the lack of scale economies and absolute health and safety directives, public utilities have other institutional constraints to maximizing efficiency for optimal financial performance. Among them is the lack of merit or performance pay mechanisms (a utility manager related recently that 50% of their staff is at the top of their pay scale, so no longer get inflationary or annual increases, let alone incentive pay). Public utilities are also governed by the Freedom of Information Act, so that board meetings are public, and all but a few privileged communiques must be disclosed on request. Constraints also include public ("low bid") purchasing requirements; bureaucratic hiring processes; and mandates to use in-house support services, such as vehicle maintenance, regardless of their internal pricing, service, or quality of work.

OPENING SKIRMISHES

Public utilities reacted to news of the privatization trend in several ways. Professional organizations like the American Water Works Association (AWWA), the Water Environment Federation (WEF), their research arms (AWWARF and WERF), and the Association(s) of Metropolitan Water and Sewer Agencies (AMWA and AMSA) funded tools to help public utilities become competitive and understand private firm behavior and tactics. Their efforts have included case study collections, toolkits, benchmarking databases, best practices guides, peer-assessment programs, a host of special conferences, and, eventually, leadership institutes (in one case, in partnership with a prominent business school).

Meanwhile, the Reason Foundation and the U.S. Conference of Mayors, among others, disseminated information about the potential benefits of privatization. A 1996 Reason Foundation report criticized Monterey County (California) for hiring a consultant-advocate, insinuating that it is inappropriate for government agencies to attempt to be competitive: "It is as though government-owned water companies are adopting defensive strategies . . . to stop takeovers from occurring and to protect jobs of entrenched management" (Neal et al., 1996, p. 1). In 1996, the Joint Economic Committee of the U.S. Congress issued a staff report entitled, "The $7.7 Billion Mistake: Federal Barriers to State & Local Privatization," which claimed that such barriers cost those governments about $7.7 billion per year.

As public utilities deepened their understanding of the competitive threat, private companies (water and sewer operations companies, developers, and consortia) behaved in ways that made them tough to compete with. They appealed directly to elected officials with promises of large savings in capital and operating costs (perhaps most effectively via the U.S. Conference of Mayors' Water Development Council, which gave them direct access to mayors of large cities). The Water Development Council's "top ten" candidates in 1996 for likely privatization included New Haven, Philadelphia, Tulsa, New Orleans, San Diego, and Oklahoma City (Mestayer, 1996). In some cases, companies offered large up-front equity (cash) payments as an incentive for signing long-term contracts. This combination of access to elected officials and short-term cash dovetailed nicely with what Micklethwait and Woolridge, in *The Witch Doctors*, call "the desperate craving of politicians for a magical solution" (1996, p. 307). And politicians, directly or indirectly, run the public utilities.

Public water and sewer agency managers (members of AWWA, WEF, etc.), on the other hand, were used to solving problems at the staff level and then making their arguments (as the technical experts) to elected officials for approval. In essence, the private companies' mode of operating was perceived as doing an "end run" around utility general managers. And the stakes were high. Losing control or ownership of a utility is usually an "all or nothing" competitive

outcome; most public managers did not face losing market share, or some customers, but the whole operation (except for very large systems, in which operations of one of a network of several facilities could be privatized).

Countering the tactics and offerings of the private sector soon became a ral-
lying cry among municipal utilities, and their consultants (primarily, environmental engineering firms) began thinking about how to position themselves to
help their clients become more competitive. Client needs fell into two categories:
(1) "technical" advice (*what* to change in the water and wastewater process,
design, and operations) and (2) process-oriented, organizational advice (*how* to
manage change and make the transition to a more competition- and efficiency-
focused culture).

"TECHNICAL" CHANGE CONSULTING

Technical help in becoming more competitive/efficient was a need articulated
by public sector clients. This first phase of consulting opportunities generally
comprised services such as competitive gap analyses, comprehensive efficiency
studies, qualitative and quantitative benchmarking, coaching in the development
of competitive bids, and design of new technical cross-training programs for
plant personnel. Most of the top engineering consulting firms were at least somewhat prepared to help their utility clients with this kind of competitiveness effort.
Common recommendations made in the technical change consulting studies included upgrading information systems, increasing automation, reducing staff
(e.g., through layoffs, attrition, cross-training), and improving energy efficiency,
as well as removing some of the institutional barriers to efficiency (including
lack of incentive pay, scale economies, purchasing strictures, etc. as discussed
above). Ironically, the threat of privatization enabled many utilities to throw off
some of these long-standing and onerous institutional burdens by convincing
policy makers that they could not hope to compete fairly, on a "level playing
field," within their traditional constraints.

THE CONSULTANTS

Engineering consulting firms soon realized that competitiveness consulting
(both technical and organizational) was an opportunity to expand into new business areas with existing clients. Prominent management consulting firms didn't
seem to be actively pursuing public utility clients (at any rate, they were not
visible in noticeable numbers in either utility journals or conferences). Management practices that were commonplace in the private sector (such as skill-based
pay, "360-degree" evaluations, and cross-training of operators and maintenance
crews) were news in the utility business.

The field of design engineering, the "bread and butter" of the engineering
firms, had become more competitive in the past decade (some use the term

commoditized, although that is surely an overstatement). Even so, head-to-head price competition had become more important in winning project assignments than the traditional differentiators of track record, relationship, and design innovation. If this trend continued, profits would drop over time. Many clients perceived the top four or five engineering firms in a given area of expertise to be approximately equally qualified, making selection based on price justifiable.

The firms speculated that if privatization of utilities became widespread, their traditional public sector client base could evaporate, leaving them to fight over private clients, who are known to be price-sensitive (and occasionally acquire "captive" firms to do their engineering).

Finally, the conventional wisdom among engineering firms was that the organizational change consulting field was more profitable than traditional engineering consulting (perhaps by a factor of two to three times) and less risky from a professional liability standpoint.

However, there were uncertainties that went along with expanding into this new territory. Change consulting, whether it is the technical type or the potentially more profitable (but less understood) organizational one, had its own risks. Most firms realized that providing change consulting of both types has inherent risks to the development of long-term client relationships—clients sometimes resist and resent advice on how they can operate and manage more efficiently and effectively. Engineers began to have the extremely unpleasant experience of negotiating with valued clients about the wording of their reports (which become part of the public record) on inefficiencies and cost-cutting opportunities. As a result of this understandable squeamishness, at least one firm has an internal policy not to "sell" technical change consulting to clients, but to provide the services if asked. Other firms had effective unwritten internal "understandings" that this kind of consulting was not to be promoted in certain offices or geographic areas.

By the late 1990s, the privatization rhetoric became so heated that there was pressure to "take sides" in the privatization war. Some consulting firms tried to claim the high ethical ground by stating that they were "independent" (i.e., would not work for private utility companies and consortia), and implied that such work involved an unavoidable conflict of interest. Independence claims came in the form of highly visible campaigns (complete with American flags and Revolutionary War imagery) and the creation of "municipal advocacy" practices that tried to make it clear which side of the conflict the firm was claiming to be on. Other firms openly joined private-sector consortia to provide the design and operating services that large projects require. Those firms took the position that municipal clients needed private-sector expertise to do battle with the private sector and that they had internal "fire walls" to prevent conflict situations. Still others avoided weighing in on one side or the other, hoping that the rhetoric would die down.

THE CHANGE CHALLENGE

The engineering firms that decided to go into the organizational change consulting field have faced a steep learning curve. At the onset, even recognizing the difference between technical and organizational change consulting was an evolution in thinking. Firms' decisions to incorporate a new set of people, skills, and values into their organizations presented an array of challenges, which fell into three categories: strategic, marketing, and management.

Strategic Challenges

Engineering consulting firms had a number of choices to make in the strategy realm. The most basic was whether to offer organizational change consulting services at all. To the extent that the need for organizational change consulting was unarticulated by clients, potential demand was hard to gauge. A senior engineering firm manager pointed out that in decades of experience managing a wide range of client problems and issues, the need for this type of consulting had *never* been raised by a client.

The question of whether organizational change (and technical change) consulting is fertile ground is one that firms continue to struggle with. Even (perhaps especially) those that made the most visible and expensive commitments will continue to ask themselves questions about whether the excursion into such foreign territory is working (by metrics such as profitability expectations, among others).

The second challenge was *how* to enter the organizational change field in which there were four obvious choices: retool existing staff, hire people with the desired skills, form strategic partnerships with specialist firms, and merger/acquisition. All four strategies have been adopted by major engineering firms, and the jury is still out on whether and how they are succeeding.

Marketing Challenges

The need for technical change management was articulated early on by public utility clients. However, the need for assistance in managing organizational change has lagged behind. This may be in part because of the technical, water and wastewater treatment process orientation of traditional public utility clients. Engineering firms that wanted to provide change consulting have had to make clients aware of an unarticulated need, learn and introduce a new vocabulary, and make compelling arguments about the value of such services. And if that wasn't tough enough, there remained the tasks of convincing clients that their engineering firm was indeed qualified to provide those nontraditional services and that they were worth significantly higher rates than engineering work.

In some firms, access to their own major clients has proved to be a stumbling block. Project managers who had a low comfort level with organizational change consulting (and its pricing) found ways to undermine attempts to approach their valued clients with the new, unproven set of offerings. Some engineers were simply uncomfortable in what they saw as quasi-personal discussions with clients about leadership development and executive coaching.

Another challenge has been leveraging existing utility-manager relationships to gain access to top-level municipal executives and elected officials, who are often in the decision-making loop on large management consulting projects but don't recognize the firms' names or reputations. However, the hiring of lobbyists (or well-connected door-openers) by engineering firms is increasingly common, and so this may prove to be a less significant hurdle over time.

Management Challenges

In addition to the strategic and marketing challenges, the problems of managing the new business segment internally have been daunting. The underlying reason is that many of the firms simply lack experience (and even a conceptual vocabulary) in organizational, process, or change consulting. That fact manifests itself in several challenges.

Overcoming Skepticism and Resistance

As organizations, engineering firms have traditionally placed the highest values on scientific, quantitative skills and training. Not surprisingly, establishing credibility for organizational consulting in those firms has been an uphill battle. Words like "touchy feely," "non-technical," "softer side," and even "soup du jour" are commonly used in engineering firms when referring to fields or disciplines that they believe to be non-quantitative or non-scientific (like organizational change consulting). Internal resistance took many forms, including opposition to hiring management consulting staff at higher salaries than those prevailing for engineers of comparable experience. The skepticism with which many engineering firm staff (at all levels) tolerated internal management seminars and training in the past was a good indication of how they would react when that material became part of their company's portfolio. The fact that organizational consulting was expected to yield higher rates and profits struck many as high irony, since it was seen as having so little intrinsic value.

Managers' anxiety levels rose when they thought about selling those "soft" (but expensive) services to their most important clients (it is, after all, the larger and wealthier utilities that can entertain the notion of using change consultants). Their resistance was not without cause; many utility executive clients are engineers by training, too, and have similar notions about the value of non-quantitative fields and expertise. In one attempt to make change management look more quantitative, the popular *Thinking, Getting, Staying Competitive* handbook (AMSA/AMWA, 1998, p. 6) provided a formula:

$$\text{CHANGE POTENTIAL} = \frac{\text{Urgency} \times \text{Vision} \times \text{Solution}}{\text{Time}} > \text{Resistance}$$

Building Competency

The first-order communication task was that of explaining to engineers and "technical" consultants exactly *what the new services were*. Most engineering firms and engineers had very little experience as consumers of management consulting; how were they to explain what it was they were proposing to do for clients? Requiring all managers to read Johnson's *Who Moved My Cheese?* (1999) (as one engineering firm recently did) was a starting point, but there was a bigger disconnect to be addressed. Engineering and environmental sciences work generally was, at least at some phase, as tangible as drawings, reports, change orders, visual presentations, and other similar materials. The new services appeared to be something very different and outside their comfort zones: workshops, surveys, "interventions," executive coaching, and leadership development.

Engineers' discomfort was not only with the foreignness and low credibility of the new consulting services; it extended to their role as client managers. Being effective required them to move from Schein's expertise or doctor-patient intervention model to a more process-consulting one (Schein, 1999), and they lacked a conceptual framework and vocabulary for talking about or making that transition.

A related challenge was determining "good" from "bad" organizational change consulting and providing the kind of quality control that engineering work was subjected to. Some simply assigned the task of quality advising to whatever executive-level engineer seemed motivated and willing to take it on. One firm hired its senior managers' executive coaches. This provided some familiarity and a sense of safety at top levels, but executive coaching seemed exotic to mainstream engineers and clients and has not been easy to market to public-sector clients.

Finding a Fit

Perhaps the most difficult challenge has been finding a place (literally and figuratively) for the new business segment within existing firms. This problem mirrors the strategic positioning decisions described earlier. Firms whose policy was not to "sell" organizational consulting but to offer it when requested sent an unmistakable signal to staff that the services were optional and not strategically important. On the other hand, firms that trumpeted their new capabilities and profit expectations sent a mixed, and perhaps unintended, message to traditional engineers that their training and skills were worth less to the organization and clients. Partly because the two disciplines are perceived as being so different, integration was fraught with difficult tradeoffs.

Some firms have struggled with what to call the new business area and have switched acronyms several times, sending a rather tentative message about the enterprise. It is not uncommon for engineering firms to lack the job classifications for employees in the new business areas; more than one prominent firm classifies every employee (including the board of directors) as either scientist, engineer, or technical or administrative staff member.

Although organization charts are not widely available for many of the prominent environmental engineering firms, web searches provide an indication of where organizational consulting falls within the firm's structure and priorities. For some web sites, the user must drill down several levels or do a site search to find organizational, change, or management consulting services. One site lists "management consulting" and "organizational development" among several other (technical engineering) areas of concentration. Another firm displays its new organizational consulting division prominently on its home page, but the second-level information is described as "under development" (missing).

Finding People and Resources

The challenge of finding staff and/or firms to team up with to provide the new portfolio is still such a new problem that it's difficult to say much about what firms have done. There is little doubt that the general lack of comfort with the subject area of organizational consulting, and lack of standards for judging quality come into play here. Compounding this problem is the fact that for the new offerings to command the high hourly rates (and profit margins) that engineering firms hope for, it is expected that it will be difficult to sell "retooled" engineers and scientists to provide those services.

A review of 10 leading national environmental consulting firms' web sites revealed that although six made various claims about offering management, organizational, or change consulting services, only one of the six mentioned recruiting outside of the traditional engineering, scientist, architectural, and other "technical" disciplines on their web site. Even the firm whose web site claims a "50% annual growth rate" for its management consulting group does not list management consulting as an area for which they are recruiting (only engineering, architecture, design-build, project development [marketing], and corporate are listed).

SUMMARY OBSERVATIONS

What can we conclude from this story about two industries (utilities and engineering firms) trying to change, with the latter trying to change into change consultants? Clearly, it's harder than it looks—internal and external challenges are formidable and values-based.

Although many of the top firms have attempted to meet the needs of municipal clients who face competitive challenges, the range of those services, their strategies for providing them, and their institutional commitment vary a great deal. Again, this is borne out by visiting top firms' web sites. Some feature organizational change consulting services prominently, others make them hard to find, and still others attempt to cover the new base with old material—by "spinning" traditional engineering project descriptions to mention any organizational component, however marginal.

Even though it is too early in the game to be making odds (at least for this author's risk appetite), there are a few lessons that have been learned about ways to mitigate the problems described in this chapter.

Assess the Culture/Communication Gaps Early and Plan to Meet Them Head-on

Several of the challenges (comfort level, skepticism, passive resistance) are at least somewhat culture- or values-based. This is especially true for firms that plan to sell new services to current clients because buy-in by existing client managers is critical.

In engineering firms, there is a widespread lack of understanding of what organizational change consultants really do, in part because those consultants explain what they do in their own language, concepts, and terms. One consultant estimated that 95% of the firms' staff had no idea why the firm was pursuing organizational change consulting.

How does this play out? When organizational change experts describe what kinds of consulting they do, the engineer-scientists listen politely, but nobody asks the follow-up question that is on everybody's mind: "Yeah, but what is it *really? What does it look like? Why would our clients want it?*" In informal discussions after the meeting is over, it becomes apparent that *nobody got it*, and so the story that the new subject matter is incomprehensible (touchy-feely) is propagated. One engineer observed that "everything we see is refracted through the lens of the status quo." Put another way, don't count on people to use their imaginations; they may not see how an "early success story" really maps on to their set of projects and clients.

The first-order answer is to accurately assess the culture and values gap, perhaps through translators who are not inculcated in the dominant culture and values and who can work with staff to identify the major disconnects of language, values, and assumptions. Train the new consultants in the fundamentals (especially the barriers) of the background culture so that they have the benefit of a cultural "cloaking device."

These communications strategies also need to be worked through with the client community (also largely engineers, but in a municipal-government culture) to lay the groundwork for gaining acceptance and awareness of the needs that organizational change consulting can address.

Plant the New Division in Fertile Soil

Of course, the definition of fertile soil differs from organization to organization. One engineering firm established its new organizational change consulting unit within its already-nontraditional, but established, financial services. In that context, the new unit was not as foreign to its surroundings (or vice versa), and the financial services practice had already gained some acceptance as a nontraditional division. It was hoped that this would lower the barriers for the new consulting practice, which employs "almost no engineers," according to one of its members.

Be Honest about the Risks as Well as the Opportunities

Skepticism feeds on half-truths. Change represented as a "slam-dunk" instantly raises red flags, even if nobody admits to seeing them. If problems are dismissed or not really addressed, they don't go away—they show up in the emperor's wardrobe.

If Necessary, Redefine Success for the New Venture

The bulk of engineering firms track chargeable ratio, booked work, revenue, and profitability as key performance measures. New ventures often need some room to maneuver around traditional benchmarks. It is especially difficult for established engineering firms to relax those standards when their core design services are still growing and profitable. People who have been successful according to those traditional measures may argue that "it ain't broke." This argument will eventually wear down support for a new venture when made repeatedly and at the right times (like incentive compensation time).

Keep Your Ear to the Ground

In traditional consulting engineering firms, resistance is rarely visible. Learning to listen, look, and think carefully about alignment of interests and fiefdoms may be the best way to find out if subtle (but effective) barriers exist. The new consultants, especially if they come from outside the firm, may not see or accurately understand these dynamics.

Many additional observations could be added here, but they would be premature at this stage. In fact, at least one firm has an organizational change practice that does not yet appear anywhere on its web site; the vast majority of the firm's staff doesn't even know it exists. Skeptics predict that the fact that engineering firms are still run (at the top levels) by engineers will inevitably limit the growth, support, and potential of this type of consulting. Others are confident that, at least for some firms, the move will be successful—and well worth the trouble.

It will be interesting to follow the development of these new offerings; their integration into the cultures, structures, and services of engineering organizations; and the eventual response (if any) by more mainstream management and organizational consultants.

REFERENCES

American Water Works Association (AWWA). 1996. *Competitive challenges facing public utilities*. Denver, CO: AWWA.

Association of Metropolitan Sewerage Agencies, Association of Metropolitan Water Agencies (AMSA/AMWA). 1998. *Thinking, getting, staying competitive: A public sector handbook.* Washington, DC: AMSA/AMWA.

Donahue, J.D. 1989. *The privatization decision: Public ends, private means.* New York: Basic Books.

Johnson, S. 1999. *Who moved my cheese?* New York: G.P. Putnam's Sons.

Mestayer, K. 1996. Conversation with Michael Gagliardo, Water Development Council staff, February.

Micklethwait, J., & Woolridge, A. 1996. *The witch doctors: Making sense of the management gurus.* New York: Times Books.

Miller, R.K. et al. 1995. *Contract operations and municipal water/wastewater privatization.* Norcross, GA: Future Technology Services.

Neal, K. et al. 1996. *Restructuring America's water industry.* Los Angeles: Reason Foundation.

Reason Public Policy Institute. 1999. *Privatization 1999.* Los Angeles: Reason Foundation.

Schein, E.H. 1999. *Process consultation revisited.* Reading, MA: Addison Wesley.

Chapter 10

Data Processing to Knowledge Management: Are Information Technology Professionals Still Addressing the Same Change Management Issues?

Gigi G. Kelly

INTRODUCTION

It is clear that the twenty-first century will bring new challenges to the world of information technology and to the people who work in this field. During the past five years, we have seen a major revolution occur with the introduction of the dot com business world. It started with a whimper, expanded with such great enthusiasm and unimaginable growth, and has now halted to a slow crawl. In this chaotic and often unpredictable business environment that we are all confronted with, the people delivering information technology (IT) solutions must persevere and deliver IT solutions for real business problems. This can be a daunting task in these uncertain times. Although the IT work force faces many challenges and obstacles today in this business world that is operating at Internet speed, many of us in the IT work force often sit back and wonder, has anything *really changed* in the IT profession from 25 years ago? Aren't we, as IT professionals, still trying to gather requirements, develop programs, and implement systems that meet the end-user's expectations?

To start this exploration of what, if anything, has changed for the IT professional, I pulled some of my old textbooks and IT manuals from my archives in the attic. I actually still have my first Fortran programming book, *Fortran for Humans*. I always wanted to know if there was a *Fortran for Monkeys* or a *Fortran for Non-Humans*. I sit here and think, why didn't I create the *Fortran for Dummies* book? It is true that programming languages have evolved over the last 25 years, and IT programmers have had to retool their programming skills to create dynamic web pages and deal with the world of object orientation; however, the fundamental skill set of good programming still relies on many of the basic programming skills that were developed in the 1960s and 1970s. These skills included being trained in the programming language and understanding how to turn program specification into code that will instruct the computer to do what you want it to do. However, in today's programming environment many new automated tools can be used to assist the programmer to more efficiently construct the design and code the requirements.

Although computer automated software engineering (CASE) tools had their origin in the early 1980s, it is only recently that the promise of automated design (AD) tools have become a reality. The development of new tools and programming languages that are much easier to use is certainly exploding in today's software market. Students in elementary schools are learning to develop and publish their own web sites with little or no programming skills. Gone are the days when programmers used green bar report layout paper with 132 blocks across to lay out the report and precisely create the code that would produce this very basic report. Programmers and end-users can now dynamically create a layout of the report, and with little programming, this simple report can be produced. Furthermore, making changes to the layout does not require a monumental effort by the programmer. But while this is true for basic requests, getting the correct data for the report and making a complex report is still often beyond the grasp of an end-user, and the experience of a good programmer is required. Programming language and design tools are surely two areas that will continue to change and evolve in the future. Although many programmers in the 1970s and 1980s were DOS, COBOL, and CICS gurus, these same people have had to retool their skill set since the 1990s to learn, for example, LINUX, XML, and HTML. Yet, there still exists a tremendous amount of legacy code where the COBOL genius is worth his or her weight in gold. The future will continue with the introduction of new programming languages and new operating systems that will hopefully simplify the development effort and provide powerful capabilities to solve business problems. However, I envision a good programmer will always be employed. In afterthought, I am not quite ready to throw away my *Fortran for Humans* book.

Another book that I found extremely interesting was *A Guide to the Successful Management of Computer Projects* written in 1978 by Hamish Donaldson. In this book, Donaldson provides a framework for IT project management, which includes:

- Getting a good start;
- Structuring project responsibilities;
- Establishing clear ground rules;
- Selecting the right projects; and
- Choosing the project manager.

Getting a good start on an IT project is even more important today than it was 20-plus years ago due to the compressed time frame in which end-users want their projects completed.

Donaldson points out that "Systems are run by people and the relationship is complex. As a result things are not always what they seem" (Donaldson, 1978, p. 2). This advice is clearly applicable for today's IT development environment. Before beginning any project, understanding the complex relationships of the business' mission and operations can assist the IT professional in developing a system that is truly going to meet end-user expectations and add value to the business. As much as "getting a good start" sounds like common sense, this is much more difficult for many IT shops than it should be. Often the technical issues associated with creating a new system are the easy issues to resolve; it is the people issues that pose the greatest challenge for IT professionals to understand and address. Furthermore, IT professionals are routinely accused of wanting to exercise power over users, as Markus and Bjorn-Andersen (1987) note: "IT professionals exercise power over user behavior by creating organizational structures and routine operating procedures that give them formal authority over users or foster user dependence on them for important resources" (p. 501). Examples of IT failures are numerous, and I am sure that everyone has a story to share. The creation of a simple system can seem like a mountain to climb. Creating an integrated business system can make sending a man to the moon sound easy. One integrated business systems area that has received a tremendous amount of press is the implementation of enterprise resource planning (ERP) systems. Unfortunately, many of these ERP systems are doomed from the start as illustrated in the following example.

ERP—NEW SYSTEM WITH SAME OLD PROBLEMS?

In the 1990s many companies realized that their current legacy systems were becoming obsolete and were not Y2K compliant. Furthermore, many core business systems such as financials, logistics, and services such as human resources and project management had been developed one system at a time, often by different vendors, and had been patched so many times that it was becoming impossible to make changes without significant time and cost investments. In general, these systems shared neither a common architecture nor compatible operating systems, thus making it even more difficult to try to integrate the information from the various systems. To address these problems, software vendors, such as SAP, Oracle, and JDEdwards, rose to the occasion and developed ERP systems. Selecting and implementing an ERP system is not an easy job, and often consultants are required to assist in this long and arduous process.

The success and failure of an ERP system implementation is not significantly different from most large-scale system implementations, although I believe that many senior level business executives were led to believe that the panacea for IT systems had arrived with ERP systems. Business executives and personnel are no longer that naive (and if they are, they are destined to either have major cost and time overruns or complete failure when attempting to implement an ERP system). In my research with ERP systems, I am reminded over and over again about the real stumbling blocks for success. One large manufacturing business summarized their experience as a time of promises, phantoms, and purgatory.

They were promised that they would finally have integrated systems and that managers would easily be able to input their information and quickly receive meaningful information back from the system. If they wanted to sort by region or by product, this would be as simple as selecting a button. Furthermore, the integrity of the data would be such that one could believe it and not have to spend hours verifying it. This would allow managers the time to focus on value-added business activities.

Unfortunately, the phantoms that existed in the system development process and continued during the implementation phase created an environment where success would be virtually impossible. Although money was spent on getting the software and hardware, the time and personnel resource budgets that were necessary to gather and understand requirements and then transform these requirements into the system were severely lacking. Not only were key people required to do their 9-to-5 job, they also had to find time to participate on the ERP project. But there were only so many hours these individuals could work before there were diminishing returns on their contributions. Furthermore, it quickly became apparent that the true issue with the new ERP system was *change*. Regardless of how appealing the promises from an ERP system are, few companies are prepared to make the drastic process and cultural changes needed to reap the benefits. The ERP system could not make people change their tendency to protect their information and their turf. A new corporate culture would be necessary to foster this type of information sharing. These changes would have to start at the top with senior management and would have to be instilled in the people who worked for these managers. The first sponsor for this ERP system had the vision; however, his tenure on the project lasted less than a year. The ownership of the project was passed around and no true ownership currently exists.

Now, this company is living in limbo. A commitment has been made to finish the ERP implementation. The project is over budget and behind schedule. However, this company has recognized the monumental change management effort that is going to be necessary for successful implementation and is addressing the ownership issue. In the meantime, the users of the various systems continue to work and look forward to a truly integrated system.

As Donaldson pointed out in 1978, it is critical for the project team to consist of participants who have a vested interest in the success of the project. It is crucial that a team be composed of end-users, IT staff, and strong leadership who are committed to success and will maintain involvement and expend the needed resources. Furthermore, defining the right problem or opportunity to maximize the value added by the project takes an effort by all parties. Getting departments to truly commit human resources to the project can be difficult when many companies are laying off employees, and employees are already working 40-plus hours a week to get their primary job completed. Management has to intervene and make sure the right people with the right skills are given the necessary time and appropriate awards to ensure that team members understand their significant role in the success of the project.

Some new issues have arisen since Donaldson wrote his book on project management. Project team members are no longer located in offices next door to one another. People must be able to contribute to the virtual environment that has been created over the past decade. Exactly where does the water cooler exist in this virtual space? People must become users of new tools that have been developed to support this virtual collaboration, and these collaborative tools are going to be requirements in businesses and a mainstay for consultants in order to deliver IT systems in the future.

Given the increased reliance of IT projects on group interaction and the fundamentally frustrating problems that groups must contend with, it is not surprising that much time and effort has been spent to improve the efficiency and effectiveness of group interaction. During the first 30 years of the computer age, research institutions and major corporations explored the application of computer technology to improve individual productivity. More recently, the research and development focus has shifted from the individual to the group, and "team-based" computer technology and software are currently receiving much attention. System developers and academics have been working together to develop computer systems that assist and facilitate efficient team meetings and decision making, with a primary concern to facilitate a transformation from meetings where you plan work to meetings where you do work. Many advances have been made in team-based computer support, also know as collaborative technologies.

Collaborative technologies can encompass everything from e-mail to meetingware and include such things as calendar managers, meeting schedulers, document managers, work-flow managers, and "white board" products that provide workflow for electronic meetings. Since the term "collaborative technologies" is used to define a wide variety of team-based software applications, the industry has categorized collaborative technologies tools on two dimensions: time and place.

Collaborative technology applications can support teams that are in the same location or in different geographic locations. Additionally, collaborative technologies can also support teams that are working at the same time or at different times. These two dimensions produce four possible combinations (see Figure 10.1).

The primary goal of same time collaborative technologies' tools is to promote the overall efficiency and effectiveness of group work (Post, 1992). During the late 1980s primitive computer software products were developed to accomplish this. Since that time, sophisticated software systems have been developed and are currently on the market. The technology is usually referred to as group support systems (GSS) but has also been called group decision support systems

Figure 10.1
Collaborative Technology Taxonomy

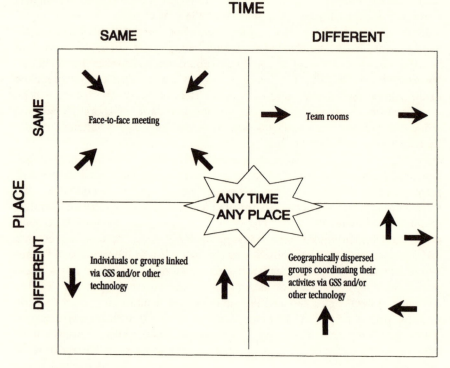

Source: adapted from Johansen et al., 1991.

(GDSS), electronic meeting systems (EMS), and collaborative work support systems (CWSS). GSS are computer-based systems designed to enhance team functioning and improve a group's ability to perform the activities assigned to it in a *meeting* situation (Bostrom, Van Over, & Watson, 1992; Dennis, George, Jessup, Nunamaker, & Vogel, 1988). Group support systems were developed, in part, in response to some of the inefficiencies inherent in group creative problem-solving processes (Nagasundaram & Bostrom, 1995). There are two broad categories of software (i.e., meetingware), based on geographical and temporal distribution, which are specifically designed *to improve meetings and decision making* within a group:

1. *Same time, same place* high-end systems that attempt to reinvent the meeting process, also referred to as meetingware.

2. *Same time, different place* tools that help groups improve communications, such as computer conferencing systems that extend meeting rooms by letting participants discuss issues without having to sit together.

Using meetingware during the development process for IT projects has proved very helpful in soliciting and documenting requirements in significantly less time than previous traditional meeting formats. There are different types of meetingware systems available.

Although same time/different place technologies are definitely a growing phenomenon and will be discussed next, face-to-face meetings are still the mainstay of today's business and are one of the most natural forms of communication. The computer technology used to support such face-to-face meetings is collectively known as group decision support systems (GDSS).

GDSS tools assist in the performance of many typical meeting functions: brainstorming and brainwriting, issue organization and analysis, alternative evaluation, voting, and policy formation functions (Post, 1992). The technology enables facilitators to poll meeting participants, capture large amounts of verbatim feedback, do statistical analyses of voting and polling results, and create detailed reports (Clark & Koonce, 1995).

There are three distinct classes of GDSS (Watson & Bostrom, 1991). Each class has a different effect on a group meeting. The simplest class of GDSS is the keypad-based tool. Most of us are familiar with "polling the audience" on *Who Wants to Be a Millionaire*. In this configuration, each group member has a keypad and the meeting facilitator has a workstation. Typically, the group would use the tool for voting. The keypad, used to enter numeric responses to questions, is similar to a calculator. The results are displayed on a public screen so that all group members can see the results. Since entering items on the keypad tool is easy to do, the tool can be used frequently throughout a meeting as new issues arise. It is important to note that many of the keypad systems perform much more sophisticated functions than simply gathering the votes.

For example, a keypad system might be used in a group that needs to agree on two of five areas to which funding will be allocated. The five areas could be entered into the system and a pairwise comparison of the items performed. Group members would then select the item from each pair that they felt was more deserving of funds. Once all items had been voted on, the results could be displayed on the public screen for all group members to view. Discussion could continue or the meeting could end. Other types of voting available on most keypad systems include ranking and rating. People choosing to abstain from voting would simply not enter a response on the keypad.

More sophisticated keypads have been developed. These pads allow members to choose their degree of agreement or disagreement. For example, one group member might choose to agree with a certain issue but only marginally, while another group member might agree completely with the issue. There are a variety of software products on the market that support keypad-based GDSS.

The second class of GDSS is the chauffeured system. This system provides a computer workstation for the facilitator with no technology available for group members, and allows group members to discuss issues while the facilitator (the chauffeur) enters their comments into the system. The data is then displayed on the public screen. One benefit of a chauffeured system is the provision of a recording mechanism for ideas presented. Also, documenting an idea interactively while it is being presented allows for clarification between the written word and the spoken word. Examples of chauffeured GDSS include tools that allow modeling of relationships. Chauffeured GDSS are particularly dominant in Europe.

A chauffeured technology would be appropriate for groups that contain a large number of people unfamiliar with technology. Participants do not have to interact directly with the technology to gain the benefits of using it. A chauffeured system and a keypad system can be combined to provide additional benefits. For example, having identified areas of concern using a chauffeured system, the facilitator can then survey the audience using a keypad system.

The most sophisticated type of GDSS is the workstation-based system. A facilitator is usually supported by a "technical" assistant who interacts with the technology. Group members sit at computer workstations into which they can enter their comments. These comments can be displayed anonymously on a public screen. Group members may all "talk at once" because they enter their comments into the system at the same time.

Specific tools available within most workstation systems include: idea generation tools that enable participants to enter their ideas about an issue for display on the public screen; organizer tools that allow participants to gather similar ideas and comments into the group; and evaluation tools that allow flexibility in voting, such as rating, ranking, multi-criteria, and point allocation (Bostrom & Anson, 1992). Meetingware is designed to facilitate positive group dynamics and minimize or eliminate negative group dynamics. Research shows that GDSS software *can* minimize a number of undesirable characteristics of group processes, such as decisions that are biased by the presence of influential members, lack of anonymity, miscommunication, interpersonal conflict, and groupthink (Townsend, Whitman, & Hendrickson, 1995). Researchers have shown that meetingware is beneficial when the following conditions exist:

- There is significant disagreement among members (Clark & Koonce, 1995).
- There is a specific problem to solve, objectives to clarify, questions to answer (Clark & Koonce, 1995).
- There is limited meeting time (Clark & Koonce, 1995; Post, 1992; Townsend et al., 1995).
- Anonymity is desired (Clark & Koonce, 1995; Townsend et al., 1995).
- There is a need to limit either personal or organizational influence (Townsend et al., 1995).
- There is a need to address sensitive issues when information or decision making is required on those issues (Townsend et al., 1995).
- The following tasks must be accomplished: information gathering, consensus building, mission clarifying, team building (Clark & Koonce, 1995); mission development, plan-

ning and strategy, issue documentation and evaluation, assumption surfacing, stakeholder identification, policy formation, nominal group work, systems requirements, group negotiation, and idea generation (Post, 1992).

- The decision-making and information-gathering scenarios are complex (Townsend et al., 1995).
- The project is long-term or making a decision is critical to the team's success.

Research has further indicated that GDSS have helped to facilitate the following positive outcomes:

- Development of more extensive and more accurate types of information (Townsend et al., 1995).
- Increased group productivity as group size increases (Valacich, Dennis, & Nunamaker, 1991).
- Full participation of team members (Clark & Koonce, 1995).
- Equal participation (Townsend et al., 1995).
- Effective brainstorming (Valacich et al., 1991).
- Effective and thorough meeting planning (Bostrom, Anson, & Clawson, 1993; Watson & Bostrom, 1991).
- Increased likelihood of quality decisions (Townsend et al., 1995).
- Avoidance of groupthink (Townsend et al., 1995).
- Increased participant satisfaction (Valacich et al., 1991).
- Convenience and flexibility (Townsend et al., 1995).
- Higher quality decisions (Valacich et al., 1991).

It can easily be seen why these tools are very useful for IT projects. Many of the problems that IT developers traditionally face can be overcome with these tools (Kelly & Bostrom, 1998). Although most researchers have demonstrated and emphasized the benefits and potential uses of meetingware, a few authors caution, "Don't make the mistake of relying on Electronic Meeting System technology as a substitute for effective human facilitation of a meeting" (Clark & Koonce, 1995). The warning was given because the amount of face-to-face facilitation required at a meeting will vary. Some meetings, like strategic-planning sessions, demand extensive discussion. However, a brief focus group session would allow respondents more time at their terminals.

It is easy for this type of technology to disrupt or even dominate a meeting, and the use of groupware is not recommended for groups that are not computer literate (e.g., corporate executives). Extroverts may tend to "drop out" of electronic meetings because they are so dismayed with their inability to use their strong verbal skills.

Meetings should be balanced between the use and non-use of electronic mediation. Ideally, a meeting is a combination of face-to-face and electronic mediation. Tools to brainstorm and prioritize ideas may be used, but the ideas generated should be discussed in the normal way. Determining when technology helps and when it hinders is the responsibility of the facilitator.

The role of the facilitator in computer-supported meetings is critical, and the facilitator must use groupware wisely (Kelly & Bostrom, 1998). Suggestions for effective use include (Clark & Koonce, 1995):

- Expect some technophobia. The facilitator may want to give a quick overview of the equipment at the beginning and monitor participants.
- Don't be a slave to the technology. Set the stage and expectations for the session.
- Learn the technology before the session. Facilitators should learn how to best use groupware's inherent flexibility and user-friendliness to suit their own training style.
- Work with technology experts.

Below is an illustration of one company's dedication and commitment to getting the right project team assembled and providing this team with new collaborative technology (GroupSystems™) to assist in the process of defining the project and ensuring a successful outcome. This is an example in which new IT tools that exist today but did not exist 20 years ago can contribute significantly to saving time and developing a better product.

REENGINEERING FOR TOMORROW

IT teams often face the challenge of redesigning key organizational processes that are "owned" by one functional area but whose design and cost is driven by the actions and processes of many other functional areas. In this example, a multi-billion-dollar food service company that operates about 2,000 restaurants was faced with the challenge of reengineering its business communication process (e.g., mail, reports, invoices, and payments). While not particularly "glamorous," these processes are at the very heart of the corporation and critical to overall success. These processes are operated by one administrative department but are dependent upon the actions of other functional areas, which decide what communications to generate and receive.

A project team of eight core members from the reengineering group and the mailroom was formed. They began by building analysis of the current system. Here, advances in technology clearly assisted in the analysis phase. A collaborative technologies tool was used to help the group generate issues and capture the information. The room was set up as shown in Figure 10.2. Furthermore, a model was built using the collaborative technologies tools that presented a pictorial representation of the process that currently existed. By having the process captured with the collaborative technologies tools, modifications to the diagram were easily implemented and provided for an accurate starting point.

Once the model was complete, the team began investigating the processes in

Figure 10.2
GSS Meeting Room Setting

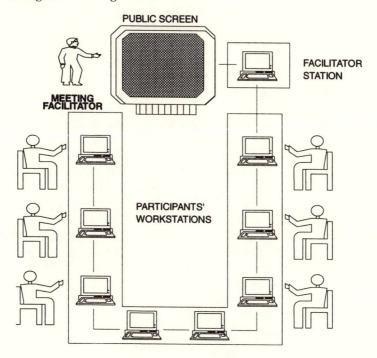

more detail. One part of the team spent a week examining the mail leaving headquarters and interviewing key managers and their support staff. On average, every day 100 overnight packages and 30,000 pieces of mail entered or left the headquarters building, 60% of which were invoices. Another subgroup investigated the amount of space used to store the paper-based records of business mail and the amount of paper discarded per day. The equivalent of two entire floors in the headquarters building (14,500 square feet) was used for paper storage. Sixteen tons of paper were discarded every month. Others performed a cost analysis on copying records and mail and on paying suppliers and employees by check rather than electronic funds transfer (EFT). All members of the core team then together performed problem analysis: identifying current problems and then solving them. This was followed by electronic exercises for breaking assumptions, future thinking, and technology analysis. These activities resulted in a large set of potential improvement opportunities, including short-term incremental actions and longer-term, more radical changes.

The next step was to seek wider participation from corporate management and the individual restaurant leaders. This company's groupware room was small, consisting of eight workstations. To accommodate the wide participation needed, the team designed a standard two- to three-hour agenda for a series of meetings with representatives from key areas in the corporation (a same place/ different time approach in collaborative technologies terminology; see Jessup & Valacich, 1993). This agenda included problem analysis, future thinking, and technology analysis. Eight groups participated: marketing, IT, finance, key administrative assistants, selected restaurant general managers, and the senior executive teams from three of the four major restaurant chains.

The initiatives identified by these groups were combined with those of the core team, resulting in a set of proposals submitted to senior management for approval. The proposals included ways to reduce communication (e.g., changing management processes to give more autonomy to restaurant general managers and regional managers), ways to eliminate paper communication (e.g., EDI, EFT, computerized reporting, computer-to-computer fax, and electronic mail), and ways to manage paper communication (e.g., optical imaging). The net effect of these changes, based on a detailed cost analysis, is an *annual* savings of several million dollars. The manager of information systems planning and leader of the company's reengineering team sees the use of collaborative technologies as "totally successful." Compared to previous reengineering projects undertaken without collaborative technologies, this groupware-based project moved significantly faster. With the collaborative technologies tools, "we did in two days what we couldn't have done in three weeks [without it]." The total costs for the groupware project (including the startup costs of buying computers, software, furniture, and training) were less than $80,000; excluding startup costs, the direct project costs were less than $35,000.

Although this case exemplifies the use of collaborative technologies in a same time/same place environment, the future use of distributive time and place are still being explored, and software is being developed to support this new and different environment. As a result of improvements in technology, people no longer need to be in the same room to have a meeting. Facilities do not have to be physical; they can be constructed in software, or "virtual" structures, that allow participants to "meet" and work together through a computer-mediated communication system (Hiltz & Turoff, 1993). These systems use computers and telecommunications networks to compose, store, deliver, regulate, and process communication among the group members and between the computer and the group. Among the types of systems that come under this heading are electronic mail and computerized conferencing systems. Electronic mail is the most common form of computer-mediated communication, but conferencing systems provide capabilities not found in mail systems. They can order and maintain a permanent database of discussions and activities related to a task and are structured to support group work. Conferences have "memberships," and different members may have different roles, all supported by software.

There are several applications currently on the market that allow same time/ different place interaction. This is an area of tremendous growth. The most popular and well-known package is Lotus Notes. Lotus Notes also allows for group conferencing, voting on issues, and support for anonymity. Lotus Notes provides a structure for people to contribute and share their thoughts. Lotus Notes and similar tools are also being used in academic settings to provide structure to support synchronous and asynchronous learning. At the College of William & Mary we use a product called Blackboard. This product allows the instructor to provide a structure for students to find information related to the class that the instructor or other students have made available. For example, notes and slides used in class can be placed out there for students to review and download. A feature exists to create groups and allow the groups to create, share, and store documents within their own defined area. Blackboard was used to facilitate a class project for 24 groups enrolled at three different universities located in Virginia, Colorado, and Norway. The groups were required ultimately to design a web site for a small business. They had a two-month time period to complete this project. Students in Virginia were the end-users and provided specifications to the analysts located in Norway. The analysts were required to create specifications and to get the end-users to sign off on the developed specifications before they were given to the developers in Colorado. The end-users ultimately had to sign off on the developers' work. Although Blackboard has the ability for synchronized creation of documents, due to the time differences, 95% of the work was done in an asynchronous mode. Those groups that developed a structure for communications and followed a defined project plan where significantly more successful in the final product. Many of the students commented that they had never worked in this type of environment before and were somewhat uncomfortable not being able to meet face-to-face with their colleagues. However, after continual use of the asynchronous tools and e-mail, most students found that they were able to adapt to this environment, and many found the process much more efficient than their traditional face-to-face group projects. There were a couple of students, however, who were adamant about not liking to work in this virtual environment. Given the fact that most of these students have grown up with technology, it is easy to understand why it is much more difficult to get those of us who are older and steeped in our traditional methods of communication to change and participate fully in the virtual communication world.

Another example of using asynchronous communications was described by a consultant who spends considerable amounts of time working on requests for proposals (RFPs). Often companies will put out an RFP for a project that they would like consultants to bid on. In order to complete the RFP many different people with different expertise commonly need to contribute to the final product. Normally, this would mean playing telephone tag and faxing documents all over the universe. With the development of a Lotus Notes database of completed RFPs, it becomes much easier to determine if you already have a similar project that can be used as the outline for a new RFP. It is also much easier to have the different contributors e-mail their contributions in the required format. The effort to combine the pieces has been tremendously simplified, and the time for completion has been reduced to months in some cases and hours in others.

Although asynchronous collaboration tools can be useful, there are some drawbacks. One of the biggest issues facing individuals today is information overload. On any given day, I easily receive 100 e-mails. How do I determine which ones should be read first, which ones require action, and which ones should go straight to the trash can? Tools to sort through the e-mail mania need to be developed to assist the recipient. Businesses and people are just at the beginning of learning how to exploit collaborative technologies.

Expanding the use of collaborative technologies beyond a communications tool is taking form in the world of "knowledge management" (KM). An entire field of is evolving to determine the best way to capture and share the intelligence that lies within and among employees.

KM, like many of areas of IT, is not a new phenomenon. It is, however, a very difficult concept to implement and even more difficult for companies to measure the value added by a KM system. On a common-sense level, people agree that sharing information and lessons learned from mistakes is a great idea and one that will lead to great learning; however, human egos prevent many people from admitting that they were wrong, let alone share the details associated with the incident. And if we figure out how to do something better than someone else or if we hold that required piece of knowledge that will make a project a success, why would we want to give away the power we possess by being the uniquely knowledgeable individual? For people to share what they know, an infrastructure must be in place in a business that will promote and reward employees who do not hoard their knowledge but are willing to share what they know, both the good and the bad. Trust among employees and management is paramount for knowledge management systems to be successful in a business.

In the virtual world, creating the environment that facilitates and builds trust can be difficult. The ability to create a shared space is important for effective collaboration and is essential for building a successful system (Schrage, 1995). Watson, Bostrom, and Dennis (1994) discuss three levels of group output that convey the process of creating a shared space and understanding: sharing opinions, shared opinions, and shared mental models (see Figure 10.3).

At the first level, sharing opinions is an exchange of information. This is accomplished through e-mail and having individuals contribute to a system. Although one may assume that this is an easy task, often individuals are unwilling to share what they know with others. Knowledge is power and power is lost when others know what I know. A new culture has to be established and individuals must be rewarded for allowing this new paradigm of organizational learning to begin. At the second level, shared opinions represent a shared understanding and shared priorities of the opinions exchanged at the first level. For an IT organization, this can be seen when end-users realize that not all systems can be built simultaneously and they work with IT personnel to best meet the needs of the organization. Individual issues are prioritized in relationship to the larger organizational issues. Finally, shared mental models explicitly

Figure 10.3
Levels of Group Output

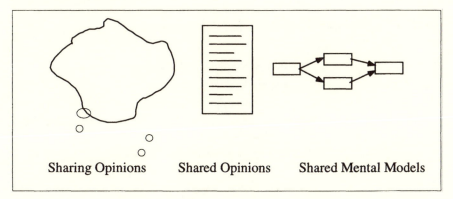

Sharing Opinions   Shared Opinions   Shared Mental Models

reflect an understanding of the relationships of the shared opinions. A system that accomplishes this final integration of information and understanding among the users of this system has truly transformed an organization into a new learning environment. This is still a rarity in business today. Although the foundation for this type of transformation is being developed, this will have to reanalyzed in the future to determine if systems truly succeed as promised.

The large IT consulting companies such as Accenture, Pricewaterhouse Coopers, and KPMG are recognized for their sophisticated KM systems. However, KM systems are not unique to the consulting industry. Many businesses both large and small realize the needs and benefits associated with KM systems. In his book *The Knowledge Management Toolbook*, Amrit Tiwana (2000, pp. 32–33) identified several key drivers (see Table 10.1) for companies to pursue KM systems.

I recently had a gentleman approach me at one of my son's lacrosse games and ask if I could meet with him to discuss the turmoil his company was in and going to continue to face in the future. Although I knew this gentleman through our kids, we had never discussed business before. He had learned about my background through the grapevine and was in dire need of assistance. I am constantly reminded that the old-boy network is alive and well. I agreed to meet with this gentleman to discuss what he saw as his problems. As I listened to him speak for about an hour, it became clear to me that because of upcoming retirements in his company and the tremendous business growth that was occurring, his company needed to think about a strategy for a system. Although this gentlemen had not heard of KM before, I used the key drivers outlined in Table 10.1 to help him understand why a KM system was needed. I also explained to him that one of the hardest issues in KM is the cultural change that must take place within an organization. After we spoke, the senior management team of the man's firm met and agreed that the company needed to pursue the

Table 10.1
Drivers Associated with Knowledge Management Systems

Knowledge-Centric Drivers	• The failure of companies to know what they already know
	• The emergent need for smart knowledge distribution
	• Knowledge velocity and sluggishness
	• The problem of knowledge walkouts and high dependence on tacit knowledge
	• The need to deal with knowledge hoarding propensity among employees
	• A need for systemic unlearning
Technology Drivers	• The death of technology as a viable long-term differentiator
	• Compression of product and process life cycles
	• The need for perfect link between knowledge, business strategy, and IT
Organizational Structure Drivers	• Functional convergence
	• The emergence of project-centric organizational structures
	• Challenges brought about by deregulation
	• The inability of companies to keep pace with competitive changes due to globalization
	• Convergence of products and services
Personnel Drivers	• Widespread functional convergence
	• The need to support effective cross-functional collaboration
	• Team mobility and fluidity
	• The need to deal with complex corporate expectations
Process-Focused Drivers	• The need to avoid repeated and often expensive mistakes
	• Need to avoid unnecessary reinvention
	• The need for accurate predictive anticipation
	• The emerging need for competitive responsiveness
Economic Drivers	• The potential for creating extraordinary leverage through knowledge
	• The quest for a silver bullet for product and service differentiation

development of a system. Although they are only at the very beginning phase, a good foundation has been developed for the success of this project.

As illustrated in the discussion above, and in stark contrast to many of the development projects today, the user's role in IT has changed considerably over the last 25 years, and I believe dramatic changes will continue in the future. Gone are the days when the user only knew that the computer filled an entire room where people in white coats worked and performed some type of magic on a "black box." The introduction of the personal computer in the early 1980s has forever changed for businesses that mystical quality that endured with the mainframe computer. Although personal computers can be found on almost every desk in most offices and laptop computers are gathering tremendous amounts of frequent flyer miles, it is the Internet that has revolutionized users' attitudes toward technology. I realized that computers have made an inroad into our everyday life when my 80-year-old father received his first computer for his birthday and now logs on every morning to check the news, weather, and e-mail. Of course, there still is the concern of the haves and have-nots due to the cost of computers. This will continue to be an issue in the future: how do we avoid a new technology discrimination factor? Some answers are already appearing. The Bill Gates Foundation and many other business and philanthropic organizations are trying to assist in reaching the mass population so all can have access to the Internet and the world of information technology, and elementary and secondary schools are investing heavily in IT to educate all students on its value.

CONCLUSION

There have been some dramatic changes in IT over the last four decades. Changes that were considered only science fiction and simply not possible a few years ago are reality today. The technology to communicate with anyone, anywhere is truly a phenomenon that is changing the world in which we live. Businesses are having to react in real time and have to build for a future that will be in constant change. What has not evolved as quickly are the people issues that surround the development and use of IT. We still struggle with ill-defined requirements and systems that are over budget and behind schedule. There are underlying and fundamental issues that IT and businesses have yet to come to grips with, including the fact that change is still not easy, that people still don't want to change, and that better methods for change management for IT are still needed.

REFERENCES

Bostrom, R.P., & Anson, R.G. 1992. The face-to-face electronic meeting: A tutorial. In R.P. Bostrom, R.T. Watson, & S.T. Kinney (eds.), *Computer augmented teamwork: A guided tour.* New York: Van Nostrand Reinhold, pp. 16–33.

Bostrom, R.P., Anson, R.G., & Clawson, V.K. 1993. Group facilitation and group support systems. In L.M. Jessup & J.S. Valacich (eds.), *Group support systems: New perspectives*. New York: Macmillan, pp. 146–168.

Bostrom, R.P., Van Over, D., & Watson, R.T. 1992. The computer-augmented teamwork project at the University of Georgia. In R.P. Bostrom, R.T. Watson, and S.T. Kinney (eds.), *Computer-augmented teamwork: A guided tour*. New York: Van Nostrand Reinhold.

Clark, J., & Koonce, R. 1995. Meetings go high-tech. *Training and Development*, 49 (11): 32–38.

Dennis, A.R., George, J.F., Jessup, L.M., Nunamaker, J.F., Jr., & Vogel, D.R. 1988. Information technology to support electronic meetings. *MIS Quarterly*, 12(4): 591–624.

Donaldson, H. 1978. *A guide to the successful management of computer projects*. New York: Halsted Press.

Hiltz, S.R., & Turoff, M. 1993. *The network nation: Human communications via computer*. Cambridge, MA: MIT Press.

Jessup, L.M., & Valacich, J.S. 1993. *Group support systems: New perspectives*. New York: Macmillan.

Johansen, R.D., Sibbet, S.B., Marting, A., Mittman, R., & Saffo, P. 1991. *Leading business teams: How teams can use technology and process to enhance group performance*. Reading, MA: Addison-Wesley.

Kelly, G.G., & Bostrom, R.P. 1998. A facilitator's general model for managing socio-emotional issues in group support systems meeting environments. *Journal of Management Information Systems*, 14(3): 23–44.

Markus, M.L., & Bjorn-Andersen, N. 1987. Power over users: Its exercise by system professionals. *Communications of the ACM*, 30(6): 498–504.

Nagasundaram, M., & Bostrom, R.P. 1995. The structuring of creative processes using GSS: A framework for research. *Journal of Management Information Systems*, 11(3): 89–116.

Post, B. 1992. Building the business case for groupware. In *Proceedings of The Twenty-Fifth Annual Hawaii International Conference on System Sciences*, Vol. 4. Los Alamitos, CA: IEEE Society Press, pp. 34–35.

Schrage, M. 1995. *No more teams! Mastering the dynamics of creative collaboration*. New York: Currency Doubleday.

Tiwana, A. 2000. *The knowledge management toolkit*. Upper Saddle River, NJ: Prentice Hall.

Townsend, A., Whitman, M., & Hendrickson, A. 1995. Computer support system adds power to group processes. *HR Magazine*, 40(9): 87–91.

Valacich, J.S., Dennis, A.T., & Nunamaker, J. 1991. Electronic meeting support: The groupssystems concept. *International Journal of Man Machine Studies*, 38(2): 74–86.

Watson, R.T., & Bostrom, R.P. 1991. Enhancing group behavior with a keypad based group support system. *Human Resources Development Quarterly*, 2(4): 333–354.

Watson, R.T., Bostrom, R.P., & Dennis, A.T. 1994. Fragmentation to integration. In P. Lloyd (ed.), *Groupware in the 21st century: Computer supported cooperative working toward the millennium*. Westport, CT: Praeger, pp. 29–39.

Chapter 11

The Balanced Scorecard: New Strategy Applications in Business-to-Business Commerce

William J. Mea, Theodore L. Robinson III, and James W. Handlon

INTRODUCTION

The Internet and business-to-business (B2B) and business-to-portal (B2P) commerce is the fastest growing area of the economy and is transforming the way organizations operate and manage. However, effective strategic planning in Internet-era businesses has taken a back seat to aggressive expectations—a fact most evident in the light of Internet company net value meltdowns. While traditional indices of value and strategic capacity may no longer apply in the same way they did in the industrial era, many organizations in the new economy fail to apply rigorous metrics in the same way to drive strategic direction. Such companies put themselves at peril of failing when they ignore fundamental steps for building and executing solid strategy with corresponding metrics. In these conditions it is the responsibility of consultants and change management specialists to help company leaders make wise decisions about their strategy. This chapter's objective is to update concepts from the balanced scorecard and apply them to the corporate context in the digital economy. We examine a number of basic issues in strategy when applying the balanced scorecard technique to companies, especially those engaged in B2B and B2P commerce. We propose new scorecard perspective options. We believe the addition of the new perspectives will help consultants assist companies to build more stable e-business organizational models and provide a more innovative approach to building and implementing strategy.

The chapter begins by providing a quick review for understanding the nature and importance of B2B companies. This is followed by a basic synopsis of strategy. Next we look at how a scorecard is traditionally constructed in real life. We propose additional perspectives such as the value of strategic alliances and internal/external communications as critical components, which must be understood in a new way in the "digital" era. Throughout the discussion we contrast old rules with new ones when applying the scorecard and also provide principles for applying the scorecard to companies in the digital economy with a particular focus on B2B. We also present general case examples of how to effectively apply the scorecard and contrast these with examples of others who have failed to apply these principles. The chapter closes with a summary of lessons learned.

BUSINESS-TO-BUSINESS COMMERCE

B2B commerce is defined as economic transactions conducted or originating electronically over Internet protocol (IP) networks, which provide more security and reliability than the public Internet. During the past 30 years investment by organizations in information technology (IT) through computers, software, networking, telecommunications, and enterprise resource planning (ERP) applications has focused on automating internal processes (Weller, 2000). The Internet provides a platform more robust than electronic data interchange (EDI) for companies to conduct cost-effective and ubiquitous commerce. The real-time many-to-many link presented by the Internet enables buyers to connect to customers, suppliers, and other members of their supply chain—the set of sequential activities that brings product to market. B2B commerce offers opportunities for increasing revenues, controlling costs, improving customer service, and reengineering workflows. It also increases opportunities for efficient management and enhances effective communication with customers, suppliers, and partners. New deployments of B2B e-commerce solutions through e-marketplaces enable the "frictionless" flow of information, payment, and products between businesses. The key advantage that e-businesses offer is the opportunity to quickly remove steps that do not add value in a supply chain.

Despite the current lull in e-company growth, B2B commerce is expected to accelerate worldwide over the next few years with projections reaching $1.3 trillion by 2003. The United States is expected to lead this global growth because approximately 85% of business is conducted between businesses and the Internet is firmly entrenched in many sectors. There are a number of areas in traditional business where B2B commerce provides recognizable benefits. Online procurement, which in the past has been highly fragmented and paper intensive, presents a key opportunity for B2B commerce because Internet-enabled processes can unify and quickly deliver solutions for data-heavy processes. In sales, web solutions can be applied to lower customer support costs, increase customer knowledge, and increase sales force capabilities. In inventory management, companies can quickly find buyers and sellers for their surplus equipment and stores through online auctions. In human resources (HR) and financial function areas, electronic hubs can greatly improve the management of benefits administration and financial transaction controlling functions.

From the perspective of participants, B2B commerce presents many new opportunities. Buyers are able to reduce inefficiencies and streamline their supply chains, electronify their catalogs to speed the search for needed parts, remove paper- and facsimile-based systems, and markedly decrease their overall costs. Suppliers, by developing electronic catalogs, can eliminate paper-based processes, create new markets, and develop integration points with their customers that improve their forecasting systems. Consumers gain through increased bargaining power as organizations compete for their business, intensified customer retention–focused service and support, and reduced searching for the required products.

An e-marketplace is the B2P form of e-commerce that acts as a third-party agent whose chief objective is to facilitate transactions between groups of buyers and sellers in a many-to-many/community relationship. In effect, the B2P is a private network or portal for conducting e-commerce. Examples of these B2P e-marketplaces are Exostar in the defense/aerospace industry and Avendra, led by Marriott in conjunction with Hyatt, Hilton, and Club Car of America, for the hospitality industry. The benefits they provide are lower trading costs, streamlined purchasing, and reliable access for aggregating goods for sale. Revenue is generated through transaction fees for connecting the parties and brokering transactions, subscription fees for membership to the site (allowing free transactions), or hybrid models that use both approaches. Four e-marketplace models predominate—catalog, auction, exchange, and community. The catalog form aggregates products or services from multiple points to provide low-cost distribution for sellers and one-stop shopping for buyers. Auctions are a venue for sale of one-time items such as excess inventory. Exchanges provide a channel for the sale of commodities. A community focuses on a specific subset of buyers/sellers to provide content of particular interest to match the interests of particular groups of specialists to increase their involvement and leverage knowledge and improve products (Lief, 1999).

DILEMMAS IN B2B STRATEGY

There is a downside to B2B, as most of those who invested heavily in Internet stocks during the summer of 2000 can attest. Executives often do not know clearly what they are trying to achieve or how to get there. This is especially the case in the Internet business space where a focus on clever ideas, new technology enablers, seeking "first mover advantage," or adding "a unique product" have come before any consideration of the practicalities of generating income. Irrational messages included the notion that one could build a valuable business by giving things away, that attracting eyeballs and stickiness (the ability to retain participants) would lead to success, and that consumers would put up with inconvenience for "cool experiences" and new technology tools (Perdue, 2001). Now that numerous e-businesses have lived out short lives born in over-hyped expectations and "vastly inflated market caps, the survivors are dancing to a different beat: the steady cadence of cold, hard numbers" (Ince, 2001, p. 68).

In their encounter with upheaval, a number of B2B companies have learned difficult lessons about conducting online business, and "as the dust settles, one of the clearest lessons is that the fundamentals . . . are becoming more important than ever" (Wilde, 2001, p. S1). In the "flight to stability" managers are beginning to recognize that a comprehensive 360-degree enterprisewide view of e-business is required to produce predicable financial returns. The strategic goals for both brick-and-mortar and online businesses are to (1) create integrated, technology-linked platforms straddling online and offline functions and (2) establish and operate synergistic business "partnerships" and affiliated organizational business activities that leverage the capabilities and marketplace penetration capacity of the affiliated group of companies as a combined entity. Well-constructed strategic plans enable corporations to be marketplace victors rather than victims.

While some B2B companies have initial concerns about strategy and even build a scorecard, many think of it as a cursory startup event for the senior management. According to Kaplan (2001), while perhaps 60% of large companies use a balanced scorecard at some level, most continue to focus on lagging indicators, particularly those associated with financial measures. They need to focus on customer retentions, quality, market share, growth, and environmental measures. Few implement scorecards tied to strategy. Fewer still take the next steps that are required. In order to be successful in articulating and implementing strategy, the scorecarding process needs to drive continuous improvement, not simply serve as an academic exercise (Kaplan, 2001).

STRATEGY BASICS

Many change consultants, while grounded in process and organizational development, are less familiar with principles of strategy and the financial imperatives that drive an organization's direction. Strategic management formation (or planning) is a process for developing an organization's entrepreneurial activities that lead to growth, renewal, change, or transformation. The key activities include:

- Establishing the vision, mission, and goals;
- Assessing the business environment;
- Evaluating organizational capabilities;
- Determining highest impact actions effecting success;
- Creating and fashioning the strategy; and
- Ensuring successful implementation.

This process is supported by analysis of the value chain and its integration points, evaluation of the company's structural compatibility and balance with options (Peters & Waterman, 1984), and assessment of opportunities and threats (including strategic partnerships needed) within the proposed framework (Porter,

Figure 11.1
Overview of Perspective Inputs and Relations

1980). Strategic implementation is the means by which an organization achieves its long-term objectives and translates strategy into planned actions on an appropriate time line.

THE BALANCED SCORECARD

Many consultants, especially those with financial services backgrounds, employ the Business Balanced Scorecard (Kaplan & Norton, 1996a) as a change lever to help organizations build the cornerstone of their strategic management system. It is used as a means to translate an organization's vision into operational actions. It provides a balanced approach for uniting strategic, operational, and organizational perspectives in planning (see Figure 11.1). It offers guidelines for integrating performance management into strategy, organization, and operations components. In translating the vision into these components, the organization's behavior is guided, the components are linked in meaningful ways, and strategy is operationalized in ways that are significant to the organization's members. In actual practice, it provides a concrete guide to decipher what is often an infrequent academic exercise conducted at the executive level and gives substance to action planning and metrics that can be cascaded throughout an organization. In brief, it presents a guide to bridge strategy to action (see Figure 11.2). Identifying and delivering needed partnerships/affiliations may be somewhat unpredictable in reality, but knowing the full value of "fit" and "future potential value" of the defined strategic partners/affiliates is central to executing the actions required to fulfill the strategy.

Consultants assist their executive clients with implementation of the balanced scorecard beginning with a translation of the vision and strategy into a comprehensive, yet digestible, set of goals and performance measures across a balanced set of perspectives. These perspectives include financial, customer, internal business process, and innovation/learning perspectives (see Figure 11.3). Questions of vision ask: "Where do we need to go in the future?" Questions of strategic

Figure 11.2
Strategic Management Process—High Level

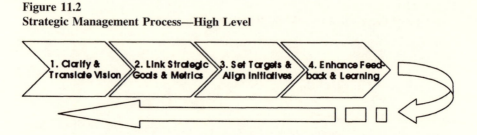

objectives ask: "How are we going to reach our goals?" "What partners/affiliates do we need to create a sustainable, competitive marketplace position?" Questions about critical success factors (CSFs) ask: "On what do we need to perform well in the market?" Questions about key performance indicators (KPIs) ask: "What should we measure to know how we are tracking toward success?" Implementation results from cascading goals into practical targets, critical performance indicators, and group/individual performance goals. The action of communicating practical goals and monitoring achievements is presumed to drive change throughout an organization so that its members are more market-oriented and have complementary objectives united to the strategy.

HOW TO BUILD A SCORECARD

While each company must endeavor to build its scorecard in a way that works best for it, we can offer some general steps and guidelines for the process. The major activities commonly employed to build a scorecard are summarized in Table 11.1. Additionally, a description of the value provided by the steps and the forums or methods that can be employed to build that step are displayed. In constructing this approach we have translated Kaplan and Norton's (1996a) original high-level approach into actionable process steps. Readers who may be interested in greater detail about the evolution of the scorecard are referred to the articles by Kaplan and Norton in the references at the end of the chapter (1993, 1996b, 2001).

Clarifying and translating the vision involves developing an initial foundation of consensus about what a company's market orientation means in real-world terms. In terms of activities, this means conducting meetings with the chief executive officer and other senior leaders of a company to clarify what is the desired outcome of developing the scorecard as well as priorities among strategy action plans (fundamental approach to market advantage) and strategic thrusts (major goals the organization needs to achieve). It also means developing initial understanding around the meaning of performance drivers, targets, and the organization's priorities for customer, internal business process, learning, and financial perspective outcomes.

Linking strategic goals and metrics involves taking the next step to get clarity

Figure 11.3
Strategic Management Process—Time Line and Perspectives

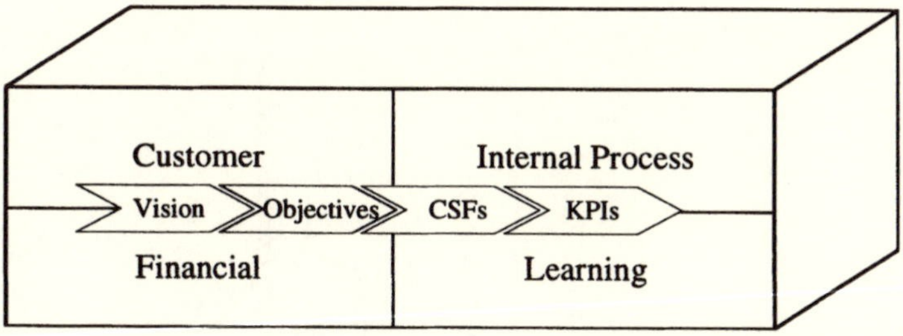

and focus on the realities of what the organization should be achieving in the future in the market(s) in which it chooses to operate. During the interplay of facilitated meetings, clarification on the balanced scorecard can be built among the top leaders for the direction of the future, for critical focus markets in which they plan to play, for the realities of conducting planning while producing, and for building sense of unity for the senior management team.

Setting targets and aligning metrics involves activities to integrate the business plan with managers lower in the organization. This creates a reality and planning structure around which understanding can be built. It also lays the foundation for helping leadership communicate with managers and supervisors on priorities, on what should be measured, and on which focus areas should have most re-sources. In terms of customers, it helps the company identify no more than four critical success factors (CSFs—qualitative imperatives describing a criterion of success) and associated key performance indicators (KPIs). To develop KPIs one must ask how the company will know it is achieving a particular facet of success and how to measure that facet appropriately. CSFs and KPIs are de-veloped for each perspective. The scorecard is completed with targets set for each KPI and with confirmation by a board of directors.

Enhancing feedback and learning involves the deployment of the scorecard to become a cornerstone for the management system by which the company can plan, learn, and modify its behavior as directed by the strategy embedded in the scorecard. This gives companies the "capacity for strategic learning . . . and thus enables companies to modify strategies to reflect [strategy in light of perform-ance]" (Kaplan & Norton, 1996b, p. 77).

Additional Scorecard Perspectives to Consider in B2B

In practice, we find that there are shortcomings in presuming that traditional scorecards meet the needs of Internet-era companies. While this approach offers some useful guidelines for uniting action, it falls short in the areas of selecting and managing strategic partnerships/alliances and providing effective means for external and internal strategic communications. We believe that more criteria

Table 11.1
Balanced Scorecard Approach: Integrating Performance Management into Strategy, Organization, and Operations

Activity	Value	Forums and Methods
Clarify and Translate the Vision		
• Establish level for BSC	• Builds clarity about objectives with most critical sponsor	• CEO meeting
• Establish intent with top management	• Builds support and understanding up front for the initiative and identifies potential issues	• Initial senior leadership interviews
• Set objectives, vision of four perspectives, key performance drivers, targets, priorities	• Clarifies direction and commitment	• Introductory executive workshop
Link Strategic Goals and Metrics		
• Document strategies (including partnerships needed)	• Provides clear "black-and-white" presentation of ideas on which agreement is built	• Documentation
• Develop leadership consensus	• Ties together understanding of cause and effect relations, worthy targets, and metrics	• One-on-one discussion with leaders and key managers
		• Follow-up executive workshop
		• Draft document

208

Set Targets and Align Metrics

- Tie in with managers
- Finalize CSFs and metrics and final scorecard for each of the perspectives (customer, process, learning, and financial)
- Confirm with board of directors

- Gets input into CSFs, metrics in use, and candidate metrics
- Sets and rationalizes metrics and validates ownership
- Builds support from a stockholder perspective

- Focus groups and interviews
- Leadership-management workshop
- Workshop/meeting

Enhance Feedback and Learning

- Develop and execute communications plan (including defining the few, but critical messages)
- Roll out the scorecard
- Align initiatives
- Enhance the system

- Clarifies key messages, stakeholders, and timing
- Ensures that the organization is engaged
- Provides rationalization of initiatives already in place
- Provides uniformity and an infrastructure for integrating strategy for the long term

- Standard communications already in place, town halls, intranet
- Conduct training
- Embed into group and individual scorecards
- Management reviews and planning sessions
- Fit into performance management and bonus system
- Tie to HR systems

need to be added over and above the four traditional perspectives. Therefore, we would add two additional perspectives: (1) strategic partners/alliances and (2) communication.

Strategic Partnerships and Alliances

Strategic partnerships and alliances are critical pillars upon which Internet businesses must rely in our new e-commerce world for effective planning and execution in delivering value across the supply chain. Internet companies must have distinct competencies and market focus, yet they often lack financial and technical resources to execute against their customer needs. In-house performance of non-core business activities is often not an option (Simchi-Levi, Kamisky, & Simchi-Levi, 2000), especially in markets that change quickly. Even if internal resources are available, other companies may be better suited to perform tasks that support a company's core competencies. Acquisitions are an option, but speed dictates effective use of partnerships.

Strategic alliances are multifaceted targeted partnerships between synergistic organizations aiming at cooperatively sharing at lower risk and potentially increasing rewards for both. Sharing goals through strategic alliances can lead to effective commitment of resources and development of new creative options through sharing of ideas. In evaluating the benefits to be realized through a strategic alliance (Lewis, 1990), it is vital to evaluate how the alliance supports issues such as improving market access, growing customers and marketplace penetration, creating new sources of revenues, augmenting operations cost and/or efficiencies, or adding to technical potency. Related issues include pooling expertise to explore opportunity, increasing capacity for organizational skills/learning, adding value to products, or enhancing financial strength. These issues are not orthogonal and represent overlapping considerations.

Alliances can be formed to leverage business capabilities as a whole, increase access to new market channels, or build critical mass required to drive operating costs lower. This is possible by partnering with well-recognized companies that already have access to wider markets and are ready to support partners who can bring additional markets or add to market strength. For example, we have worked with many companies to explore opportunities to partner with B2B marketplaces that already have strength through global market reach in areas not immediately accessible to the company which seeks that access. It is intuitively obvious, for example, how pairing with Microsoft, Intel, or Dell would add market channel opportunities for a company seeking to extend brand recognition, advertising, and existing sales channels. An e-marketplace that focuses on transportation and logistics would potentially benefit from pairing with a Cargil or Archer Daniels-Midland. Exostar in the aerospace/defense industry and Avendra in the hospitality industry have achieved early meaningful successes by creating e-marketplaces (private e-commerce industry-focused B2Ps) that leverage the competitive advantages of all partners in terms of purchasing power and logistics management costs. They are proving the impact of partnerships/affiliations in capturing the value chain potentially available in a marketplace.

In addition to enhancing market access, many e-marketplaces also use strategic alliances to augment their operations. Operations may be more successfully augmented by (1) outsourcing non-core processes, (2) partnering to enable technical integration to the marketplace (on-boarding), and/or (3) aligning with other e-marketplaces to offer complementary product offerings. Outsourcing non-core processes is the least risky way of enhancing operations. Transaction-heavy functions such as payroll processing and credit verification are commonly outsourced. On-boarding companies to the marketplace often requires partnering with a technology firm or consultancy to ensure rapid integration. Partnering with other e-marketplaces enables a company to provide one-stop shopping for its customers. For example, an e-marketplace focused on heavy building materials such as concrete may form an alliance with a steel marketplace so that all of a customer's needs can be met at once. Each type of alliance increases the effectiveness of an organization's operations while allowing key resources to be spent on its core value proposition.

Adding to technical strength is one of the most interesting and risky areas for B2Bs to explore. Technology that is shared among companies can add to the technical competencies of each. In the case of e-marketplaces, the transactional engine (such as Ariba or Commerce One) creates a common, central functionality shared by all users. Back-office functions like billing, collections, accounting consolidations, and other important processes needed to complete an end-to-end e-commerce solution present special technical/technology issues to users of e-marketplaces. Other technology alliances and purchases that form the IT infrastructure building blocks for customer relationship management (CRM), accounting processes, or integration features are secondary but also critical decisions.

In many cases, where an e-marketplace has IT development as an additional focus, strategic alliances offer an opportunity to evolve into additional marketplace solutions. As the marketplace explores software capabilities in the context of market development, it is driven to build software processes that respond to its customer demands. At the same time, in the context of integration with other products it learns "sweet spot" integration points of overlap with its partners as they develop to match customer needs. As integration points in the value chain increase, each company can realize synergistic strategic opportunities that magnify potential options. This is illustrated in the Figure 11.4, where each chevron represents a software answer in a supply chain. The boxes represent integration points with other software products. Over time, provided the right market conditions, the aggregated integration points increase, represented by expanding rings, which become their own distinctive marketplace powerhouse advantage.

Strategic alliances can also provide opportunities for enhancing each company's organizational skills. In most cases, they have the added advantage of providing a safe harbor from which to learn to structure in ways that provide

Figure 11.4
Integration Points in Software Development Opportunity

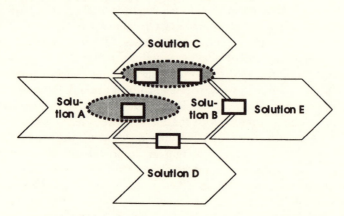

benefits to each. For example, in one B2B alliance, partners developed an organizational structure to support the allied process for which they shared responsibility. At first, as each learned about the other's weakness and as each
failed to live up to agreements on shared project time lines, tensions multiplied.
However, as each learned that they could more appropriately swap some task
responsibilities, each developed new skills in understanding requirements and
mediation, and improved their organizational structures. Moreover, they developed a professional service offering these new competencies to the market for
other noncompeting B2Bs.

Partnering to enhance financial strength is an additional consideration. With
venture capital and initial public offerings fueling the optimism about Internet
companies, little thought was initially given to the factors involved in alliances
that enhance financial strength. Many considered more traditional companies to
be poor sponsors for B2B initiatives. The quality of partnership for financial
strength is seen to be much more critical in retrospect. In a sense, the financial
stability provided by funding from *Fortune* 500 companies provides the kind of
anchor many B2Bs could have used to their advantage. For example, at one
B2B there was frequent complaining by the more progressive thinkers when the
primary financial sponsor, a global *Fortune* 50, urged the B2B to take a more
traditional approach to developing its metrics evaluating profit momentum. The
same progressive thinkers were among the most relieved when market conditions
required a retrenchment and the company survived because it was generating
"real" revenues.

In order to evaluate the comparative worth of partnerships, we suggest an
initial qualifying approach that matrixes opportunities. These opportunities
should be discussed and evaluated in a facilitated session with managers representing each of the critical perspectives—financial, customer, process (espe-

Figure 11.5
Evaluating Partnerships

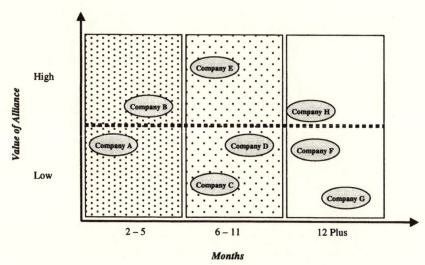

cially IT), learning, communications, and partnership. In a B2B these interests might be represented by leaders from Finance, CRM and Business Development, IT infrastructure and IT development, Human Resources, Marketing, and Sales. The first step involves prioritizing the critical factors most important to the long-term objectives of the company in forming strategic alliances. In the second step, a matrix with axes of perceived value and time horizon should be developed for each of two to three top factors. Because speed represents a critical evaluation point in B2B, consensus around time frames is a foundation for the discussion and provides the opportunity for the group to develop additional shared understanding of urgency. This helps participants focus on the reality that many of the partners one might choose to select might not exist in the future. The third step is to evaluate each of the potential partners at a high level in light of criteria. Follow-on steps would be to gather additional detailed information for discussion of business case presentations at a later date. This is illustrated in the Figure 11.5.

Communications

From our experience, communications should be considered from a strategic perspective in its own right in developing a balanced scorecard for B2B companies. In the traditional scorecard, communications is presumed to have some prominence in developmental process and in the actual substance of the scorecard strategic thrusts, CSFs, and KPIs. In Internet terms, communications has a strategic impact on success and must be addressed accordingly. We feel these concepts are inadequately addressed in the literature on the balanced scorecard. Because at its core B2B commerce involves strategic messages, we believe it should be considered from a strategic perspective. Communications occur across every dimension—technologic, person-to-person internally, and with buyers and suppliers. We will cover a small number of the critical factors in communications related to B2B that need to be strategically developed and integrated into a comprehensive understanding of strategy evaluation.

Because the pace of organizational growth and change in B2B companies is very rapid as they aggressively build to gain "first-mover advantage" (sometimes known as "Internet speed"), internal communications take on a highly critical dimension rarely required for more traditional businesses. The mode of communication needs to be both flexible and dynamic. The core/strategic messages about the values, strategy, goals, standards of relating processes, and long-term objectives need to be simple, unified, clear, and convincing.

Internal communications matter in B2Bs. When companies are staffed by workers whose core skills have been built in technical areas of rapidly growing organizations, they may not possess the key communications skills more routinely found in larger companies. On the other hand, they are also unconstrained by those same issues. For instance, effective product development requires excellent communications, both formal and informal, across functional boundaries in emerging B2Bs. If people in an organization work ceaselessly in a "heads-down mode" and fail to take the time to come away from their project tasks to communicate with others, critical opportunities may be missed. Effective B2Bs will find that building in a strategic, formal process for this communication, with associated KPIs, provides an engine that makes it possible to bring new winning products to market with greater speed and quality.

Communications with customers, either as buyers or suppliers, offers an additional area for specific focus in building and evaluating strategy. Communications with suppliers in B2B e-marketplaces offer an illustration of the importance of how the dynamics of communications can affect results. For example, in one e-marketplace a rapid effort was undertaken to build an automated registration of the suppliers of a key buyer. The tone of the initial contact by one buyer with significant leverage with its suppliers created alarm among the smaller players. Visits to suppliers by sales agents only confirmed the concerns. A major effort in strategic communications comprised of simple messages with clear content was required by the marketplace to overcome the initial "push-back."

Numerous other perspective options could also be considered for a B2B balanced scorecard. Some examples of perspectives could include the value of intellectual capital, technology in all its varieties, and communities of interest (COINs). The important point to be made is that leaders need to strategically develop, evaluate, communicate, implement, and monitor strategy in a way that increases opportunity while lowering risk.

SUMMARY

Strategy, specifically employing the balanced scorecard in B2B, offers a number of challenges that were not apparent at the exuberant launch of Internet businesses. We offer a number of lessons for change consultants from the authors' perspectives in working in the "B2B space."

Lessons Learned

Lesson 1. In B2B companies, where the future has often been built upon bright expectations rather than traditional basics, the efforts of consultants to assist companies in maintaining financial health must be complemented by the implementation of the new strategy perspectives we offer in this chapter.

Lesson 2. Consultants should help leaders keep balanced scorecard metrics to a short list, perhaps up to 20. These must be balanced among the perspectives we provide in this chapter (customer, business process, learning, financial, partnerships/alliances, and strategic communications). The balanced scorecard metrics should be line-of-sight and support strategic priorities clearly understandable to all.

Lesson 3. The quality and strength of partnerships in (1) business markets, (2) technology, and (3) non-core business-related areas can make or break a B2B. Therefore, during the consulting process a sober and balanced evaluation of alliance partners needs to take into account both the opportunities and the downside risks of companies.

Lesson 4. Effective strategic communications, both internal and external, represent key areas of focus for the success of B2B companies. Leaders must plan, execute, and monitor communications strategy and its effectiveness. Change consultants need to be particularly tuned in to using communications tools they normally use in new ways to help companies build a robust capability in this area.

Lesson 5. With the assistance of an alert change consultant, solid execution of a good strategy via an updated scorecard approach will help B2Bs navigate the treacherous waters of Internet business.

CONCLUSION

Despite the 2001 meltdown in Internet valuations, B2B commerce will grow at a dramatic pace. B2B offers interesting new and indelible models that will ultimately transform modern business. Change consultants have much to offer in translating older concepts into methods that assist B2Bs in planning their strategy. Strategic planning, when employing the business balanced scorecard for B2Bs, must be augmented by additional critical impact perspectives, including partnerships/alliances and strategic communications to be successful. In doing so, the net result of the strategy implementation process will result in a more solid and lasting foundation for success for B2Bs.

REFERENCES

Ince, J.F. 2001. Business to business: The morning after. *www.upside.com* (May): 68–74.

Kaplan, R.S. 2001. The disruptive consultancy. *Consulting* (March): 36–38.

Kaplan, R.S., & Norton, D.P. 1993. Putting the balanced scorecard to work. *Harvard Business Review* (September–October): 134–142.

Kaplan, R.S., & Norton, D.P. 1996a. *The balanced scorecard*. Boston: Harvard Business School Press.

Kaplan, R.S., & Norton, D.P. 1996b. Using the balanced scorecard as a strategic management system. *Harvard Business Review* (January–February): 75–85.

Lewis, J. 1990. *Partnerships for profit*. New York: Free Press.

Lief, V. 1999. Anatomy of new market models. In *The Forrester Report*. Cambridge, MA: Forester Research.

Perdue, L. 2001. A bright future: After the train wreck. *Inc. Tech 2001*, 1: 51–53.

Peters, T.J., & Waterman, R.H. 1984. *In search of excellence: Lessons from America's best companies*. New York: Warner Books.

Porter, M.E. 1980. *Competitive strategies: Techniques for analyzing industries and competitors*. New York: Free Press.

Simchi-Levi, D., Kamisky, P., & Simchi-Levi, E. 2000. *Designing and managing the supply chain: Concepts, strategies, and case studies*. Boston: Irwin McGraw-Hill.

Weller, T. 2000. BtoB commerce: The rise of eMarketplaces. *Legg Mason Spring Industry Analysis* (Spring): 2–3.

Wilde, T. 2001. Evisions: Flight to stability. *Oracle Magazine*, special supplement (May–June): 1.

Part IV

New Approaches and Models for Change

Chapter 12

Changing How Organizations Manage Change from the Inside Out

Andrea B. Bear and Kathleen A. Brehony

No man ever steps into the same river twice, for it's not the same river and he's not the same man.

—Heraclitus

INTRODUCTION

I was working in the television news business as an executive producer at WLS in Chicago, an ABC network affiliate, when my friend Ellen came for a visit. Ellen had never seen a live newscast from the inside, so I invited her to join me in the control booth for a taste of chaos. My talented crew of anchors, reporters, editors, directors, producer, and others were racing to get ready for the 6:00 news that Saturday evening. There was no big, breaking story that day, but this was the height of the college football season and since ABC broadcasts college football on Saturdays, my station carried the regional game of interest. There was nothing memorable about the game itself, except for what it did to the newscast, at least in Ellen's mind. I had ridden this horse before! The rules were: if the game ran over by no more than 15 minutes, we would still go on the air with an abbreviated newscast; if the game ran longer than 15 minutes into the 6:00 hour, the network would fill the time and there would be no early local news on our station that evening. By the time we made our way up to the control room, with a luxurious 10-minute cushion before scheduled airtime, it looked fairly certain that we would have to reshuffle our show lineup and collapse the newscast to fit into the available time once that football game was over. As the top of the hour came and went, the show producer and I huddled, then he succinctly and simultaneously relayed to the technical staff in the control room, the floor crew and the anchors, "Here we go! Let's drop pages 6, 7, and 9, move up page 4, read the lead-in to the fire story as a voice over, weather is two minutes, sports gets cut to three." Every passing second required more changes as we struggled to fit our show into the time allotted, including commercials of course. Finally, the football game ended with just enough time to put us on the air, but the changes continued throughout the newscast "No time for three minutes on sports. Cut it to two." Each change that we made swept through our team like a tornado touching down here, then there, then sweeping through the streets scattering everything in its path as it cut everyone's air time and sent people scrambling for the right video, graphics, and teleprompter pages. When the anchors breathlessly signed off, Ellen turned to me looking totally drained and said, "I feel like I just smoked a carton of cigarettes. So many changes in such a short period of time. How do you do it?"

As a management consultant, I often think back about Ellen's innocent question and all the implications it holds. Change. Ubiquitous and offering opportunities for both disruption and growth, change is not an interloper to our sense of how things are "supposed" to be, but rather it is a constant in our lives and the lives of our organizations. The fact is, certain organizations deal with change better than others.

In this chapter, we will explore the relationship between change, consciousness, and ways in which vibrant organizations passionately respond to change and use its power as opportunities for growth, fulfillment, and the actualization of its full potential.

Let's start with three hypotheses:

1. Change is never-ending and ever-present.
2. Organizations that are self-aware, that is to say they are conscious, are better able to see change coming, more honest in determining how best to respond to it, and more courageous in taking action steps to capitalize on change itself.
3. The area of organizational consciousness that is most often neglected revolves around human factors—"the soft stuff."

ON THE NATURE OF CHANGE

The early Greek philosopher, Heraclitus was right when he wrote, "We cannot step into the same river twice." Just as the rushing waters of a moving river are in constant flux and change, so are we. In only a few years time, not a single cell in our bodies will be the same one that it is today. And like our living, changing bodies, organizations live and change at even larger scales. The commonly held idea that we or our organizations can remain static and predictable is both illusionary and dangerous. To resist change is futile, to embrace change as a dynamic force that allows for real growth is the only way to go.

Consider the door-to-door-salesman who refuses to embrace and adapt to the realities of the changing work force. He still hits the streets everyday, knocks on the same doors and wonders why no one's home or answering. Has he not noticed that many of the stay-at-home mothers are now working moms, and those still at home aren't inclined to open the door to strangers?

Consider what the one-two punch of the invasion of the national super-store retailers and the exponential growth of e-commerce has done to mom-and-pop shops, from office supply stores—some of us remember them as stationers—to independent bookstores to small, eclectic record stores, and on and on. Most failed to see the wave of mega-retail chains offering big volume at cut-rate prices. Economically, most could not compete. Independent booksellers, for example, lost 42% market share between 1991 and 1996. That was just about the time the Internet exploded. Most experts believe that as the e-commerce pie grows, the local retailers' slice will shrink even further. In fact, in 1998, the total e-commerce market was $7.8 billion, with only 9% earned by local stores. By 2003, it's predicted that the e-commerce market will increase by an astounding 1,400%. The market share of local stores is expected to drop to less than 6% ("Mom-and-pop online stores, 2001). These are simple, yet vivid examples of what can happen when change is ignored, not fully understood, or inadequately prepared for.

The most successful companies not only adapt to change but capitalize on its power with creativity, courage, and with an eye toward transformation. The abilities to move fluidly, react quickly, and embrace new realities should be considered as basic requirements for every organization that wishes to fulfill its mission and grow toward the future. The need for a new lens with which to see the cycles of life and business and the truth about the nature of change has never been more critical, especially in today's fast-moving world when the forces of change have intensified in frequency and magnitude. The unstoppable power of change is, in fact, an opportunity for enhanced consciousness. It's a wake-up call for honest self- and organizational-awareness and a new appreciation about the true nature of reality (including change itself).

Greater awareness and heightened consciousness make the critical difference between successful companies and unsuccessful ones particularly as they strive to adapt and thrive in our ever-changing world. Consciousness refers to a deep and honest attentiveness, a habit of mindfulness about what is true, and a willingness to open one's heart and mind to change. There's no reason to think that consciousness only revolves around what cynically has become known as the "soft stuff" (e.g., the human factors in organizational success). Generally, however, we have found that it is this aspect of business that often remains the most unconscious and the most often neglected. Perhaps these human dimensions of organizational success are often overlooked because this area is the least measurable, most personal, and most often underappreciated as a critical factor in achieving goals and maximizing profit and shareholder value.

CORPORATE CONSCIOUSNESS

The word *consciousness* itself comes from the Latin *conscius*, meaning "knowing with others, participating in knowledge, or aware of." Scholars and philosophers throughout history have argued about the nature of consciousness, its evolution, and its expression in human cognition and behavior. In spite of the academic controversy and the subtle and complex qualities of consciousness, there is still broad agreement that, using its most fundamental description, consciousness really means awareness. What do we really know about ourselves? What do we really know about the nature of reality?

More than 2,000 years ago the ancient Greeks wrote brilliantly about the importance of consciousness when they carved a mere two words into the cave wall at the Temple to Apollo at Delphi. Their instructions were simple and clear: "Know Thyself." We can define corporate consciousness then as the collective embodiment of the consciousness of the individuals within a company, organization, or team. In our understanding, consciousness embraces a variety of elements, including soul, spirit, energy, feelings, awareness, intuition and perception, emotional intelligence, the persona and the shadow, interpersonal relationships, values, attitudes, behaviors, and culture.

In spite of careful planning, creative processes, and a deep understanding of market realities, many organizations still fail to meet their goals. Why? In our experience, these failures to meet and exceed business objectives arise from the reluctance to fully know oneself and one's organization. Often there are dysfunctional attitudes, behaviors, and values that lie deep beneath the surface of awareness. It is the unconscious aspects of organizations and people that impede the way to full potential.

Think of an iceberg as a metaphor for consciousness. Then consider that nine-tenths of the iceberg lies below the surface—in the unconscious. What we know we can navigate around, like the mission, goals, strategies, structure, systems, policies, procedures, and work processes. It's what we don't know about ourselves and others that sinks organizational ships—things like values, perceptions, feelings, emotions, trust, personalities, and leadership styles.

The heady questions about consciousness asked by philosophers may seem a far cry from the everyday concerns of most organizations as they scramble to adjust to a changing world, but, in fact, the most successful and vital leaders grasp the importance of deep insight and accurate knowledge about themselves and their organization. They know that those words the Greeks painstakingly scratched onto that cave wall are as true today as they were in antiquity.

Effective leaders constantly direct their focus toward accurately understanding their organization's strategy, tactics, financing, policies, processes, systems, structures, facilities, technology, marketing, economics, global and political trends, and the list goes on. But, and this is a critical difference, great leaders, highly conscious leaders, pay equal attention to the less measurable aspects of organizational success such as values, culture, team dynamics, leadership styles, communications, and the individual personalities within their leadership teams. Their attention is directed not only outward but inward as well. They are aware of their own strengths and challenges and have made a commitment to personal growth and continual improvement as a leader. These executives are wise, indeed. In fact, conscious leaders challenge the business principles-du-jour that focus exclusively on the management of numbers (with their appealing neatness and order) rather than on people, with all their rich complexity and unpredictability.

More and more leaders are recognizing that business, especially in our fast-paced world, requires a new paradigm of organizational leadership and development in order to exploit change, build competitive advantage, and realize success. They understand that becoming conscious of our strengths and challenges—the truth about our organization and ourselves—is the first step on the path to achieving and exceeding business objectives.

Research has shown that as an organization becomes more conscious, it releases the magnificent untapped energy that resides beneath the surface, creating a container that brings out the full potential of each and every member. Conscious organizations are always creative, productive, and highly successful. Conscious organizations are spirited and their people feel respected, nurtured, and find passion and meaning in the work they do. The poet Kahlil Gibran spoke elegantly about the nature of work when it is conscious and filled with spirit, when the bigger picture is present in everyone's heart and mind. Gibran wrote, "Work is love made visible." We know he's right.

Being conscious means being present, "in the moment," mindful. Think about how many times you sit in what feels like endless meetings where attendees are barely present. Their minds and attention are elsewhere, reading the latest stack of memos, checking e-mail, or whispering into cell phones. At times like this, "out of body" experiences are no longer the curiosity described by ancient mystics (and, of course, actress Shirley MacLaine). Instead, we may wonder how to encourage "in the body" experiences, where participants are intellectually, emotionally, and creatively engaged in the tasks at hand, using the very best of their skills and personalities to solve problems and more effectively manage change. You rarely see these mindless behaviors in conscious organizations. Rather, conscious organizations value everyone's time and know how to squeeze a lot of energy and productivity out of a little bit of it. The most effective teams and organizations are both conscious and mindful; conscious leaders are not only aware, but also attentive. Technology provides us with so many new capabilities, but it can also be a distraction. When you compound the organizational challenges with greater geographic dispersion and decentralization, consciousness becomes all the more critical, especially about the human factors—the soft stuff. And while many tough executives may dismiss its value and importance, the soft stuff really is the hard work.

The more conscious we become, the more we narrow the gap between how we see ourselves and how others perceive us. And the more conscious we are, the better we know ourselves and the more we get to know others. Importantly, consciousness is not a static intelligence; it's dynamic. Consciousness is a heartfelt commitment to ongoing assessment and honest but compassionate self-analysis.

As management consultants, we have been distressed to observe that most organizations and companies, as well as most individuals, spend the great majority of their waking hours in a rather unconscious state. Individual leaders may be expert at market analysis or economic forecasts but have no insight into their interpersonal behavior or management style. Teams within organizations may get the job done, but miss their unfulfilled potential because of petty personality conflicts, grandstanding on the part of some, and a failure to cohesively gel as a force to exceed expectations. We know that one of our first tasks in working with any organization is to illuminate a secret hidden in plain sight: Achieving higher levels of consciousness releases pent-up psychological energy. The liberation of this energy leads to superior performance and increased value and satisfaction. This equation always adds up.

Time and time again, we have confirmed the hypothesis that conscious organizations are more successful at dealing with change and all its implications. It's not just because they are conscious of all of the business challenges, strategies, global trends, tactics, technology, and economics but because they are very conscious of *all* the important elements of organizational success, including the "soft stuff." When highly successful companies take disastrous actions that sour people's opinions of the company and its leadership, affect stock values, and shatter the confidence of the consumer and investor communities, don't you often wonder how these obviously very bright business executives could have made those decisions, taken those actions? "What were they thinking?" you ask yourself. We answer, "These leaders don't 'get it.' " And the "it" has to do with a level of consciousness and awareness about the social or human capital of an organization or company. In contrast then, leaders who do "get it," understand the connections between the people in organizations and the bottom-line metrics of profitability and shareholder value. These leaders know the value of building healthy environments and balancing work force performance with employee fulfillment. This observation is intuitively fulfilling—after all, we recognize how these factors affect our relationships and success in our lives outside of organizations. And empirical studies testify just how the human element is intimately interconnected with organizational success.

For example, an in-depth study of 25 enterprises—across a variety of industries—that consistently achieved a significantly higher level of work force performance bears this out. "The most compelling commonalities . . . were in the philosophical beliefs and practices shared at all levels." Leadership expert Jon Katzenbach directed the research effort, which was sponsored by McKinsey & Company, Inc. and The Conference Board. In *Peak Performance*, Katzenbach summarized these shared traits into three basic characteristics of these organizations:

- They believe strongly in each employee;
- They engage their employees emotionally as well as rationally;

- They pursue enterprise performance and worker fulfillment with equal vigor. (2000, pp. 11–12)

Recent empirical research has unequivocally shown what great leaders have always intuitively understood: When people function as vibrant teams, hone their leadership and communication skills, deepen levels of emotional intelligence throughout the organization, and empower motivation and determination by living an effective corporate culture, their companies meet and exceed even their most ambitious stretch goals. And yet as much as we know these things to be true, it takes great courage and commitment to focus on this journey to leave behind the "business as usual" mentality that has outlived its usefulness. It takes more than great courage to stay the course. It takes consciousness.

THE POWER OF CONSCIOUSNESS AND CHANGE

Heightened consciousness about ourselves and others is a powerful engine and one of the key ingredients to long-term success and high performance. And for all those who have a hard time buying into the importance of consciousness in dealing with change, the business research literature highlights a dramatic cause-and-effect relationship between a company's investment in its human capital and increases in shareholder value. What follows is just a fraction of the emerging data that supports this premise:

- Companies that create and live (or sustain) an effective corporate culture and bolster human resource practices can gain as much as a 30% increase in market value. Watson Wyatt Worldwide's (2000) survey of more than 400 companies shows "a clear relationship between the effectiveness of a company's human capital and the creation of superior shareholder returns" as calculated by its Human Capital Index—a set of 30 measures that quantify which human resource practices and policies increase or decrease shareholder value.

- A Gallup Organization survey of 2 million employees at 700 companies showed that having a caring boss is valued more than money or fringe benefits by most workers. The study also found that "how long employees stay at companies and how productive they are is determined by their relationship with their immediate supervisor" (Zipkin, 2000, p. C1)

- Eighty percent of executives worldwide believe that attracting and retaining the best people will be the overriding force to business strategy over the next 10 years. Seventy-five percent of these executives rank human performance as the clear competitive advantage over strategy and technology (Neill & Borell, 1999).

- Southwest Airlines is a perennial favorite among proponents of corporate culture and values-centered leadership. This company truly values its people and pays great attention to the "soft stuff." And today it still remains at the top of many lists, including *Fortune* magazine's *Fortune* 500, Americas Most Admired Companies, Global Most Admired Companies, and the 100 Best Companies to Work For. Southwest Airlines has experienced 28 consecutive years of profitability. It has ranked number one in fewest customer complaints for the last nine consecutive years and has maintained the best cumulative baggage handling record among major airlines as published in the Department of Transportation's *Air Travel Consumer Report*. In April 2001, the National Airline Quality Rating (AQR) ranked Southwest Airlines number three among the top 10 airlines for performance in 2000. The airline has an annual employee turnover of just 7%, and in 1997, for every 3,000 jobs available, there were 105,000 applicants. It has the best safety record in the industry and the second lowest cost per average seat mile (Southwest Airlines, 2001).

• In their groundbreaking six-year research that culminated in *Built to Last*, Jim Collins and Jerry Porras (1997) studied 18 visionary companies (visionary meaning more than successful, more than enduring, representing the best of the best in their industries) and compared them with other well-established companies in their respective business sectors. They found that a common thread among the visionary companies was that they all had and preserved a core ideology of purpose and values, while changing the processes and policies and stimulating progress. These companies excelled at aligning their systems and actions with the core ideology, developed strong leadership throughout the organization, remained flexible to adapt as the market demanded, and set huge goals for the entire company to reach for. Changes in organizations today—flattened hierarchies, more geographical dispersion, more decentralization, more autonomy, more knowledge workers as opposed to laborers and assembly-line workers—require even greater attention to values-based leadership. "The corporate bonding glue will increasingly become *ideological*. People still have a fundamental human need to belong to something they can feel proud of. They have a fundamental need for guiding values and sense of purpose that gives their life and work meaning. They have a fundamental need for connection with other people, sharing with them the common bond of beliefs and aspirations" (Collins & Porras, 1997, p. 247).

This research underlies the work we are doing with leadership teams to maximize individual and team potential for financial success. Enlightened leaders understand that in order to get more out of teams and individuals, people need to know more about themselves and one another in order to communicate more authentically and work together to achieve common ends. Enhanced communication, the authentic behaviors of successful teams, shared vision, and a common understanding of the culture and values are *the* critical ingredients in effective change management.

With knowledge as power, consciousness helps better align all the systems and practices that affect an organization. Specifically, this relates to a corporate culture in which values like trust, respect, honesty, integrity, innovation, and growth are the cornerstones. Shared information and open communications demonstrate such values and are critical components of what workers expect in healthy work environments. They must be embedded in the myriad systems and polices of an organization, including recruitment, hiring and retention, promotion, performance review, compensation, and benefits. The hierarchical structures of yesterday have given way to more flattened organizations of empowered employees, with top-down and bottom-up leadership. And because of the long hours people spend at work today, value for individuals may relate to the family-friendliness of a company (i.e., flexible work hours, on-site day care, wellness programs, fitness centers, etc.).

The satisfaction of employees engenders loyalty and commitment. But there is an interesting twist in the data. A recent study of 5,000 U.S. households shows that American workers are less satisfied with their jobs today than they were five years ago. In fact, that data shows that less than half are happy with their jobs. And it's the baby boomers (aged 45–54) who are the least content (only 47% expressed satisfaction with their jobs). High expectations, fast-paced work environments, and coping with constant change are thought to be the cause of the decline in job satisfaction. Workers see and hear about the mega-bucks earned by CEOs and dot com executives and feel they aren't getting their fair share of the pie, according to The Conference Board, the worldwide business and research network that conducted the study. In addition to financial rewards from their jobs, today's employees look for their jobs to provide "friendships, family support, community, and sense of identity." Unmet and unrealistic expectations lead to dissatisfaction (Caudron, 2001, p. 34).

BUILDING CONSCIOUS ORGANIZATIONS

It's quite easy to talk about being conscious and extremely difficult to stick with it consistently, and for the long-term. As in most of life, it is far easier to "talk the talk" rather than "walk the talk." And that's true both for individuals and organizations. Based upon a burgeoning empirical business literature and our professional experiences, we are convinced that consciousness lies at the very heart of the elements needed to effectively manage change, achieve superior performance, create continuous improvement and learning, enhance work force fulfillment, and affect other measures of success. In an effort to bring together a wide-range of critical factors, we have designed a model to capture some of the fundamental aspects of consciousness that lead to individual and organizational success. We call this "C Your Way to Full Potential" (see Figure 12.1). Our model incorporates Change, Culture, Commitment, Communication, Compassion, Creativity, Courage, Competency, and Coaching.

Our "C-Model" is intended to be fluid and spark your thinking about new ways of looking at your organization and your personal leadership skills and philosophies that give direction to positive change. As always, insight is an important and critical first step, but insight without action will not change a thing. In plain words Confucius summed this up nicely: "The man who stands on a hill with his mouth open will wait a long time for a roast duck to drop in." We can't emphasize the importance of taking action any clearer than that!

Translating your insights into specific plans of action that can and will be implemented is the essential next step. Because every organization and every person has a different starting point, the priorities of these elements will be different for each organization, team, and individual. The amount of work on

Figure 12.1
"C" Your Way to Full Potential

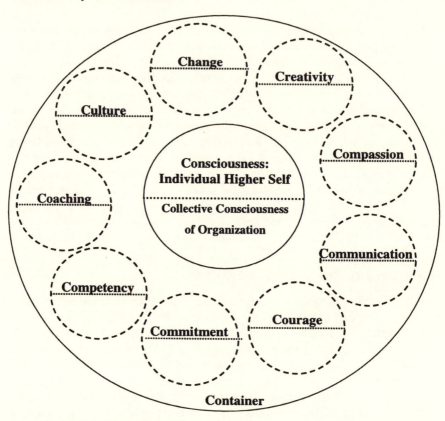

each of the aspects of consciousness depends on you and what clear and specific steps you take to make changes in yourself and your organization.

Think of our "C Your Way to Full Potential" model as a sphere, much like the simple structure of an atom (let's think about 8th grade physics here and ignore the science of quantum mechanics!). With consciousness as the nucleus, the facets of consciousness are like the electrons in orbit around the nucleus. The container is like the atom's shell (the outermost area of the atom's influence). All of the elements of consciousness (as depicted by the circles around the container's perimeter) move about in various relationships to one another, expanding and contracting. Each takes on various sizes representing its relative importance to a particular organization or individual. For example, perhaps your organization possesses tremendous competency, but the culture resembles a command-and-control operation. Or maybe you're a conscious coach who communicates openly, but you struggle with constant change and leave creativity to the artists. Each aspect describes both the individual and the collective and can therefore be used for both personal and organizational gap analyses, individual and collective development plans, and team-building strategies, to name a few examples. The container thus forms the background as well as the sum total of the "consciousness" within the organization itself. The sum total of consciousness of individuals and the organization as a whole, in fact, creates the container.

Breaking open and exploring each of the expressions of consciousness reveals a rich bounty that holds massive implications for organizational success. In what follows, we offer a fundamental description of each aspect of consciousness, relate it to change management, and leave you with a few ideas to consider on your individual and organizational journey to heightened consciousness and, thus, to phenomenal success in spite of the never-ending vicissitudes of business.

Culture

This refers to the environment or atmosphere that is created or exists within a company or organization. We've all heard the phrase "the way we do things around here" and understand it to mean a certain set of expectations and standards that people share and that creates the work environment. Elements of culture include values, attitudes, and behaviors; instincts; feelings; perceptions; history; leadership style; group dynamics; and alignment of all the systems, strategies, structures, policies, procedures, and actions of the organization and individuals with the chosen values and culture.

- Walk around your organization. Look and listen. How does it feel to be there, work there? What is the tone? Do people appear happy and collegial or do they have an "I can't wait until Friday (or 5:00)" attitude? How do *you* feel at work?

- Ask the people in your organization to express the feelings and attitudes they experience during their workday. Ask them to help you understand what you can do to improve their work experience, their productivity, and their creativity. Important hint: Ask people at *all* levels of your organization.

- Examine the values that are actually lived out in your organization. Make a list of adjectives that describe the working relationships in your group. Better yet, ask others in your group for that feedback. Consider an anonymous questionnaire or suggestion box that will allow people to tell it like it is without fear that their opinions may have negative consequences for them. If the anonymous approach offers more honest and fruitful suggestions, you should ask yourself, "Why can't my co-workers say this to my face?"

- Carefully analyze how and if the values expressed in your organization will be an asset or a hindrance to the realization of your stated business objectives.

- Look at organizational systems and structure (performance review, bonuses, hierarchy, etc.) and determine if they are aligned with the values and culture. For example, if your organization says it values teamwork, then how does that fit with the existing bonus or merit system?

- Look at your stated values (e.g., teamwork, customer service) and honestly appraise how well you are living the values (personally and organizationally). List action steps that will close the gap between the idealized and real expression of those values. Then take those steps . . . everyday.

- Look at your leadership style. Ask other people to describe your leadership style to help you see blind spots. Are you flexible with using a variety of leadership styles based upon the demands of a wide range of management/leadership situations?

- Successful organizations are ones that exude ethics and integrity at every turn. They are built on concepts of teamwork and the assumption of goodwill. The leaders of vibrant organizations share the accolades and take full responsibility for the failures. How do you stack up?

- How do people treat each other in your organization? How about you? Are you or your organization contaminated with any "isms" (e.g., racism, sexism, ageism, ableism)? Look carefully at your personal beliefs and attitudes and not just your overt behavior. People will always know what you hold in your heart. Remember the old adage, "What you do speaks so loudly, I cannot hear what you are saying."

- What are the stories, the myths, and legends that inform your organization? Who are the heroes in your company? Do they serve your business objectives? Are they true?

Change

Since this chapter and book are about change and change management, this expression of consciousness can best be summed up by saying change is omnipresent; the more conscious people and organizations become the better they are in managing, even capitalizing on, change and all its implications.

- Anticipate and prepare for it. Don't allow change to sneak up from behind and surprise you. Develop a plan for change. Consciously ask the why, what, who, how, where, and when questions. Why must we change? What are the forces for and against change? What are the changes needed to bridge the gap between the real and the ideal states? Who will be impacted by the changes (employees, customers/clients, shareholders, vendors, etc.)? How will the changes be implemented—in terms of process, resources, communications? Where should the change be implemented—organizationwide or in certain areas of the company? And when is the optimal time to introduce the change and when do you implement a program to reinforce and support the change?

- Learn from it. Conscious organizations and individuals encourage continuous learning. Learning from change and how you handle it provides valuable lessons for the next major change that's right around the corner. What three things do you do really well in dealing with changes in your personal life and how can you apply those strengths to organizational change? What are your three worst fears about change in your organization? How would you triumph over those fears?

- Enjoy it. Treat change as a new game, a new adventure, rather than as a natural enemy. The chaos of change requires creative thinking, behaviors, and actions just to keep your head above the wave of change and avoid being caught in the undercurrents.

Humor stimulates creativity and provides positive energy—a much-needed resource for managing change.

- Improve how you handle it. Managing change is an art. Some leaders are born with great natural talents and proclivity toward change. Others leaders become masters after great study and experience. Either way, the best change leaders consciously work at dealing with change better, faster, smarter, and kinder. When you improve from one change cycle to the next, you create a nimble and resilient organization, one that's good at traversing the minefields of change and bounces back stronger from each change.

- Deal with it! Ask yourself what might happen if your or your organization resists change, best and worst case scenarios. The most skilled change leaders understand the value of change and know not only how to deal with it but also how to capitalize on change for organizational and personal growth and development.

Commitment

Emotional investment in a shared vision and a commitment to the values, along with the consistent and measurable operationalization of those values (walking the talk) is vital to raising corporate consciousness and thriving in the swirls of change. Dealing with change requires a commitment of personal energy from each individual in the organization. And to get individual commitment, the organization and its leaders must demonstrate their commitment with investments in the resources devoted to help individuals understand the change, appreciate its value, and become champions of the process.

- Examine the organizations and your personal commitment of time and resources to change efforts. Do you consciously create an environment that is conducive to change? Do you instill confidence in your staff or team and commit to helping them succeed?

- Look at how well you follow through on commitments. Are you consistent? Can others count on your support and commitment? What about your colleagues, staff, and top leadership?

- Assess how well you live the values and demonstrate a commitment to the vision and mission, citing specific examples. Are there times you don't live up to the agreed-upon values and if so, why? Get feedback from others.

- Look beyond the "letter of the law" into its spirit. How well do you perform in this regard? How well do your colleagues perform in terms of their commitment?

- Examine how well you inspire others to share the commitment. Do colleagues and staff line up in support of change efforts and willingly disrupt the status quo? Conscious leaders commit to long-term change efforts and provide a sense of passion and emotional conviction for the vision, mission, and goals of the organization.

Communication

We both have spent significant segments of our professional careers in various aspects of communications, so we're very tuned in to both the verbal and nonverbal dimensions and how they impact relationships. When people are unconscious of how others respond to what they say and how they say it, there is no opportunity for authentic and genuine communications, and ultimately real relationships between individuals and teams cannot happen. We call this the *pebble and boulder conflict*: what the unconscious communicator thinks may have the impact of a pebble, may to the recipient crush like a two-ton boulder. Personal filters, perceptions, and assumptions often distort what we hear or how we say it.

The fact is that effective, clear, and honest communication is not always easy. Talking is easy, communicating requires greater skill. And it requires listening, a skill that precious few seem to master. As Saint Francis of Assisi so wisely observed, it is important to "seek first to understand, then to be understood." People don't care so much that you agree with them as that you hear them . . . and listen.

Today, the challenge of effective communications is compounded by more and increasingly complex channels. The good news is that there's so much more information available. The bad news is that there is so much information! Conscious communications in the new economy means e-relationships, not just e-business or e-mail, and it calls for a timely response, not a knee-jerk reaction.

The integration of verbal and nonverbal communications is a critical component of conscious communications. When there are too many disconnects (to use a term appropriate to the Internet age) between what someone says and what he or she does, the organizational ship is cast into dangerous waters filled with confusing and often conflicting messages. We often overlook the reality that nonverbal behavior accounts for 98% of interpersonal communication. Conscious communications means greater attention to consistency of message, both the verbal *and* nonverbal components.

- Look carefully at how you communicate. Are you always honest, authentic? Is information clearly conveyed to the people who need it? Are commitments honored? Look at how others communicate. Do honest and direct communications characterize your organization or is backstabbing and gossip the prevailing interactive style? How do people respond to your communications?

- Randomly ask four people to give you honest feedback about your communication style? Are you clear? Do you say what you mean? Can they trust what you say? Are you kind in your communications? Are you assertive, aggressive, or passive most often?

- Examine your own mixed messages—especially when there is a disconnect between your verbal and nonverbal communications. Ask Human Resources to arrange to videotape you while you are communicating to another individual or a group. Then review it with the same passion that a professional athlete looks at the tape of the championship game or match.

- Do you inspire as well as inform in your spoken and written word? If not, why not?

- Technology is great, but do you have face-to-face time with people in your organization, your staff, your boss? Practice the "yellow test": print out your schedule for the past month and use a yellow highlighter to mark the times when you had a satisfying, real conversation with a colleague.

- Are you a good listener? An old Persian adage reminds us that: "The Creator gave you two bright eyes, two lovely ears, and only one mouth so that you can listen and look twice as much as you talk." Good advice. How are you doing with those proportions? When you listen, do you make eye contact? When you listen, are you fully present, fully mindful, or are you going over a list of all the things you have to do today?

Courage

Like the Cowardly Lion in the *Wizard of Oz*, perhaps a medal validating our courage is the right idea. The dictionary defines courage in terms of mind and spirit, giving one the capacity to face danger, fear, and the unknown. It takes great individual and collective courage to doggedly pursue heightened consciousness and embrace the forces of change in organizations. And as the pace, magnitude, and very nature of change changes, courage is the mettle (and metal) in your armor as you charge ahead to successfully exploit change. Without courage, raising corporate consciousness is like pushing a boulder up a mountain. We find that many executives are very courageous about risk-taking and business decisions. But, when it comes to delving into the unknown (the unconscious) about oneself or the organization, leaders often lack the courage to be open and honest with themselves and others. As psychologist Carl Jung said, "The most terrifying thing is to accept oneself completely."

- How do you react to difficult (especially unexpected) changes in the course of business? Look at your reactions both cognitively *and* emotionally. How would you describe them?

- How do your team, supervisors, and direct reports react to change? Open a discussion among your people. Ask these questions and carefully consider what you learn.

- Discuss possibilities. NASA has a history of asking questions framed as "What if this happens?" For it is only through the exploration of the unexpected that they have learned to build life-saving and mission-rescuing redundancies into their systems. You may not be navigating a flight to the moon but the process of exploring *all* potential realities and outcomes will put you into the "forewarned is forearmed" camp, and that is necessary if your organization is going to grow and prosper through all the changes it will inevitably experience.

Creativity

In her book *Awakening at Midlife*, Kathleen Brehony wrote, "Creativity is more than an occasional good idea. It is an attitude toward life, a way of expressing inner reality by bringing it into our outer world. It incorporates innovation, new perspectives, passion, humor, playfulness, joy, and inspiration" (2000, p. 245). Seeing creativity as an attitude, a habit, is critical to encouraging it. We misstep when we mistakenly limit creativity to the artists. Creativity is a natural attribute for the human species, but often we get in its way by refusing to take risks or appear foolish. Creativity is the ability to see things in new ways and uniquely solve problems, and is an important source of energy for individuals and organizations to manage change. This is especially true when the next change—the one that's right around the corner—is left to our imagination.

- Look at your own thinking process. Do you allow yourself to think outside the box? Are your solutions unique, powerful, and new or are you stuck in patterns that fail to realize your full potential?

- Brainstorm (formally or informally). Allow all kinds of "out of the box" thinking to creatively realize business objectives. After a wide range of possible solutions—including off-the-wall ones—is generated, then, and only then, ask questions about how effective and practical each of those may be. In short, creativity is a two-stage process: idea generation and, only then, assessment.

- Inspire and reinforce creative solutions throughout your organization by building a vibrant and respectful environment (container) in which individuals feel safe to express their imagination. For example, Yahoo!, the global Internet communications and media company, has been known to hire yahoos, but no bozos! Have fun.

- Albert Einstein said, "I am enough of an artist to draw freely upon my imagination. Imagination is more important than knowledge. Knowledge is limited. Imagination encircles the world." Who are we to second-guess Einstein?

Compassion

The word "compassion" is from the Latin and literally means, "to suffer with." When you have compassion for others, you're better able to appreciate the challenges others face and give them help when they falter. When compassionate leaders must criticize, they specifically criticize the act (or lack of action) and not the person. When you have compassion for yourself, you learn from experiences, disappointments, and failures rather than beat yourself up about less than perfect performance. You learn from your mistakes. Compassion means recognizing the humanity within the people in your organization, their strengths and weaknesses, commonalities and differences. Compassionate organizations ride the waves of change with more heart and soul. Without compassion, change becomes a calculated and cold process.

- How do you really feel about other people? How do you feel about the nature of people and work in your organization? Do you believe they work hard and want to do a good job? If not, why?

- Practice self-compassion which is self-love coupled with self-discipline. What does the voice inside your head say to you when your performance is less than perfect? If you listen quietly, you will have a great opportunity for self-growth as a person and as a leader.

- Compassionate leaders are generous with their time, spirit, energy, and resources. Do you acknowledge the hopes and dreams of people at every level of your organization or are you a snob who believes that the value of another human being is predicated on their level in the organization or their ranking of overt success?

- Do you follow the "Golden Rule" (treat every other being as you would like to be treated) in every aspect of your behavior and attitudes? If not, why not?

- Understand and use the power of positive reinforcement. When you must criticize, criticize the act (or lack of action) and not the person.

Competency

Today's hyper-competitive job market, even during record-low unemployment rates, demands a certain level of competency and skill. Conscious organizations create learning environments and provide the right resources and training for growth in professional competencies and leadership skills.

- Make a list of the specific professional skills that are required for your position. Then sort this skill list into two columns: "Got 'Em" and "Need 'Em." Be honest with yourself about these lists. Then design specific action statements to immediately begin to acquire the skills that you are lacking and set stretch goals for the skills that you have.

- Ask each member of your organization to construct the same kind of list described above. Help each one develop specific action plans to acquire the skills needed for success.

- Think expansively and creatively about the skills that will be necessary in the future. Begin now to develop those new competencies.

- Consider other critical competencies. Think about the *emotional intelligence* (EI) that you exhibit and that is expressed within your organization. EI is a type of social intelligence that involves the ability to monitor one's own and others' emotions, to discriminate among them, and to use the information to guide one's thinking and actions. Honestly look at your relationships with your co-workers. Are you liked? Respected? How do people see you? How do you feel about them? If you cannot assess this on your own, ask for feedback, work with your human resources professionals to conduct a 360-degree evaluation. Most importantly, make a commitment to know more about yourself and your professional relationships (chances are this feedback can also help your personal relationships as well). Simply put, emotional intelligence is "people skills" and should be considered to be as important as any other competency upon which the success of your organization depends.

- With regard to honestly appraising your competencies, ask yourself the following questions: Do you recognize your own emotions and their effects? Do you know your own strengths and limits? Do you have a strong sense of your own self-worth and capabilities? Do you keep disruptive emotions and impulses in check? Do you maintain high

standards of honesty and integrity? Are you flexible in handling change? Do you strive
to improve or meet a standard of excellence?

- Make a commitment to follow a path of compassionate self-enlightenment. Learn about
yourself and your competencies through feedback, reflection, introspection, meditation,
and self-analysis. Get help through a personal coach or therapist if need be.

Coaching

Coaching is all about full potential. Good coaches inspire people to think they
can; great coaches inspire people to think they can and do. Conscious organizations have a coaching mind-set and leaders at all levels who possess a passion
for building the capacity of others. Baseball manager Joe Torre (currently with
the New York Yankees) says he tries to understand what motivates other people.
Torre explains, "Some players may be critical of a decision I make, but I'm
more into 'Why they did it?' as opposed to what they said" (Useem, 2001,
p. 66). Organizations that excel at handling the forces of change take advantage
of their internal coaching resources and institutionalize mentoring as part of the
corporate culture.

- Put formal coaching activities in place to help make coaching the norm. If you don't
have any formal coaching or mentoring processes, we highly recommend that you put
some in place.
- Consider your own coaching style, as well as the prevailing style within your organization? Describe each in five words or less.
- Do you have a method for measuring coaching success? If not, how will you know
how you are doing? An unaimed arrow never hits its mark, according to the Zen
masters.
- Help people in your organization to set stretch goals, develop action plans to achieve
those, and provide feedback and reinforcement for success. These are the fundamentals
of coaching.
- Be bold in your expectations for yourself and your team. People will invariably live
up to whatever is expected. As a leader, a big part of your job is to help your team
imagine that. Keep your standards high and fair. Stretch your goals. Let your spirits
soar. Life is not a dress rehearsal.

CONCLUSION

In this chapter, we have attempted to cover a great deal of ground in short
order. A truly in-depth discussion about the nature of individual and collective
consciousness would fill many volumes, with many more still to be written as
we learn more about the full potential of the human experience and how best
to actualize it. Our experiences as organizational consultants (and as human
beings, we might add) have shown us quite clearly that a commitment to "Know
Thyself" is the single most important first step that any individual can and must

take in order to grow beyond the quotidian, to live a meaningful life, and to bring spirit back into the world of business.

Carl Jung once observed the simple yet profound relationship between truth and change. In *Mysterium Coniunctionis*, he wrote: "All true things must change and only that which changes remains true" (para. 503). And so it may be that the greatest gift of change in its ever-spiraling cycles is new opportunities to explore the truth about ourselves and our organizations, to grow beyond what we are into what we might become.

The German philosopher Arthur Schopenhauer (1974) gives us a tangible metaphor for understanding the unconscious aspects of life and the importance of its examination. He likened life to a piece of embroidery. He says, that at first we see only the "right" side of the embroidery, its surface, its public face. Of course, it appears beautiful and perfect. But then, in order to learn and grow, we must turn it over and study the "wrong" side for it is only here that we can see how it is actually put together. It's not nearly so lovely but it is far more instructive as we now can see the way in which the threads have been worked together (1974, p. 102).

Conscious organizations maintain a passionate commitment to better understand how the embroidery threads are put together, striving always to courageously and fearlessly know more about themselves, capitalize on their strengths, and fix the disconnects and gaps between where they are and where they are aiming. And it is with this warrior spirit, this clear and focused desire for truth that they boldly go beyond the mere management of change and instead use this force to spur them toward unrivaled growth and success.

Finally—and we can't overstate this—don't wait to make changes until there's more free time (there never is) or until the market turns more favorable. The natural tendency in many organizations is to hold off on nonrevenue generating, "feel-good" efforts, especially when changes have thrust them into challenging times. Like reluctant dieters who keep pushing forward the start date in their calendars ("I'll stop eating potato chips *next* Monday"), we waste time and opportunity while wishing and hoping for the optimal moment to begin. There is no optimal moment. The time to begin is now. Goethe said it better than we, when he wrote: "Whatever you can do or dream, you can begin it. Boldness has genius, power, and magic in it. Begin it now."

It's hard enough just keeping up with the pace and magnitude of change today, so don't compound things by trying to get new results with the same set of tools and strategies. We believe the ultimate competitive advantage is heightened individual and organizational consciousness on the journey to high performance and the realization of full potential. Conscious, aware organizations and leaders approach change with greater openness and honesty and passionately respond—not simply react—to it, prepare for it, grow from it, and endure. During lean times and feasts, nourish the people, the culture, the spirit, and the soul of your organization. Pay attention to the "soft stuff" and it will pay off on the bottom line.

REFERENCES

Brehony, Kathleen. 2000. *Awakening at midlife*. New York: Henry Holt.

Caudron, Shari. 2001. The myth of job happiness. *Workforce* (April): 32–36.

Collins, James C., & Porras, Jerry I. 1997. *Built to last: Successful habits of visionary companies*. New York: HarperBusiness.

Jung, Carl. 1963. *Mysterium coniunctionis*. CW 14. Princeton, NJ: Princeton University Press.

Katzenbach, Jon R. 2000. *Peak performance: Aligning the hearts and minds of your employees*. Boston: Harvard Business School Press.

Mom-and-pop online stores: A thing of the past? 2001. *BusinessWeek Online*, http://www.businessweek.com:/ebiz/.

Neill, Terrence V., & Borell, Martin H. 1999. Maximizing your return on investment in human capital. http://www.accenture.com/xd/xd.asp?it=enWeb&xd=ideas/outlook/6.99/over_human.xml.

Schopenhauer, A. 1974. *Parerga and Paralipomena: Short philosophical essays* (E.F.J. Payne, trans.). Oxford: Clarendon Press.

Southwest Airlines. 2001. http://www.southwest.com/.

Useem, Jerry. 2001. A manager for all seasons. *Fortune*, April 30, pp. 66–72.

Watson Wyatt Worldwide. 2000. The Human Capital Index™: Linking Human Capital and Shareholder Value Survey Report.

Zipkin, Amy. 2000. Management: The wisdom of thoughtfulness. *New York Times*, May 31, pp. C1, C9.

Chapter 13

Change: Build It In, Just Like Quality!

William I. Sauser, Jr. and Lane D. Sauser

INTRODUCTION

For several decades now we have used as our basic premise when teaching "change management" Lewin's conceptual model: unfreeze-change-refreeze. This has served us well, but now it is time to rethink the model, which implies that "change" is a process imposed upon a "steady state" norm. It is evident that in today's competitive work environment, change is the norm, while "steady state" is illusory or, at best, a fleeting, temporary state. The management of quality took a great leap forward when we abandoned our old paradigm of "inspecting for quality" and replaced it with an effort to "build quality in" through Total Quality Management (TQM) and other such schemes. Rather than a "steady state," quality was viewed as something that can be improved continuously through incremental processes. This same reconceptualization needs to be applied to the change management process.

Recognizing that change is a continuous process has implications for the way we manage change. No longer is it appropriate to consider organizational change as a project or event—with a beginning and an end—to be managed, but rather we must consider change management as an ongoing aspect of the leader's job. What are the implications of this viewpoint for the way we teach change management in our colleges of business and in our continuing professional education programs? How can we refocus ourselves to consider change as the natural state of things, and thus an element of our environment to which we must continually adapt? How might we inculcate this viewpoint into those we are preparing to lead our organizations in the future? These are a few of the questions that will be examined in this chapter.

FIVE KEY ASSERTIONS

This chapter is built around five key assertions regarding organizational change: (1) The most successful organizations in the long run are those that (continuously) adapt to changes in the competitive environment. (2) The forces for change in the competitive environment are manifold and continue to build at an accelerating rate. (3) It has become essential to manage change as a continuing process, not as a discrete event or even a series of discrete events. (4) We must adopt a philosophy of "continuous organizational change" to mirror the adoption of the philosophy that has revolutionized quality management, "continuous quality improvement." (5) This will require a new breed of manager, one who understands change and seeks continuously to adapt the organization to its dynamic environment.

How do we prepare such managers—this "new breed" to which we refer? Based on our experience as change consultants as well as academic instructors, we offer several suggestions to address this critical question. Let us begin by examining briefly each of our five assertions.

Assertion One: The Most Successful Organizations in the Long Run Are Those That (Continuously) Adapt to Changes in the Competitive Environment

This is not a new idea. In fact, Lawrence and Lorsch (1967) and Schon (1967) were making this point in their seminal writings over three decades ago. The need for organizations to adapt to their competitive environment in order to succeed in the longer term is now a recognized underlying principle in theories of both organizational design (Nystrom & Starbuck, 1981) and strategic management (Guth, 1985). As the competitive environment changes, organizations must also change if they are to survive and thrive. In fact, as Drucker (1954) pointed out years ago, one of the key factors in effective management is the ability to sense environmental change and take steps to position the organization to capitalize on this change.

We teach that it is not enough simply to *react* to change; instead the effective manager must *anticipate* change, or even better, be the *creator* of change. It is far better to have your competitors scrambling to react to the changes *your* organization has made (to adapt to the competitive environment) than to be among the pack seeking to follow the leader. These days, the race goes to the swift, and it is the strong who survive.

Assertion Two: The Forces for Change in the Competitive Environment Are Manifold and Continue to Build at an Accelerating Rate

This assertion has been the theme of a number of recent "best sellers" in the business book market (e.g., Brown & Eisenhardt, 1998; Drucker, 1999; Kelly,

1998; Strauss & Howe, 1997). Certainly the theme "rings true" to those of us in the modern workplace. It seems that the pace of our work continues to increase as we move faster and faster to survive in the brutal globally competitive marketplace. Here are five examples of change we are facing in our modern times and some of the stressors associated with these changes (Sauser, 1999b).

Organizations under Siege

Fueled by intensified global competition, increasing customer sophistication and demands for improved quality at lower prices, and a growing cynicism toward big business, government, and labor, we have witnessed of late a major attack on many of the venerable old institutions and organizations of the past. Government, universities, the military, financial institutions, major manufacturers, utilities, and mainline churches have all become targets for scrutiny and change. "Downsizing" and "reengineering" have emerged as worldwide trends for large organizations as a result of intense global competition and its attendant needs for efficiency. These days, even experienced technicians and managers are losing their jobs as organizations seek to streamline operations. This has led to considerable insecurity and stress among groups of workers who were protected from such pressures in the past.

A Technology Explosion

The seeming explosion of new technology which has entered the workplace has affected all of us. Personal computers, fax machines, scanners, cellular telephones, fiber optics, radar detection systems, graphics design software, the Internet, web pages, and all the other new wonders we are experiencing can be quite intimidating to those of us who still have trouble programming our VCRs! Yet new technologies enter the workplace daily, in wave after wave, version after version. Trying to keep up with technology, use it effectively, make cost-efficient decisions about its deployment, and the like are issues that are straining even the most sophisticated employees and managers. Securing our information and protecting our technological investments and sensitive data are growing problems for many of us. New technologies are wonderful, but they can be challenging and stressful as well.

Standards, Laws, and Procedures

Most of us value playing by the rules, and seek diligently to comply with the law, with professional standards, and with regulations and specified procedures, which we see as the rules of the game. Staying in compliance, though, becomes difficult when the rules are constantly changing. This is the way of life for many managers and employees these days: new statutes and administrative rules, new case law, new professional standards, and revised organizational policies and procedures are issued every day as the pace of change in the workplace accelerates.

Time Compression

"The check's in the mail," we used to say, knowing that would buy us a few days' time. But first with overnight delivery services, then fax machines, then e-mail, everything sped up. Now we can be buzzed, beeped, paged, and prodded no matter where we are or what we are doing. As the means of communication have become more efficient and the exchange of messages has stepped up in time dramatically, we often feel as if time has become compressed. Some employees and managers are feeling considerable pressure to do more and more, faster and faster, and are beginning to break under the strain.

Litigiousness

Our nation is strong due in part to our freedom to seek justice and reparations in the courts. This constitutional right is dear to all of us. However, most readers will no doubt agree with us that the mood of litigiousness which pervades our society today can make the task of management—and even employment—at times very unpleasant. We must constantly be on guard not to say or do anything offensive lest we find ourselves in court as a defendant in a lawsuit. "Working in a fishbowl" can be tiring and annoying, and we frequently hear fellow managers express their private frustrations with being constantly vigilant in all they say and do.

Altogether, these five factors—which are just a sampling of the *many* political, economic, demographic, and technological changes we could identify and list—can make our jobs as managers very daunting. They are affecting not only the competitive environment we must face, but also our stamina for facing it. Implications for our fifth assertion will be considered below. However, we now turn to the third assertion on our list.

Assertion Three: It Has Become Essential to Manage Change as a Continuing Process, Not as a Discrete Event or Even a Series of Discrete Events

Those of us who have worked for years in the field of change management consultation have come to appreciate the value of Kurt Lewin's pioneering work in this area. Consultants have assisted organizations to bring about effective change by following Lewin's (1951) three steps of "unfreezing, moving, refreezing." Hellriegel, Slocum, and Woodman (1992, p. 734), drawing upon the work of Cummings and Huse (1989), describe these three steps as follows:

Unfreezing usually involves reducing those forces maintaining the organization's behavior at the present level. Unfreezing is sometimes accomplished by introducing information to show discrepancies between behaviors desired by employees and behaviors they currently exhibit.

Moving shifts the behavior of the organization or department to a new level. It involves developing new behaviors, values and attitudes through changes in organizational structures and processes.

Refreezing stabilizes the organization at a new state of equilibrium. It is frequently accomplished through the use of supporting mechanisms that reinforce the new organizational state, such as organizational culture, norms, policies, and structures.

Far be it from us to critique Lewin's time-proven theory, but we must quibble with the concept of "establishing a new state of equilibrium," which the third of Lewin's steps, "refreezing," implies as necessary for organizational change to be successful. If our second assertion is correct and change in the competitive environment is arriving at an ever-increasing rate, it may not be useful—or even possible—to speak of stabilizing an adaptive organization into a state of equilibrium. In fact, our very point is that the competitive environment is changing so rapidly that seeking to maintain stability in such an environment is actually *counterproductive*. While we are not advocating here a sense of anarchy or chaos, we do argue that "seeking stability" may not be the healthiest strategy for an organization desiring to compete successfully in today's ever-changing environment. Instead, we are advocating (in our fourth assertion) a philosophy of "continuous organizational change."

We change consultants have thrived for some time now by assisting organizations to "work through" discrete organizational changes. Typically we have treated such change efforts as "projects," and have managed them as though they had a distinct beginning, middle, and end. We celebrated each successful "ending" of a change project by congratulating our clients (and ourselves), collecting our fee, and leaving the organization's management team with the task of guiding the "changed" organization.

We submit that this is no longer good enough. We submit that our role as change consultants has shifted from (1) guiding our client's leadership team through a successful change project to (2) building into our client's leadership team the capacity to guide organizational change as a continuous process. As we build such capacity within the client's leadership team, we better prepare the client organization to survive and thrive by adapting continuously to its changing competitive environment. No longer can we afford to conceptualize successful change management as a discrete event, or even as a series of discrete events; we must now realize that our task is to assist our individual clients not in "managing change projects," but in building their own capacity to create and drive change within the organizations they lead. It is this "new breed" of manager who will lead the successful organizations of the future. Suggestions on how to produce this "new breed" of manager are offered below following discussion of our other two assertions.

Assertion Four: We Must Adopt a Philosophy of "Continuous Organizational Change" to Mirror the Adoption of the Philosophy That Has Revolutionized Quality Management, "Continuous Quality Improvement"

Prior to the "TQM Revolution," most manufacturing firms had elaborate quality control units whose job was to inspect completed products and reject those that did not meet established quality standards, sending the culled pieces to the "rework" section or the scrap heap. Similarly, "customer complaint" offices were commonplace in service organizations; here customers could complain about the poor service they may have received and the organization could take steps to "put things right." Customer satisfaction has long been known as a key to customer attraction and retention, so these organizations were "doing the best they could" to meet quality standards using the paradigm of the times.

All of this changed, however, with the advent of the Total Quality Management (TQM) concept that resulted from the work of such pioneers as W. Edwards Deming (1986), Joseph M. Juran (1979), and Philip B. Crosby (1979). Total Quality Management, also known as Continuous Quality Improvement (CQI), is based on a driving philosophy: To make commitment to total quality operations "a way of life" within the organization (Schermerhorn, 1999, p. 34). Schermerhorn asserts that the Malcolm Baldridge National Quality Awards standards (listed below) indicate "the full extent of the day-to-day commitment that is essential to gaining competitive advantage through a commitment to total quality" (pp. 34–35):

• Top executives incorporate quality values into day-to-day management.

• The organization works with suppliers to improve the quality of their goods and/or services.

• The organization trains workers in quality techniques and implements systems that ensure high-quality products.

• The organization's products are as good or better than those of its competitors.

• The organization meets customers' needs and wants and gets customer satisfaction ratings equal to or better than those of competitors.

• The organization's quality system yields concrete results such as increased market share and lower product-cycle times.

    The "passion for quality" that world-class firms have built into their organizational philosophy, systems, and day-to-day operations has resulted in immense quality improvements across the globe. By adopting TQM/CQI principles into their day-to-day operations, many organizations—private sector, public sector, and voluntary—have become far better positioned to compete in today's market environment.

    We submit that a similar set of "continuous organizational change" principles might also be formulated and adopted by those organizations seeking to assure world-class adaptation to the changing market environment in which they must compete. At a minimum, we argue that organizational leaders consider adopting the following ideals for themselves and the people they lead:

• Incorporate within the culture of the organization an appreciation for the need for continuous adaptive change to thrive in the dynamic competitive environment we face today.

- Reflect this principle—this need for continuous organizational change—in day-to-day operations and decisions made at all levels of the organization.
- Build within the organization's human resources a capacity to recognize environmental change and a desire to adapt successfully to such change.
- Reward those employees (at all levels) who guide the organization into successful adaptive change.

Organizations that follow our suggestion to adopt these principles will quickly discover the value of our fifth assertion.

Assertion Five: This Will Require a New Breed of Manager, One Who Understands Change and Seeks Continuously to Adapt the Organization to Its Dynamic Environment

We have now reached the crux of the matter: Adaptive organizations employing the principles of continuous organizational change we advocate above must be led by a "new breed" of managers—those who understand, appreciate, and use the concept of continuous organizational change as they fulfill their day-to-day responsibilities within the organization. How are we to prepare this "new breed" of managers? That is the question we address in the next section of this chapter.

PREPARING A "NEW BREED" OF MANAGERS

As educators of tomorrow's leaders, this question has been foremost on our minds. How indeed are we to prepare capable leaders for adaptive organizations? What must we include within our college curricula? What must we incorporate into our programs of continuing professional development for managers? How might we upgrade the change management skills of the "rank and file" employees of the organization striving to maintain a leadership position in today's ever-changing competitive environment?

We must admit we do not have all the answers! We do, however, have a few suggestions that might stimulate our readers to seek their own answers to these important questions. We have organized our thoughts under three headings: (1) college curriculum requirements, (2) continuing professional development, and (3) mastering change personally. We turn our attention now to these three topics.

College Curriculum Requirements

We are interested here not so much in the *structure* of the management education curriculum as the content and approach employed within the curriculum as it pertains to developing the capacity to manage change. Clearly the curriculum must address the factors that are driving change in the modern competitive environment. Students must be exposed to the dynamics of our political, economic, and cultural systems. They must understand how environmental and demographic factors influence our everyday lives. They must gain an appreciation for the power of technology and the blinding speed at which information is transmitted throughout the world. Biological, agricultural, psychological, and sociological factors must also be taken into account as we build a "change management" capacity within the future generation of organizational leaders.

Methods of instruction must be dynamic and must challenge our future leaders to embrace change as a necessary part of all we do. Cases, group projects, brainstorming exercises, debates, discussions, and even lecture sessions must reflect the changes we are facing in today's competitive environment. Critical thinking and the desire to question and seek new answers must be outcomes that we strive to reach in our management training curricula. It is no longer acceptable (if it ever was) to teach "the status quo." Our lessons must stretch our students far beyond the present. We must challenge them to think beyond current bounds, to expand horizons, indeed to "invent the future."

Continuing Professional Development

And what of our current generation of leaders? Must we wait for them to "step aside," or are there possibilities for enhancing their change management capacities as well? Surely our leaning toward the latter option does not surprise our readers! We assert that there are a number of ways we can build a capacity for effective management of change into our current workforce. One such technique, providing workshops on mastering change personally, is discussed in detail below. Before we address this topic, however, we mention several other ideas for employee development.

One technique we have found very valuable is to invite employees from throughout the organization to participate in "strategic planning" exercises. Katz (1974) has argued that as one moves up the organizational hierarchy, the mix of necessary managerial skills shifts, such that *conceptual* skills (the ability to think analytically and achieve integrative problem solving) *increase* in importance while *technical* skills (the ability to apply expertise and perform a special task with proficiency) *decrease* in importance. (Katz's third category of skills—human skills—are important at every level of management.) Frequently our continuing professional education programs focus primarily on technical and human skills; too often we fail to build the conceptual skills necessary to effect success in the higher levels of management. Yet it is these conceptual skills, we believe, which are essential for success as a manager of change.

Sauser (1989) showed how participation in "strategic planning" exercises can help build employees' capacity to conceptualize and to design programs for organizational change. These workshops (not necessarily intended only for "top management" but inclusive of all levels of the organization) can teach employees how to identify and predict changes in the competitive environment, analyze the organization's capacity to adapt to these changes, determine strategic objectives, and prepare plans of action to guide progressive organizational change. Allowing employees broad exposure to strategic planning exercises, whether "for real" or moot, can be an excellent way to develop the "new breed" of manager we spoke about above.

Other techniques for developing change management capacity include team project assignments (especially when the team "crosscuts" functions and levels of hierarchy), exposure to futurists and their writings, "brainstorming" sessions, quality circles, scenario planning, and simulation exercises. We recommend that these be built into programs intended to develop managerial talent among the current work force.

Of course, we need not neglect the importance of other human resource decisions when building an organization's capacity to sense the need for and implement adaptive change actions. When selecting potential managers, attention should be given to applicants' ability to adapt easily to change, experience in leading change, and potential to facilitate or resist change. As continuous change management becomes more and more important as a driving management philosophy, selecting for management positions those applicants who are more comfortable with change becomes essential. This same argument applies, of course, to promotion decisions, training and development decisions, placement decisions, and the like.

We must teach our current managers how to make every day-to-day decision with an eye toward how the decision will help the organization adapt to the ever-changing competitive environment. After all, it is well and good to have a strategic plan that calls for sweeping organizational change, but it is as this plan is translated into day-to-day *decisions* that it becomes fully implemented and absorbed into the organization's culture. If the intent is to create an organizational culture that embraces the need for adaptive organizational change—and acts upon that organizational value—then it is necessary that the culture appreciate and reward those employees and managers who are willing to take actions in accordance with that value. Notice how these comments align with the "principles of continuous organizational change" listed under our fourth assertion.

Mastering Change Personally

Sauser (1999a) recently described a comprehensive program to become a better *personal* manager of change. Four "tips" discussed in that paper for working proactively with change are summarized below. They can easily be incorporated into change management workshops and programs of a variety of forms.

Tip One: Raise Your Antenna

We often wall ourselves off from important information by employing selective perception, habit, and specialization/dependence to keep ourselves from being exposed to ideas we might not want to hear. While this is human nature, it is not a good strategy for mastering the forces of change. Instead, we should seek to *broaden* our sources of information, even to the point of risking some fear to explore ideas heretofore unknown to us. By raising one's antenna and seeking broader information that might signal oncoming change, a manager will have a distinct advantage over those who tend to isolate themselves. Here are a few suggestions in this regard.

Become aware of your situation. What is going on in your immediate situation? Don't know? Then you'd better take steps right now to find out! What is the mission of your unit? What is the purpose of your job? What are your key responsibilities and assignments? What does your supervisor expect of you? What obstacles stand in your way? What resources do you have at your disposal? How well are you performing? How does the citizenry view the importance and effectiveness of your unit? What changes are blowing in the political winds? If you are unable to answer questions like these, you had better begin immediately to "do your homework," for you are in a prime position to be overwhelmed by unexpected forces of change.

Read broadly. Reading is a good, quick way to gain information. We recommend broad reading—reading that stretches horizons and helps one gain facility with previously unfamiliar ideas. Read the newspaper, perhaps a news magazine or two, some classics, a few biographies and histories, some fictional novels, some fantasy and science fiction, and some nonfiction books on current topics. You will be amazed how ideas from a variety of sources like these will open your mind to new ways of thinking, thus increasing your adaptability when change is needed.

Set up a network. One excellent way to broaden your access to knowledge is to set up a network of friends and colleagues, all of whom keep one another informed of important happenings and tidbits of news. We're not advocating here a "gossip grapevine" of false information, but rather a set of informed individuals who care enough about one another to share valid information which may be helpful to all. Civic clubs, professional associations, and other such groups are a natural foundation for networking, and are typically employed for this purpose with excellent results.

Find out for yourself. Specializing in a particular field and depending on others for information and help in less familiar areas is a natural human behavior. It works well, *as long as those upon whom you depend give you accurate information.* Unfortunately, not all persons can be counted on to supply the truth. When you are in doubt about the validity of information you have received, *find out for yourself.* Do an independent investigation of the situation and see if the facts support what you have been told.

See the forest and the trees. Which is more important, the "big picture" or the details? Why waste time pursuing that question; instead, seek out both types of information! Don't become so involved with the details that you miss the overriding concept, but also don't get so enamored with "the big picture" that you ignore important details. Too many people have been harmed by their failure to "read the fine print." The key here is to *balance* your information-seeking behavior and your interpretive thinking. Pull back and see the forest, but also step forward and examine closely some of the trees.

Look for trends. This is the point of seeking information—to spot the trends that may be signaling change on the horizon. Look for seemingly isolated facts that begin "fitting together" like the pieces of a puzzle. When you think you have spotted a trend, begin to investigate it carefully and to project into the future the changes that trend may bring for the way you do business. Gather broad information, ponder it carefully, search for trends, project what is about to happen, then plan your moves accordingly. Don't just react to change, anticipate it and prepare for it.

Spot the perfect wave. We are not surfers, but those who are skilled in this sport tell us, "The key to a good ride is to spot the perfect wave, then go!" The whole point of raising our antennas and searching for trends is to spot that perfect wave. When you see a wave of change coming your way, prepare yourself for the ride. We'll look at this idea in more detail below as we consider Tip Four.

Tip Two: Build Your Skills

Adapting to change frequently requires the effective use of all your acquired skills. In some—perhaps most—cases, adapting to change will call for the use of skills which you might not yet have mastered, or even begun to acquire! Since successfully dealing with change does require the use of many skills, it is important to build as many of them as you can before their use becomes essential for organizational survival. No one wants to be "caught short" in a crunch time. Here are some ideas to consider.

Keep on learning. There's a saying we like: "When you're through learning, you're through." The point of this saying is that we must always keep learning in order to survive in a changing world. Prepare yourself for a lifetime of learning, for that is what is necessary for success these days.

Consider taking refresher training in your area of competence. Enroll in a college course which interests you, even one "not for credit." See if your professional association offers training sessions and workshops. Look into correspondence or "distance" education. If circumstances allow, pursue an advanced degree. If college is not an option, broaden your reading and personal study as described above. Join a group of others with similar interests and learn from them; form a discussion group or study team. Read a technical manual or recent review of research in an area of interest to you. The point is to keep your *learning* skills fresh; learning how to learn is too valuable a lesson to allow it to atrophy over time.

Embrace technology. One of the most important lessons to learn is to stop fighting *against* technological change, and instead to embrace it and learn how to use it for your own benefit. Technology is expensive; and yes, technology seems to change all the time, with newer devices and models being released everyday. Some "labor saving" devices may not actually be helpful in your circumstances, but how will you know what helps if you never try anything?

If you are uncomfortable with new technology, try it out in the privacy of your own home, or in the presence of those you know to be trustworthy friends and teachers. Computer manufacturers and other purveyors of new technology have learned that "user friendly" devices are much more popular with those who have not "grown up" in the information age, thus they are now designing hardware and software with great appeal due to ease of learning and use. If you can become at ease with new technology such that you are not afraid to try it out and innovate with it, you can become a role model for others seeking to master change. If you are having trouble "getting the hang of things," seek the assistance of another person who seems naturally skilled in this area. By learning from one another, we break down interpersonal barriers and gain respect for one another's talents.

Try some new things. The point of this idea is to break ourselves out of our old habits, our routines. Mastering change often requires new skills and ways of thinking. You can sharpen your ability to adapt to change by proactively trying some things you have never done before. If you haven't done so before, go to the theater, the library, a nearby manufacturing plant, the zoo—something new. Travel, learn a new language, play some new games, visit a new place, make some new friends, study a new subject, learn a new skill—these are all valuable ways to prepare oneself to adapt to change.

Discover your hidden gifts. Each of us has been given talents and gifts. Wouldn't it be a shame to live your whole life in ignorance of some special talent you may have, and to let it go to waste? Once you have discovered hidden gifts and talents, you can turn them into new skills to add to your portfolio. The more skills you have, the more valuable you will be in a world that demands flexibility in adaptation to change.

Tip Three: Use the Power of the Force

Kurt Lewin (1951) helped us to understand the concept of "force field analysis" and to employ it in the context of creating change. Basically, Lewin taught us that the "status quo" represents a situation in which forces for change are equal to forces against change. When one or the other forces is strengthened or weakened—*or changes direction*—change will begin to occur. Thus an analysis of the force and direction of vectors for and against change can help us predict the speed and direction that change will take. Armed with this knowledge, we can then begin not only to prepare for change, but actually to *shape* change. By deploying our own forces strategically, we can *influence* the direction of change and use it for our own benefit. The ideas presented below represent a "step by step" approach to applying Lewin's theory. By following them, we can indeed "use the power of the force."

Marshal your muscle. Changing the momentum of a powerful force for change requires the expenditure of your own energy, so the first step is to assess and gather your own forces, or "muscle." What knowledge, skills, and abilities can you bring to bear? What key information do you have? Who are your allies, and what strengths do they possess? What other forces might you rally to your cause? Now is the time to marshal them, to bring them near to hand. The more "muscle" you can marshal, the better your chances for shaping the direction of change. Here is where the time and energy you invested in following Tips One and Two begins to pay off.

Don't fight change head on. Trying to fight change head on is like standing in the path of an oncoming freight train—you will likely get plowed under, or will certainly be injured beyond repair. This is not the winning strategy. Even if you can "hold off" change for a while, its superior momentum will likely weaken you and wear you down to the point where you will eventually be swept along in its path. Instead, use your imagination to mentally picture the oncoming force of change, and to determine in what direction you would like to see it move.

Know where you want to go. Imagine in your mind the direction you would like to see the forces of change take you. Envision your destination, your ultimate goal. Is there some way you can combine your own energy with the forces of change so that you can be "swept along" to exactly your intended goal point? If you can envision a way, the next point is to "make it happen."

Be like a football offensive lineman, a sumo wrestler, a ballet dancer, a martial artist. What do these skilled athletes and artists have in common? They know how to apply their own energy to that of a moving body, thus sending that body in a new direction. All have demonstrated their practical understanding of force field analysis—they have marshaled their own muscle to direct another body into a predetermined desired direction. This is how one masters change.

Steer the forces of change. With a minuscule movement of her wrist, a woman can steer her big, powerful sports car. She knows where she wants it to go, and is able to use her driving skill and sense of direction to harness that powerful vehicle to take her wherever she wants. She has mastered the forces of that vehicle; she is "in the driver's seat." This is our own challenge in becoming masters of change: We need to put ourselves into the driver's seat.

Be a responsible driver. Let us end this section with a plea for ethical behavior. Once you have become a master of change, you will have at your disposal powerful forces that can be used for great good or great harm. We deplore those who use their power to hurt others. Seek to be a responsible driver of change; never use the power of the force to inflict harm on others.

Tip Four: Surf the Waves of Change

This brief tip is simply a recap and summary of the ideas presented above, but this time building upon the analogy of the surfer. Our purpose here is to remind our readers that being a change master can—and should—be fun.

Spot the perfect wave. Be on the lookout for a good ride. Don't let the perfect wave pass you by, but don't sit still in the ocean waiting forever if you see an exciting wave rolling your way. You can't have fun surfing if you spend all your time watching. *Get into position, then go.* What more needs to be said? Let's go!

Ride the wild surf. Jump on your board and ride that wild surf! Don't let it intimidate you. Go for it!

Have fun on the way. After all, isn't this why we came to the beach? If you're not having fun, get out of the game.

Paddle out for more. Even the perfect wave eventually breaks against the shore and is no more. Don't despair, just paddle out for another! This is the key to enjoying yourself as a change master. There's always another wave, another opportunity to use the force for your own fun and for the benefit of others.

CONCLUSION

We have argued in this chapter that change must be reconceptualized as a continuing process, not as a discrete project to be managed with an eye toward establishing a "steady state" of equilibrium for the organization. We have built our argument around five key assertions: (1) The most successful organizations in the long run are those that (continuously) adapt to changes in the competitive environment. (2) The forces for change in the competitive environment are manifold and continue to build at an accelerating rate. (3) It has become essential to manage change as a continuing process, not as a discrete event or even a series of discrete events. (4) We must adopt a philosophy of "continuous organizational change" to mirror the adoption of the philosophy that has revolutionized quality management, "continuous quality improvement." (5) This will require a new breed of manager, one who understands change and seeks continuously to adapt the organization to its dynamic environment.

We have proffered four principles organizational leaders should consider adopting as ideals for themselves and the people they lead: (1) Incorporate within the culture of the organization an appreciation for the need for continuous adaptive change to thrive in the dynamic competitive environment we face today. (2) Reflect this principle—this need for continuous organizational change—in day-to-day operations and decisions made at all levels of the organization. (3) Build within the organization's human resources a capacity to recognize environmental change and a desire to adapt successfully to such change. (4) Reward those employees (at all levels) who guide the organization into successful adaptive change.

Finally, we have suggested three techniques for building within the current and future work force the capacity to lead organizations as they change to adapt to the dynamic competitive environment they are facing: (1) Create within college curricula multiple and varied opportunities to encounter and master change in the organizational environment: (2) Establish continuing professional development opportunities for current employees so they too may become change masters. (3) Develop personal mastery of the forces of change.

By following these suggestions, we hope our readers can learn (1) how to build an appreciation for change into the culture of their organizations, and (2) how to lead their organizations toward more effective adaptation to the dynamic competitive environment in which they must thrive. Our thesis? Change: Build it in, just like quality!

REFERENCES

Brown, S.L., & Eisenhardt, K.M. 1998. *Competing on the edge: Strategy as structured chaos*. Boston: Harvard Business School Press.

Crosby, P.B. 1979. *Quality is free*. New York: McGraw-Hill.

Cummings, T.G., & Huse, E.F. 1989. *Organization development and change*, 4th ed. St. Paul, MN: West.

Deming, W.E. 1986. *Out of crisis*. Cambridge, MA: MIT Press.

Drucker, P.F. 1954. *The practice of management*. New York: Harper & Row.

Drucker, P.F. 1999. *Management challenges for the 21st century*. New York: Harper-Business.

Guth, W.D. (ed.). 1985. *Handbook of business strategy*. Boston: Warren, Gorham, & Lamont.

Hellriegel, D., Slocum, J.W., Jr., & Woodman, R.W. 1992. *Organizational behavior*, 6th ed. St. Paul, MN: West.

Juran, J.M. 1979. *Quality control handbook*, 3rd ed. New York: McGraw-Hill.

Katz, R.L. 1974. Skills of an effective administrator. *Harvard Business Review*, 52(5): 90–102.

Kelly, K. 1998. *New rules for the new economy: 10 radical strategies for a connected world*. New York: Viking Press.

Lawrence, P.R., & Lorsch, J.W. 1967. *Organization and environment*. Homewood, IL: Irwin.

Lewin, K. 1951. *Field theory in social science*. New York: Harper & Row.

Nystrom, P.C., & Starbuck, W.H. (eds.). 1981. *Handbook of organizational design*, Vols. 1 and 2. New York: Oxford University Press.

Sauser, W.I., Jr. 1989. Strategic planning as a management development tool. *Journal of the Alabama Academy of Science*, 60: 29–38.

Sauser, W.I., Jr. 1999a. Riding the wild surf of change. In M.H. Abdelsamad & E.R. Myers (eds.), *Business issues for the new millennium*. Proceedings of the 1999 SAM International Conference. Corpus Christi, TX: Society for Advancement of Management, pp. 97–105.

Sauser, W.I., Jr. 1999b. Staying sane in an ever changing world. In R.R. Sims & J.G. Veres III (eds.), *Keys to employee success in coming decades*. Westport, CT: Quorum Books, pp. 199–222.

Schermerhorn, J.R., Jr. 1999. *Management*, 6th ed. New York: John Wiley & Sons.

Schon, D.A. 1967. *Technology and change*. New York: Delacorte.

Strauss, W., & Howe, N. 1997. *The fourth turning: An American prophecy*. New York: Broadway Books.

Chapter 14

Creating a New Kind of Conversation: A Consultant's Role in Building Sustainable Change in the New Economy

Ann C. Baker

INTRODUCTION

Imagine a beautiful coastal city, full of history and southern hospitality as well as an exceptional natural environment of water, beaches, marshes, birds, and exquisite sunlight that reminds you of the light that inspired the Impressionists painting in southern France a century ago. Add to this picture the most historic part of the city at the end of a peninsula jutting out into the water with beautiful old homes on narrow streets, inviting neighborhoods with trees and gardens, a park at the tip of the peninsula surrounded by blue water glistening in the sunlight. Living in these neighborhoods are many of the most influential people in the community representing many professional, political, and business leaders as well as some of the oldest families who have lived in the area for generations.

Another face of the city is an increasing majority African-American population, severe disparities in socioeconomic well-being, an economy that depends heavily on tourism and has recently lost one of its largest employers, heightening concern about the economic well-being of the area, and an increasingly diverse population and its attendant frictions among what are referred to as the "come-heres" as opposed to the "been-heres"—the distinction between people who "recently" moved into the area and those whose families are deeply rooted in the historical fabric of the city.

The long-standing complaints from people in this historic neighborhood—about tourists who wander into their gardens, leave litter along the way, knock on their doors asking to use their bathrooms, traffic jams on their narrow streets with more and more cars and horse-drawn carriages offering tours of the historic district—are increasingly coming to the city's mayor and City Council members in the form of irate letters, phone calls, conversations on the street and at social functions, and so forth. Similarly, business leaders, especially those whose financial well-being depends directly or indirectly on the tourists, are also clamoring for assistance from the mayor's office. Members of the City Council, representing diverse neighborhoods, are increasingly bringing their competing constituents' complaints and frustrations to their meetings and conversations with the mayor and city staff. And as with all disputes, the history that each party brings to the conflict legitimately intensifies their anger and sense of being wronged and not being heard—yet again. A crisis mentality begins to prevail.

WICKED PROBLEMS

This scenario is a classic "wicked problem" as described by Jeff Conklin and William Weil, one where there "[1] is an evolving set of interlocking issues and constraints, . . . [2 there] are many *stakeholders*—people who care about or have something at stake in how the problem is resolved. This makes the problem solving process fundamentally [a] social [process] . . . [3] The constraints on the solution, such as limited resources and political ramifications, change over time . . . [and 4] Since there is no definitive Problem, there is no definitive Solution" (Conklin & Weil, 1995). Unlike a "tame" problem that can be addressed linearly with sequential, predicable steps, a "wicked" problem requires an opportunity-driven approach that pays attention to *learning* rather than trying to find the *right answer* or trying to *be right*.

The *new economy* presents endless wicked problems. It is characterized by:

- Stakeholders with differing world views (Burrell & Morgan, 1988; Fambrough & Comerford, 1998; McWhinney, 1997; Pepper, 1942), thought worlds, and experiential histories;
- Rapid and continuous change;
- Increasing ambiguity and less predictability;
- Complex webs of interests and influence;
- Multiplicities of expertise needed concurrently requiring collaboration among people from vastly differing paradigmatic backgrounds with profession-specific vocabularies and working styles;
- Conflicts emerging out of differing perspectives about goals, priorities, expectations, appropriate and best means to work on tasks and to accomplish goals, etc.; and
- Multiple technologies that are rapidly changing, unevenly available to diverse populations (for example, too expensive for many individuals, smaller organizations, non-profit organizations, smaller towns, poorer communities, etc.), and variously acceptable among the constituencies that do have access to them (for example, people who resist changing their ways of doing business or communicating, people who feel unable or unwilling to learn how to use new technologies).

ORGANIZATIONAL CONVERSATIONS

Addressing wicked problems and achieving sustainable change in the new economy requires the recognition that *conversations* among these vastly differing stakeholders are imperative. According to Alan Webber (1993), formerly a managing editor/editorial director of the *Harvard Business Review* and a founding editor of *Fast Company*, "the most important work in the new economy is creating conversations. . . . But all depends on the quality of the conversations. . . . Conversations—not rank, title, or the trappings of power—determine who is literally and figuratively 'in the loop' and who is not" (p. 28). The new economy is dependent upon the ease, frequency, and quality of conversations within and among organizations and communities.

Building upon the work of many people such as Alan Webber and David Whyte (1996), a poet who consults with many of the most successful global organizations, I am calling for a new kind of conversation in organizations and in communities—*conversational learning*. Because the quality of conversations is so critical, the nature, intentions, and contexts surrounding conversations need to improve, leading to the role of the consultant vis-à-vis change in the new economy.

Although conversational learning involves many dimensions, in this chapter I am focusing especially on the role of the consultant in the reframing of two primary ideas—*change* and *differences*. Each of these words is simple and may on the surface appear to be easily understood. However, at the heart of reframing the meaning of change and differences lie foundational components to assist clients in creating sustainable change in the new economy. And the consultant's work originates and is shaped by the worldviews, thought worlds, and paradigmatic orientations (Burrell & Morgan, 1988; Fambrough & Comerford, 1998; McWhinney, 1997; Pepper, 1942) that he or she brings to the work.

Reframing change involves recognizing change as an ongoing given in organizational life and becoming adept at greeting it as an opportunity for learning, improvement, and departure from the status quo. It means becoming flexible enough to live with ambiguity and letting go of the need to predict and the illusion of having control.

Reframing difference involves recognizing that differences are also increasingly a part of organizational life and greeting them as catalytic resources for learning, change, and improvement as well. It means not avoiding or reacting to or becoming alienated from people and ideas that seem different.

The predisposition of most people in Western cultures is to think linearly and to approach organizational work with an efficient plan to address issues and tasks in ways that have been proven successful and that are likely to offer predictable outcomes. This kind of approach, which Conklin and Weil (1995) suggest is appropriate for "tame" problems, and which I suggest was appropriate for industrial economies and highly routinized tasks, is not adequate in the new economy.

Although the new global knowledge-intensive economies have dramatically changed the dynamics within organizations, the underlying assumptions of most managers and of many organizational consultants have not evolved and too often have not even been questioned (Argyris, 1994, 1997; Brown & Duguid, 1991, 2000). For example, consultants often gather data for organizational diagnosis through surveys, assessment instruments, and interview protocols designed by white, well-educated, middle- or upper-class people (most often men) whose native language is English and who have lived most or all of their lives in the United States. Underlying assumptions guiding the gathering of data, the kinds of questions asked, and the measures of success, for example, may be culturally incongruent and misunderstood by many of the people from whom responses are needed. These problems are inherent in pluralistic economies even when the research efforts are designed by experienced and well-educated researchers because their education and experience is also often embedded within this same homogeneous culture and its attendant assumptions, which have seldom been questioned. Without intentional efforts to include people from diverse cultures, races, ethnicities, and so forth (i.e., continuously seeking differing perspectives), it is impossible to consider the vast obvious and subtle differences embedded in unchallenged assumptions (Argyris, 1994, 1997), leading to ineffectual data being used to guide organizational change efforts.

A conversational learning approach is especially advantageous for consultants in change efforts in the new economy that so often involve:

- Recognition of differences as essential for the continuous learning required;
- Collaborative learning among people with differing worldviews, skills, areas of expertise, vocabularies, and so forth;
- Increasing dependence on group/team work to represent the wide range of expertise and insights typically needed;
- More integrated efforts that enable systemic, rather than symptomatic, changes focusing on capacity building within the client system;
- Proactive, rather than reactive, change efforts that anticipate changes and recognize them as opportunities;
- Multiple, and highly varied, sources of media available to accommodate diverse working and learning styles, to accommodate the necessity for asynchronistic interactions, and to have access to the most appropriate tools and technologies for the work at hand; and
- Soliciting input from others to ascertain the most appropriate medium for tasks rather than using a one-size-fits-all approach and having facility with a wide range of technologies such as face-to-face, small and large group, structured and unstructured virtual contexts, and so forth to offer the client system.

TOURISM PROJECT ILLUSTRATIONS

Let's return to the city project with conflicting interests about tourism, vis-à-vis the need for creating a new kind of conversation. The stakeholders' positions about whether to encourage or discourage tourism were embedded in generational lessons passed down to them from such diverse families as those of

- Former slaves.
- Former slave owners.
- Middle- and lower-class Caucasians whose families had lived in the area for generations.
- People from "the North" and other "come-heres" who either did not have, or were perceived by some to not have, a substantial understanding of the complexity of the experiential histories of the region, histories that naturally helped shape people's current perceptions and positions on issues.

The city staff and its progressive mayor created a diverse ad hoc advisory board composed of people from all possible stakeholder groups, such as residents of the most affected neighborhoods; small and large business owners; craftspeople (usually African Americans) who sell their products largely to tourists; publicly elected officials at the local and state level; people with expertise about traffic flow, environmental issues, tourism patterns, and so on; Chamber of Commerce leaders; blacks and whites, young and older. Most of the people selected to participate on the advisory board had strong, well-known, and deeply entrenched positions about what the city should do to address the issues. I was brought in as a consultant to facilitate the board's work, which was to develop a five- to 10-year tourism plan for the city that would hopefully address the concerns of the competing constituencies and be adopted by the City Council through the passing of city ordinances.

There were many unexamined assumptions (Argyris, 1994, 1997), as is typical, that could limit the capacity for the kind of learning needed among the ad hoc advisory board members. Some of these included their varying preferences and expectations about how decisions should be made; appropriate styles for speaking and presenting themselves; who, if anyone, could be trusted; whether the group should get down to business immediately or should spend some time getting to know one another first; and who had power and who did not have power as well as perceptions about sources of power (i.e., positional, personal, authority, political, influence, demographic). For example, some of the residents whose families had lived in the historic neighborhood for generations and whose families had often been the community's political and business leaders unconsciously came into the group with the sense of entitlement that accompanies unexamined white privilege (McIntosh, 2001). On the other hand, while some of the African Americans on the board were initially reluctant to speak, others were vocal and bolstered partially by their awareness that African Americans' historical lack of influence was rapidly changing as demographic changes increasingly made it easier to affect change.

Although this case does not involve the *virtual* dimensions so often associated with the new economy, it does include all other primary characteristics of the new economy such as multiple stakeholders, rapid changes (such as the loss of the largest employer in the community, changing technology, the changing availability of federal funds, etc.), complex overlapping interests and issues, requirements for diverse professional expertise, and conflicts fomenting from centuries of misunderstanding and pain. This case also includes dependence upon the most sophisticated expertise about traffic patterns, environmental concerns, demographics, tourism trends, and so forth.

One example of the interlocking webs of interests involved business owners whose businesses were related to tourism and who also either lived in the historic neighborhood or whose close friends and families lived in the historic neighborhood, causing them to feel pulled in opposing directions. Another common example of the interlocking webs involved the previous formal and informal relationships among the ad hoc advisory board members, the city's staff, council members, and the mayor, all shaping the historical experiences that each person brought into this particular project.

CONVERSATIONAL LEARNING

Given such a consulting situation, how is conversational learning relevant? How can a conversational learning approach contribute to the consultant's capacity to reframe people's perceptions of change and ways of responding to differences? What does conversational learning involve in a consulting engagement? To address these questions, initially a brief conceptual description of conversational learning will be given followed by specific examples of how these ideas were used in this case. The chapter will conclude with a brief summary of the role of the consultant in encouraging and supporting a new kind of conversation that catalyzes the continuous learning necessary for sustainable change in the new economy.

The concept of learning used in this chapter is one that is grounded in experience and is described by David Kolb (1984) as "a process whereby knowledge is created through the transformation of experience" (p. 41). Conversational learning eludes precise definition. Yet, some parameters may be helpful as a guide. Much of the spirit of our meaning of conversational learning rests in this message from Howard Stein (1994):

To listen is to unearth rather than to bury. It is to feel rather than to be compelled to act. It gives us all greater liberty and responsibility in our actions. . . . The heart of listening deeply . . . is attentiveness to others' voices . . . the capacity for surprise in the face of any and all planning. Serendipity is readiness and playfulness in the face of surprise . . . incorporation of the astonishing into the ordinary, the refusal to hide behind a shield of routine. It is a willingness to be moved, changed . . . letting go of control. (p. 111)

To support the kind of listening that Stein is describing, creating receptive spaces for conversations is essential. When these safe receptive spaces in organizations and in communities are created and held sacred, people can learn to listen deeply to their own inner voice and to the voices of others—to listen in the spirit of learning, of being surprised, of being willing to slow down and reflect upon new possibilities, and of letting go of control.

To create sustainable change around the wicked problems that permeate organizational and communal life in the new economy, these kinds of conversations are essential to facilitate the reframing of how people conceive of and encounter change and differences. Conversational learning requires many substantial shifts in thinking for most people including:

* Listening to others with the intention of learning with them;
* Reflecting intentionally to gain more understanding of the complexities of organizational life using Schon's (1983) model of the reflective practitioner;
* Moving away from assuming there is one way of thinking (either/or) toward assuming that there are multiple legitimate and viable perspectives and possibilities of any situation;
* Moving away from assuming there is a right answer or a right approach toward placing more value on trying to learn from the multiple perspectives of as many other people as reasonably possible; and
* Avoiding reactive behavior by becoming highly proactive in anticipating change and finding ways to learn from different perspectives.

ROLE OF THE CONSULTANT IN A CONVERSATIONAL LEARNING APPROACH

Now let's consider the implications for the consultant in creating this new kind of conversation among people in organizations and communities (Brown & Duguid, 1991, 2000; Wenger, 1998). How would the consultant's work look different? What competencies and skills would be necessary? My intention in this section is to list some especially relevant implications and then describe them with illustrations of a few ways that I used them in the city's tourism project.

While in no way conclusive, some of the implications for the role of the consultant include things that typically apply in consulting engagements but have a special slant when a primary intention is to create a new kind of conversation that promotes learning and sustainable change efforts. These include:

* "Doing one's own personal work first."
* Preparing the soil (i.e., the context, the space, the people—to build as much psychological safety as possible).
* Attending with special care to *beginnings*.

- Broadening and sharing the worldviews (Burrell & Morgan, 1988; Fambrough & Comerford, 1998; McWhinney, 1997; Pepper, 1942) and experiential histories (people's stories) among stakeholders who will be affected by the change efforts.

- Emphasizing reflection as an essential part of learning and working to improve the quality of reflection.

- Emphasizing the relational, social dimensions of change in the new economy—thus, transforming the notion of conversations and relationship building as essential to the work rather than a divergence from work.

- Building competence and confidence among people for asking questions that delve below the surface, for constructively grappling with differences and conflicts, for staying engaged with differing perspectives even when one's instincts are to avoid or react, and for being able to recognize when and how to allow differences to emerge and be explored and when and how to set appropriate boundaries.

- Proactively creating, with the client system, new patterns and routines that will anticipate change opportunities and will enable and support continuous conversational learning.

Many of these approaches function like overlapping layers of a textured fabric that serve to make it more durable, since the use of one will often reinforce or strengthen the intentions of several others. Therefore, many of the descriptions below are grouped by similar content and also highlight some of these overlapping uses. For example, many of the illustrations of ways to broaden and share worldviews and experiential histories were used in the beginning of the city tourism project to prepare the context and prime people to work together collaboratively.

Self

"Doing one's own personal work first" is one of the guiding principles of responsible, professional consulting. In other words, knowing our strengths and shortcomings, being honest with ourselves, continuously striving to increase our self-awareness, seeking and listening to feedback from responsible peers and colleagues, knowing our own personal "hot buttons" and how to anticipate and deal with them responsibly, being able to work from a centered place of a commitment and guiding clients to find their own paths forward rather than falling into the pattern of imposing our ways upon them are all part of "doing one's own work." Yet, to enable a substantial reframing of change and differences, to model conversational learning, to guide clients toward developing their own competence in conversational learning, and to authentically prepare them for the possible tumultuous short-term organizational consequences and resistances to this approach requires consultants to be on a lifelong journey of doing their "own personal work." This approach is not "business as usual" because it calls for *listening to learn* and *ongoing changes*, not just in the client system but also within each of us as consultants.

Without having a fairly well-developed self-awareness and acceptance of one's own self, it is difficult to listen deeply to others in ways that are open to being surprised and hearing new possibilities. Without the calming effect of an authentic acceptance of multiple perspectives, it is difficult to help the client system create safe environments that seek alternative and perhaps competing perspectives. Without an ability to anticipate change as an opportunity for positive movement, it is difficult to help the client be proactive about organizational changes. Without openness to learning from the differences in others, it is difficult to guide clients to embark upon conversations that raise differing perspectives and to remain engaged with them when the inevitable tension surfaces. Without an understanding that remaining engaged constructively with differing perspectives is an essential part of systemic change, it is difficult to stand shoulder to shoulder with clients to assist them in developing their skills of constructive engagement in conflict.

Preparing and Beginnings

Preparing the soil is a metaphor that may be the quintessential image that encompasses the message of this chapter. Whether in initial interactions with the primary client, with individual participants, groups, or external associates of the client system, the preparation of the soil—the context, the space, the people—may be the single most indispensable part of the process.

Without a receptive space to hold and sustain conversational interactions and relationship building, the question asking and risk taking associated with learning will be curtailed. Without a strong sense of psychological safety (Edmondson, 1996, 1999; Schein, 1999), differences will not surface directly in ways that catalyze learning. Instead the differences typically will covertly lead to unconstructive behavior like:

- Avoidance
- Reaction
- Alienation
- Passive-aggressive behavior

All of these drain energy and resources from organizations and their primary missions and tasks.

While trust and safety are easy to destroy by a judgemental comment, a broken promise, or a lie, the rebuilding of that trust and sense of safety can take endless energy and time. On the other hand, attending in the beginning of new projects, new groups, and so forth to carefully and consistently strive to create a shared sense of trust and psychological safety takes far less time and effort in the long run. And acknowledging and taking responsibility for less constructive behavior and talking about it in the group can make the inevitable human foibles much less destructive and offer potent teachable moments. Thus, from the first contact with the client system to each additional new beginning of the work, the consultant has powerful opportunities to model and help others recognize the potential of being able to venture into conversations and relational interactions that can create new ways of knowing and understanding that would never have been possible without trust, safety, and those connections (Gadamer, 1994).

In the tourism project, at my initial meeting with the city planning staff before I was hired, I was very candid about my values and approach as a consultant, in order to begin trying to establish a relationship of trust and respect. I told them that I needed to be able to interview each member of the ad hoc advisory board confidentially prior to the board's first meeting. I indicated that I could not undertake the work without the opportunity to learn the perspectives of each board member one-on-one and without the commitment for several days of trust- and relationship-building work with the board members before the task of developing a plan was begun. I explained my fundamental consulting approach using conversational learning, although I did not actually use those words.

Once hired, I strived to enter the interview with each board member with the assumption that I was there to learn from that person, who had a valuable and legitimate perspective, and that I was there to begin to build a relationship with her or him based on mutual trust and respect. At the beginning of the interviews, I assured each person of confidentiality and also let him or her know that I had an agreement with the city that I would not be asked to share any identifying information about anyone's perspectives, statements, and so forth. Therefore, I hoped to be perceived as an independent neutral in potentially volatile circumstances.

At the first meetings of the board, each agenda item was carefully chosen again to prepare the context and to begin the work in ways that would most likely support collaborative conversational learning. I introduced myself and had people introduce themselves by sharing a bit about their hopes and expectations for the group's work. I paid close attention to the words and possibilities that were said, and those that were not said as well. I made careful mental notes to revisit themes that I wanted to reinforce and comments that I thought might need to be unobtrusively reframed later.

I talked very briefly about my hopes and expectations with the intention of beginning to help people develop some jointly shared superordinate goals that would call forth the most generous and community-minded intentions—using what I refer to in the next section as a brief (not more than 10 minutes maximum) lecturette given in a conversational manner without notes and using frequent examples that people could relate to easily.

Also as part of the opening meeting, I asked people to imagine the ideal kinds of conversations that the group might have together and to jot down some of the characteristics of what those conversations might look like. I suggested that we jointly do some brainstorming (offering their ideas without evaluation or discussion until all ideas were on the flip chart paper) to generate together possible norms for us to use in all of our subsequent conversations. I also came prepared with ideas that I felt were important and added suggestions as possible norms. After lots of ideas were on the flip chart, we talked collectively about the items on the list and gradually worked toward gaining a consensus—an understanding that while each item might not be shared by everyone with the same enthusiasm, each item that remained on the list was one that people "could live with" as a shared norm. Fairly quickly this consensus was reached. A large poster of the list was printed and posted at all subsequent meetings of the group, and individual copies were also given to each person at the next meeting. The list of norms was revisited and slightly modified in light of people's reflection after the first meeting. This list served as the guide developed by this particular group giving the parameters of appropriate and unacceptable ways of communicating during the life of their work together.

Broadening and Sharing

One way that people's worldviews can be broadened is by listening carefully to other people's stories of their experiences, expanding the range of authentic possibilities. Stories, unlike the abstract declaration of ideas, can engage people in the possibilities of varied ways of growing up and developing in ways that may generate more empathetic and careful consideration and attention. Hearing abstract ideas, separated from personal experience, makes it difficult for some people to imagine how these ideas would be manifested in actual behavior. Also, especially when abstract ideas are presented, unless the speaker is especially attuned to his or her choice of words, tone of voice, verbal and nonverbal attitude, and so on, listeners may feel that they are being preached to, generating a reaction against the content and interfering with possible new learning and reflections. This distinction between ideas and stories is exquisitely illustrated in the following quote from Alice Walker's (1998) novel, *By the Light of My Father's Smile*. The quote is from a conversation between two of the characters in the book, one of whom is a Mundo, from an indigenous population in Latin America.

No one among the Mundo believes there is anyone on earth who truly knows anything about why we are here, Senor. To even have an idea about it would require a very big brain. A computer. That is why, instead of ideas, the Mundo have stories.

You are saying . . . that stories have more room in them than ideas?

That is correct, Senor. It is as if ideas are made of blocks. Rigid and hard. And stories are made of a gauze that is elastic. You can almost see through it, so what is beyond is tantalizing. You can't quite make it out; and because the imagination is always moving forward, you yourself are constantly stretching. Stories are the way spirit is exercised.

But surely your people have ideas, I said.

Of course we do. But we know there is a limit to them. After that, story! (pp. 193–194)

Thus, the story can stir listeners' imaginations, tantalize them to stay engaged, offer an elastic gauze-like frame within which their own worldviews can be seen and perhaps expanded. Obviously, the format and the timing for sharing stories in a consulting engagement need to be contextually appropriate and relevant, but often the consultant's all-too-frequent assumption is that the client just wants specific information, a rational approach, the most "efficient" use of time, and so forth. This emphasis, however, usually precludes time for storytelling when storytelling can serve multiple purposes simultaneously and become a high point early in a consultant's work with a new client system. The organizational learning literature (Brown & Duguid, 1991, 2000; Nonaka, 1994; Wenger, 1998) is filled with confirmation of the substantial wealth of learning potential that can emerge in the wise use of sharing of stories and narratives.

A few other ways to broaden people's worldviews include brief, easy-to-understand pre-readings to prepare people for group conversations about the readings; brief, easy-to-understand lecturettes by the consultant or by a highly regarded person either within the organization or an outsider who has credibility; and spontaneous strategic inclusion of the ideas and examples of varied worldviews in group conversations, especially when connections are made as examples to illustrate how differing worldviews are filters through which the world is seen and understood.

In the city's tourism project, after the interviews were completed, I did a thematic analysis of the interview data and then shared common and unique themes that emerged in the interviews. A commonly shared theme that ran throughout the interviews was the lack of trust people had for one another and the skepticism that people had about the possibility of the board reaching any agreements except by acrimonious close votes. Yet, another common theme was the genuine concern, appreciation, and pride that people shared for their community.

Differences, Reflection, and Learning

Generally, when people reflect upon their differences with other people, the potential for learning from the differences is increased. And the likelihood for learning is further increased when the quality of reflection improves. One of the first people to write about organizational learning was Donald Schon (1983), who also has written extensively about practitioners who reflect on their experiences and "stay in conversation" with organizational situations. These reflective practitioners are able to observe and listen intently and recognize how a unique situation is similar and different from previous ones. They are able to reflect upon intended and unintended changes to let each new situation in the organization "talk back" to her or him and serve as a possible source of learning. And Schon, as many others after him, recognized that it is in the differences among people and in the unexpected and unintended changes that the greatest potential for learning can often be found. And yet, it is also in these very circumstances that breakdowns can occur that not only impede learning but also often lead to misunderstandings, distractions from work, and lost energy and productivity.

Typically people in organizations and their consultants have limited skills and little experience with the constructive engagement with differences and the surfacing of conflict. The more limited these skills and experiences are, the more likely people are to avoid letting differences come to the surface and be talked about, the more likely people are to avoid others whom they perceive as different, and the more likely people are to become alienated from individuals and parts of the organization that they perceive as different. For example, in an organization the marketing folks, the research and design folks, and the service delivery folks often do not talk to one another, thus leading to a lack of coordination, at the least, and at the most lack of potential collaborative energy that could become an invaluable resource for new ideas and for new knowledge creation.

In the city tourism project, folks from differing and "opposing camps" on this issue had never been in the same room with one another, were reluctant to be in the same room with one another (and repeatedly asked me in the interviews if I had any idea what I was getting into by trying to facilitate this effort), and had seldom calmly listened to people who had opposing points of view on these issues. Preparing people to trust that there would be civil conversation, that everyone would be treated with respect, that each person would have a chance to be heard, and that this would not be a futile waste of their time were among the challenges that required the kind of preparation described above.

Much of the preparation took place in the interviews as I tried to listen carefully to the unique experiences and perspective of each person and tried to address their individual concerns. For example, some of the African Americans on the board had been asked to be a representative (often a token representative) on boards many times before, had given of their time and effort, and had seen no results after getting their hopes up that there would be change. With those individuals, I had to assure them that this effort would be different, putting my own reputation on the line and activating my own adrenalin at the same time— an effective stimulus for many of us as consultants, but one that creates the kind of stress we know too well.

The initial meetings (the beginnings) of the ad hoc board were also critical for helping people learn new ways of engaging around their differences so that they could *listen to learn* from their differences. The jointly created norms of conversation provided the framework for a new kind of conversation. I used gentle interventions when norms were not observed (for example, asking if the group felt we were following our own agreed upon norms and in some cases naming aggressive behavior when a more gentle approach was not effective). I tried to create a safe receptive space for conversation by letting people know up front that I would intervene whenever necessary to assure that each person was treated with respect. I asked questions and brought up topics to encourage people to talk about their differences below the surface and tried to model a new kind of conversational interaction in my own behavior. This kind of work requires that we, as consultants have had training and experience in conflict resolution, facilitation, and group dynamics; that we have sensitivity to the experiences of each person in the group; and that we have had extensive experience in recognizing institutionalized "isms" and the need to bring differences to the surface to challenge the status quo. For example, those of us who are Caucasian need to grapple extensively with the white privileges that we typically have taken for granted if we are going to have any credibility and viability in creating a new kind of conversation among diverse people.

Relational and Proactive

When change is happening in organizations and communities, it is taking place at multiple levels (i.e., at the individual level, the group level, the organizational level, the societal or environmental level). And as a consultant, being able to be proactive, rather than reactive, to the dynamics of change at each level demands a relational orientation to the change process. While an emphasis on relationships and social interactions is embedded in organizational development and in the training of most consultants, the pervasiveness of the relational dynamics is intensified in the new economy where "conversation" and collaboration are the essence of the work.

In this project, the preparation and beginnings elements were interwoven with the proactive work that was required. Recognizing and being able to track the relational dynamics that were occurring on all four levels simultaneously was one of the biggest challenges, requiring me to structure my own frequent reflection upon the work to learn from the "talk back" of each unique situation. And in the first three meetings of the board, spending structured and unstructured time to help the board members begin to build new relationships was critical.

For example, in the second meeting, we did a visioning exercise. Each person wrote words on index cards that described their ideal images for the community. These cards were then posted on the walls of the room. People were then asked to walk silently around the room reading all of the cards followed by a time of group reflection in which the conversation brought out what people noticed as they silently read the cards. Overwhelmingly, the main impression was the similarity of the images of what they wanted for their community—a transformation from seeing themselves as holding down "opposing camps" into a growing recognition that they shared more common ground than they had imagined.

CONCLUSIONS

After many meetings and difficult conversations, the project ended several months later with the presentation of a comprehensive five-year tourism plan to the mayor and City Council. The full ad hoc advisory board adopted the plan by unanimous consensus. Essentially all of the recommendations were passed as city ordinances by the City Council and signed by the mayor. The plan calls for periodic updates about every five years. As demonstrated in this project, by building the capacity for a new kind of conversation, the possibilities of creating sustainable changes can grow exponentially.

To be most effective as a consultant in creating a new kind of conversation in organizations and in communities, it is important for the consultant to be on a personal lifelong journey of increasing self-awareness, to collaboratively re-frame perceptions of *change* and *differences* into vital resources to develop experience and skills in multicultural work and conflict resolution, and to collaboratively create with the client system receptive conversational spaces imbued with psychological safety.

With the increasing complexity of knowledge intensive work in a pluralistic world, the nature, intentions, and contexts that surround conversations need to be given considerable attention—leading to an important role for the consultant vis-à-vis building sustainable change and continuous learning opportunities in the new economy.

REFERENCES

Argyris, C. 1994. Good communication that blocks learning. *Harvard Business Review* (July/August): 7.

Argyris, C. 1997. *Organizational learning*. Oxford: Blackwell Business.

Brown, J.S., & Duguid, P. 1991. Organizational learning and communities-of-practice: Toward a unified view of working, learning and innovation. *Organization Science*, 2(1): 40–57.

Brown, J.S., & Duguid, P. 2000. *The social life of organizations*. Boston: Harvard Business School Press.

Burrell, G., & Morgan, G. 1988. *Sociological paradigms and organizational analysis: Elements of the sociology of corporate life*. Portsmouth, NH: Heinemann Educational Books.

Conklin, E.J., & Weil, W. 1995. Wicked problems: Naming the pain in organizations. http://www.gdss.com/wp/wicked.htm.

Edmondson, A. 1996. Learning from mistakes is easier said than done: Group and organizational influences on the detection and correction of human error. *Journal of Applied Behavioral Science*, 32: 5–28.

Edmondson, A. 1999. Psychological safety and learning behavior. *Administrative Science Quarterly*, 44: 350–383.

Fambrough, M., & Comerford, S. 1998. Changing epistemological assumptions of group theory. Under revision for publication.

Gadamer, H.-G., 1994. *Truth and method*, 2nd rev. ed. New York: Crossroad.

Kolb, D.A. 1984. *Experiential learning: Experience as the source of learning and development*. Englewood Cliffs, NJ: Prentice Hall.

McIntosh, Peggy. 2001. White privilege and male privilege. In Margaret L. Andersen &

Patricia Hill Collins (eds.), *Race, class and gender: An anthology*, 4th ed. Boston: Wadsworth Publishing Company, pp. 95–105.

McWhinney, W. 1997. *Paths of change: Strategic choices for organizations and society.* Thousand Oaks, CA: Sage Publications.

Nonaka, I. 1994. A dynamic theory of organizational knowledge creation. *Organization Science*, 5(1): 14–37.

Pepper, S.C. 1942. *World hypotheses: A study in evidence.* Berkeley: University of California Press.

Schein, E.H. 1999. *The corporate culture survival guide.* San Francisco: Jossey-Bass.

Schon, D.A. 1983. *The reflective practitioner: How professionals think in action.* New York: Basic Books.

Stein, H.F. 1994. *Listening deeply: An approach to understanding and consulting in organizational culture.* Boulder, CO: Westview Press. Online version, PSOL CD, George Mason University.

Walker, A. 1998. *By the light of my father's smile.* New York: Ballantine Books.

Webber, A.M. 1993. What's so new about the new economy? *Harvard Business Review* (January–February): 24–42.

Wenger, E. 1998. *Communities of practice: Learning, meaning, and identity.* New York: Cambridge University Press.

Whyte, D. 1996. *The heart aroused: Poetry and the preservation of the soul in corporate America.* New York: Doubleday.

Chapter 15

Restorying and Postmodern Organization Theater: Consultation to the Storytelling Organization

Grace Ann Rosile and David M. Boje

All the world's a stage, and all the men and women merely players.
—William Shakespeare, *As You Like It*

INTRODUCTION

A woman is on her knees, hands stretched out together over her head, elaborately bowing down to the floor in an exaggerated "salaam" motion while reciting an endless monologue of "I hope this is OK, is what you want, oh great one, I am here to serve you." The person standing over her is peevishly reciting offenses on the fingers of each hand, with headshakes and rolled eyes and a patronizing righteous manner. Each person appears to be in a separate monologue. They begin to make eye contact, begin to engage a bit, and to react to each other. This scene is typical of a new form of organizational change approach using theatrics. The two characters have been chosen from groups of participants, each enacting in their own monologues a past experience of being disrespected or oppressed and also at times taking the role of the one disrespecting/oppressing them. They are matched with no regard to the nature of the internal story they enact. As they begin to interact, sometimes confusion at not getting expected responses leads them both to revert to their original internal monologues, and they communicate less and less with each other, each spinning and helplessly caught in his or her chosen role. At times, the oppressed person turns the tables and becomes the oppressor. At some point we (consultants to the group) stop the action and call for discussion from the spotlighted actors and from the observers. The vignette is both real and art/artifical, and releases a flurry of responses. We will return to this example later.

This chapter describes a use of narrative and theatrics for organizational development. We begin by viewing organizational life as a story and organizational development as a means of changing that story or "restorying." We use a seven-step process to guide individuals, groups, and organizations in their own restorying process. Part of that process involves taking apart the opposing "dualisms" (like black-white, right-wrong, etc.) which are often unconsciously embedded in organization members' language. In this dualism analysis, we use theatrics to deconstruct or analyze situations and to free organizational members to fashion liberatory responses to exploitive organizational dynamics.

In consulting to storytelling organizations, to change the organization is to change its storytelling processes and enter the realm of theatrics. We could look at organizations as theater in metaphoric ways. We could begin by saying, the way ahead in many organizations looks like a blacked-out theater, where the play has yet to begin, and a common story is not agreed upon. And others seem to have lost their story script or have a faded one, impossible to read after being recopied so many times. We could explore the theater metaphor and say that once in a while, unexpectedly, a stagehand shines a moving "follow spot" to catch an actress, poised and ready to perform a newly written story script to an enthusiastic audience. Is there a backstage where executives and staff check their story lines, adjust costumes, and wait for their cues? Our metaphor evaporates as our imaginary spotlight fades.

But what if *organizations are theater* here and there? We could look for examples of theater and explore face-to-face or virtual stages (i.e., Internet), places where a story line is made presentable as a rationale and legitimation to spectators, the customers, employees, investors, vendors, and community. In this way theater and storytelling is the full time job of leaders and many consultants.

We will explain our methods through a series of organizational consultation case stories. We include detailed descriptions of some specific structured physical activities. We have used these methods successfully in organizational development (OD) consultations as well as in undergraduate and graduate classes concerned with organizational change and development.

The structure of the chapter is as follows: First, in Part I, we introduce our concept that organizational life constitutes a story and offer our definition of the "storytelling organization." Next, in Part II we present our seven-step restorying process. We explain the process in Part III via a consultation story (The SciFi Case) which offers a broad overview of how we use this restorying process. We follow this with three step-by-step examples of theatrical restorying. Part IV is DePorres' Problem-Externalizing Approach, Part V is The Ritz Hospital Story Deconstruction Example, and finally, Part VI is Malbogat's Manipulation Walk Workshop exercise.

PART I: THE STORYTELLING ORGANIZATION

We believe consultation is about diagnosing and changing what we call the "storytelling organization" (Boje, 1991a, 1991b, 1995, 1998, 1999c. Boje, Fedor, & Rowland, 1982; Boje, Luhman, & Baack, 1999). We do not mean that organizations are *like* storytelling systems; we say they *are storytelling organizations* and ones that are increasingly theatrical, not metaphorical, and therefore call for consulting practices attuned to theatricality.

A storytelling organization is defined as a dynamic action of sequences and characters (real or imaginary) that comprise a collective memory network in performed stories, the meaning of which is revised as part of the story work of any organization. "Storytelling is the preferred sense-making currency of human relationships among internal and external stakeholders" (Boje, 1991a, p. 106). Organizations are complex patterns of stories being told, remembered, and re-storied to create not only new futures but also new remembrances of the past. Historians call it "revisionism" but it is something done by every organization.

Strategy is storying. A strategy is the organization's story of how it will enact its resources (information, people, and technology) to enact some future. Strategic management involves extensive use of planning scenarios and visioning futures—in short, storytelling (Barry & Elmes, 1997; Landrum, 2000).

In postmodern theater, employees reconstruct current organizational theater, as well as craft and rehearse scripts of change. We call this evolution the "re-storying of organizational theater in a postmodern world," the transformation of theatrics from artificial-metaphor to "authentic" inquiry, modern (professional) performance, and postmodern blurring of the boundary between actor and spectator, until the boundary between staged and real is impossible to find.

PART II: CHANGE THROUGH RESTORYING

The seven steps below demonstrate a storytelling-based strategy for change, which may be applied at both the personal and organizational levels (Rosile & Dennehy, 1998). Beginning with establishing a positive sense of identity, the questions below lead through problem identification and an assessment of positive and negative aspects of the problem. By identifying a "unique outcome" we may begin to reconceptualize past history. This new history reveals the previously hidden story of an organization or person able to overcome their problem. The final questions identify sources of support for the new story, the story of success at overcoming this problem. These steps were developed by the authors and are derived from White and Epston's *Narrative Means to Therapeutic Ends* (1990) and from other examples of restorying efforts, especially by Barry (1997), Kaye (1996), and others. These and other related references are listed in a bibliography by Boje (1997) and are available from Professor Boje at New Mexico State University.

Seven Steps for Restorying

Characterize (True Identity)

Describe the organization at its best, as if it were functioning perfectly and living up to all its ideals. (At the personal level, how might you be described by your favorite grandparent, relative, or teacher? What are your most outstanding qualities?) Create an "influence map." Influence mapping exposes:

- What is the impact or influence of the relevant persons on the problem?
- What is the problem's influence on the persons?
- What is the "state of affairs" at the onset, middle, and end of the story?
- What is the "state of affairs" we would predict for the future?
- How has the problem affected people's relationships with themselves?
- What ideas, beliefs, and so forth feed the problem?

Externalize the Problem

Tell us about a problem the organization currently faces, as if the problem were separate from any individual in the organization and is another character in the organization's story.

- The problem is the problem.
- The people are not the problem; a particular person is not the problem.
- Make the problem into a character ("overwork") that the person, as agent, can affect.
- Reduce the depressing effects of problem-saturated accounts.

Sympathize

What benefits does the organization derive from the problem? What feeds the problem?

- Identify the dualisms supporting the status quo.
- Explore the dominant side of each dualism.
- Explore the subordinate side of each dualism.
- Study the construction of dualisms—how they are two sides of the same coin.

Revise (Commitment to Change)

Explain the ways in which this problem has had negative effects. Would people really like to be rid of this problem? Why?

- Disadvantages of the problem.
- Explore the limitations of dualisms.
- Deconstruct the dualisms.

Strategize (Unique Outcome)

Tell about a time when there was a "unique outcome," when this problem was not as strong or when it was completely eliminated. Identify an existing potential to overcome the problem.

- Deconstruct the problem.
- Use "double descriptions" or alternative descriptions, so *the story* becomes "a story."
- Realize that multiple stories and outcomes are possible.
- Expand the alternative story—what thoughts and feelings, what happened before, after?

Re-historicize (Restory)

Take this unique outcome and instead of it being the exception, make it the rule, the dominant story. What evidence is there to support this "alternative" story? What might a news release say about your organization's new ability to overcome this problem? What would they say they saw in the past that might allow them to predict your success in overcoming the current problem?

- Choose the preferred new story.
- Choose the past "unique outcomes" that support the new story.
- Choose the future predictions/predictors that support the new story.

Publicize

Who would say they could already see the basis for, or that they would support, this new organizational approach that is overcoming the old problem? How might you enlist the support of these others to ensure continuing success in overcoming this problem?

- Writing letters to recognize and encourage the storyteller's efforts.
- Writing "letters of reference."
- Concretizing the "reauthoring" process.
- Providing tangible evidence of support and interest.

Next, we offer an example of using the above seven steps in a consultation setting.

PART III: RESTORYING IN THE CASE OF THE SCIFI ORGANIZATION

Following is the story of SciFi, a high-tech military-related organization of more than 2,000 people. I, Grace Ann Rosile, am the author of this story version (Rosile, 1998a, 1998b). Over a period of six months, my husband David Boje and I gathered data and conducted a four-day strategic planning organizational consultation involving the top leadership at SciFi. This is the story of how we encouraged SciFi to restory itself. The concepts of storytelling, story deconstruction, and restorying were all used throughout this process, from the initial data gathering through the consultation process and the final report. As story listeners, you will judge how successful we were. You will use your own retelling of this story to explain your conclusions regarding the validity and usefulness of our story methods.

What follows is part of the story David and I co-created with the people of SciFi, in the process of researching and consulting with them.

"I grew up never really knowing what my father did because he worked at SciFi and he wasn't allowed to talk about it. It was the same for lots of kids around here." Hearing this comment, I was beginning to understand the daily lived experiences behind the big sign we saw as we arrived for our first day of interviews at SciFi. Right there on the brick archways housing the armed guards, bold letters prohibited cameras and recording devices. First-day jitters blossomed into a moment of panic. Surely we had mentioned that we had planned to tape record our interviews, hadn't we? Later we discovered that while others in the past had been forbidden to tape record, no one objected to our doing so. Looking back, shouldn't we have guessed that in this environment of routine secrecy, communication would be a serious problem?

SciFi is a high-tech military-related government organization established at the height of efforts to bring about an end to World War II. As with most such organizations, they are highly sophisticated with regard to personnel and equipment and have high security requirements. They are governed by a complex overlaying of military bureaucracy and governmental regulations. Their environment has always been greatly affected by global military and political actions. As with most defense-related activities, the end of the Cold War brought reduced funding. But every military "hot spot" like the Gulf War brings an upsurge in demand for service and a corresponding release of government funding, which may be too late to meet crisis needs. In peaceful times, SciFi is under increasing pressure to recover high overhead costs by bringing in more revenue from private entrepreneurial ventures (i.e., using their high-tech staff and equipment for nonmilitary purposes). These efforts represent a new and as yet fairly small portion of their income. Some think that the SciFi technology is too specialized to adapt to private industry uses, at least not on a scale broad enough to replace the vast scope of their military activities. SciFi also leases space to small high-tech private organizations, which are also customers. Next to their U.S. military customer services, SciFi's other mainstay is selling their services to foreign governments. This practice is common with other branches of our government/military organizations. It is justified by noting that we retain the most advanced weapons technologies for ourselves, while selling only older weaponry against which it is claimed we can easily defend ourselves.

About two years earlier SciFi decided to become more proactive in managing its destiny by engaging in a strategic planning and reorganizing effort. Their intention was to become more flexible and more competitive and to make SciFi more "businesslike," and the plan was called "SciFi Inc." Some called it "reengineering." A small group of top people worked with a consultant to design a more businesslike, reengineered organization. Implementation of this plan was met with great resistance, resulting in seriously low morale and high perceived uncertainty. People whose parents had spent their careers at SciFi and retired from there suddenly realized they might not be able to do the same. These reactions occurred in spite of the fact that great efforts had been made to avoid any forced layoffs.

At the time of the consultation, there were differing views on the success of the reengineering efforts at SciFi. Some felt the reengineering plan was both necessary and good. Some said they would not participate in any future effort that did not build on the good work begun and yet to be completed by the first reengineering project. Others felt that the plans may have been good, but poor participation and communication with the work force made implementation problematic. Still others felt the early work was a near disaster and recommended that we not even use certain words that had become negatively associated with the earlier reengineering change program.

In retrospect, it appears the work force and most of the leadership of SciFi believed they had little or no voice in the plan or its implementation. Over 20 briefings were offered to inform and educate, but apparently personnel still did not understand the nature of, or the justification behind, many of the changes. Then David and I were brought in to begin a new "strategic planning" process. After interviewing key people, we began our consultation with a letter.

Dear SciFi Leaders,

We have finished a series of 15 interviews, each lasting an hour and a half, with the top leaders of SciFi and we want to write to tell you about our discoveries. We appreciate your openness and candor during our interviews. From those interviews we present below a summary of the results most relevant to our first day's meeting.

First, we present our general assessment of SciFi. You are the people who made possible the joke about the job that "doesn't take a rocket scientist." Your jobs do require rocket scientists, and you have, as one person said, "the best of the best." You have work areas that look like science fiction movie sets. In spite of budget cuts and the end of the Cold War, you had "scud-busters" in place and working within 48 hours during Desert Storm. People enjoy their work so much that it was reported that they cheerfully arrived at 3 A.M., for no extra pay to carry out tests. They do "just great . . . [in spite of] 1950s equipment." You are the premier competitor in your field. You are proud of your beautiful setting. You are good neighbors, contributing between $1 to $1.5 million per day to the surrounding local economies. What has disturbed this ideal scene?

According to some, this is the story of people who until very recently were the best and the brightest. They were the solution; now they feel they are treated like they are the problem. Yesterday they were the shining white knights; today they are white elephants. They were scud-busting heroes; now they are budget-busting expense items. What happened between yesterday and today?

SciFi is experiencing trouble and everyone would like to help. There was high agreement that the employees are the greatest strength of SciFi. One person described this strength as "the devotion of employees toward accomplishing the mission . . . to make things happen successfully; the most technically sound people [in this field]." These are the people who worked around the clock during Dessert Storm. Yet, these people with all their years of dedicated experience and expertise were not consulted about the SciFi Inc. plan. The approach of having over 60 people in a meeting proved unwieldly, and the strategic planning process was then delegated to three persons. Those persons were chosen for their years of experience and presumed relatively unbiased perspectives. Their recommendations went to the chief executive, who announced the plan in a series of briefings. In retrospect, it appears that the work force and most of the leadership of SciFi believe they had little or no voice in the plan or its implementation. They attended the briefings but did not understand the reasoning and justification behind many of the changes. Thus, to some, it appeared as though "yesterday we were the best work force and today we are worthless." What happened between yesterday and today were many changes, changes so rapid that one person said, "I would stop changing here" and "We are not in the status quo mode now, we are in the mode of 'where are we?' " and "It's that C word."

While everyone recognized that change is difficult and typically resisted, it is believed to be especially difficult to manage the recent changes here at SciFi for several reasons, some of which are: (1) Initial expectation levels may be unusually high at SciFi. Some employees saw their parents retire from a lifetime of service here, and they were expecting to do the same. (2) Lack of communication regarding the changes; one person suggested that even saying, "We still don't know what will happen" would be helpful communication.

Stop. As the storyteller, I will intervene now before I present the restorying recommendations that David and I presented to SciFi. I want to give you, the reader, a chance to restory this situation yourself. Below is some additional background on SciFi, followed by an outline of steps to take to restory.

Restorying

Fueling the forces for change at SciFi are an impressive series of economic, environmental, political, and regulatory pressures that are acting on a global scale. Seeking to proactively manage this turbulent environment, SciFi leadership embarked on the SciFi Inc. strategy. It is difficult to know which of the current problems stem from the above-named external pressures and which stem from flaws in the SciFi Inc. plan itself. Most comments indicated that problems were perceived to flow not from the SciFi Inc. plan itself, but from its implementation. Such problems were described most often as "communication" problems.

But almost everything is a communication problem. By examining the steps below, you, the reader, may discover how David and I, as the consultants in this story, composed the above letter to SciFi in a way that we hoped would enable them to see their situation as a story, and by seeing it as such, they would be able to restory themselves. Do you see in the letter the restorying elements listed below? (See Part II, above, for longer descriptions of the restorying steps.)

1. *Characterize.* Describe the organization at its best, if it were functioning perfectly and living up to all its ideals.

2. *Externalize.* What is the problem, viewed as separate from any individual, as an external entity?

3. *Sympathize.* What benefits does the organization derive from the problem?

4. *Revise.* Disadvantages of the problem, benefits foregone, reasons to change.

5. *Strategize.* Find a "unique outcome" from the past, even a potential, that allowed the organization to defeat the problem.

6. *Re-historicize.* Make the "unique outcome" the rule (instead of the exception) in a *new* story of freedom from the problem.

7. *Publicize.* Enlist support for the new story. Use letters, ceremony, and so forth.

Recommendation Letter

Now we go to the recommendations David and I presented to SciFi. Our recommendations also were initially introduced as a letter telling the story we saw. We attempted to lead the SciFi top management into redefining their problems as a story that can then be changed or restoried. Do you think we convinced them?

At this point we would like to make a recommendation regarding how to redefine these reported problems. We recommend a process we call "externalizing" the problem. With this approach, we do not view the problem as being due to the characteristics of the people in the organization. This step alone helps us to avoid finger-pointing and blaming and the strong tendency for attributional biases to lead us to see other people as "the problem." Instead, we look to external factors influencing the problem, and we assume that "the problem" *is* "the problem." This subtle yet powerful redefinition allows our people to be part of our solution, to again be our heroes. We plan to spend a part of the time during our first day's meeting to focus on this positive and productive way of describing problems. By revising the story of the problem ("restorying"), we escape the victim language and dynamics of the "problem-saturated" storyline. We then control the problem and have thus empowered ourselves to take action against it.

Following are some examples of "externalized" problem definitions, highlighted in capital letters. These externalized problems are the common enemy of everyone in the organization, and are not presented as caused by any particular individual or group within SciFi.

The problems cited most consistently by everyone were FEAR and UNCERTAINTY. These problems were usually perceived to be due to a HIGH RATE OF CHANGE perceived as unpredictability. Yet gloomy predictions predominate: "There is no good news; '97 will be viewed as good, later on." This leads to LACK OF TRUST, due to the LACK OF COMMUNICATION about the values behind decisions and the reasons why certain choices were made, leading to one comment that "it is all ego and politics."

Lack of communication about reasons and especially about the values behind decisions leaves those decisions open to multiple interpretations in times of uncertainty. This is compounded when goals are unclear or are not shared by all. Thus, the purchase of a new piece of equipment may be interpreted as "They value technology more than people here" or "That unit got the equipment and we did not; they are the favorites of management" or "They are replacing us with computers" or "Management wants us to have the best equipment available to help us do our jobs even better."

Even when values-oriented information is communicated, the communication may be ineffective and the message may be distorted or not received at all if the fear and trust issues have not been addressed. Otherwise, as one person put it, the impression is created of "a used car salesman, saying everything is OK, you still have your job, that (the job) would be the bone that would make it OK. That ain't enough!" Even the promise of continued employment may be interpreted as belittling employees' reasons for working there: "It's not just for the paycheck; we care about more than that."

Recognizing these fears and concerns as the common, externalized enemy, allows us to work together to overcome them.

Conclusion

I interrupt again, not to present my conclusions but to invite you to create your own. After days of wrestling with understanding the various aspects or parts of their problems, the SciFi top management group was floundering. They had steadfastly resisted all attempts to get them to restory themselves. On the morning of the last day, David showed a video of a business case example of a turn-around. On overheads, David showed how SciFi could adopt a strategy along similar lines. The impact was dramatic. They saw the light. "That's us! We're just like the company in the video! We want the same plan. Let's just adopt what is on David's overheads!" They were saved, and David was their savior. Could we have just used the video, and skipped this story stuff? I believe our days of work allowed this group to understand the elements of their story, and the video model then triggered their ability to restory. What's your story? Next, DePorres demonstrates a method for externalizing the problem and making it a character in the organizational story.

PART IV: DEPORRES' PLAY-FUL PROBLEM EXTERNALIZING APPROACH

For the past several years we have been teaching storytelling organization practices to Pepperdine and Benedictine University doctoral students. One Pepperdine student, Daphne DePorres, applied what she learned to her consulting work (DePorres, 2000). We obtained Daphne's permission to share her exercise with you (see Figure 15.1). It demonstrates how to "externalize the problem" as characters in a play.

DePorres used restorying in consultation work with an agency that served victims of abuse. Interestingly, organization members described many of their own organizational problems in terms of abuse of power, almost as if the clients' presenting problems were becoming internalized in both the fabric of the organization and in the lives of its individual members. DePorres addressed the

Figure 15.1
Daphne DePorres' Problem Externalizing Exercise

Goal of This Exercise: Better understanding of—not necessarily agreement on—the issues/problems facing the organization's functioning.

Purpose: To explore power, to see what it's all about, to gain a greater understanding of how power exists and plays itself out here at this organization.

Instructions:

• In this exercise, each organizational member will be assigned a role, based on data gathered from the organization about the problem.

• The purpose of the assignment of roles is to enable the maxim, "the people are not the problem, the problem is the problem."

• Diverse and competing opinions are WELCOME during this process!

Specifically, today's goal is to have a better understanding of *Power*, *Power Struggle*, and *Casualty of Power Struggle*. The exercise is based upon interviews with the staff.

Step One—Pre-work: Who Are You?

The exercise begins with a simple question written on flip chart paper, Who Are You? "When I think of power, I think _____" (fill in the blank).

Flipchart: When you speak, you must be in role, until notified otherwise.

When you speak, for example, say, (example) "As Power Struggle, _____," You are not speaking as yourself, or a staff member. You are speaking from the position of one of the three roles. Later in the afternoon, we will shift into a dialogue about these three things at [organization], but for now, you're bringing what you know about the three from any facet of your life.

"Power"—Who Are You?

• What does Power look like? Describe its physical body. What colors does it wear? What styles of clothing does it like? How does it smell? What are Power's usual behaviors?

• How does Power speak? What is Power doing when it's not speaking? Who does Power report to? Who does Power hang out with?

"Power Struggle"—Who Are You?

You need to discuss these questions as a way of getting to know who Power Struggle is.

• What does Power Struggle look like? Describe its physical body. What colors does it wear? What styles of clothing does it like? How does it smell? What are Power Struggle's usual behaviors? What do Power Struggle's actions look like? How does Power Struggle speak? What is Power Struggle doing when it's not speaking? Who does Power Struggle report to? Who does Power Struggle hang out with? Who are Power Struggle's friends?

"Casualty of Power Struggle"—Who Are You?

• What does the Casualty of Power Struggle look like? How do I feel? What do I look like?

• How do I stand? How do I communicate? How do I try to get power? How do I contribute to your hold on me?

(continued)

Figure 15.1 (continued)

Step Two—The Interview Process: "Questions for Power, Power Struggle, and Casualty of Power Struggle" from the Interviewer

Power

- What do you look like? What else do you look like? How do people recognize you? Power, what are your strengths? Why do you exist? How do you help this organization accomplish its mission? Power, how are you misunderstood? Why don't people like you?

- Do you have friends? How do you make friends? How do you make enemies? What do you want people to understand about you that they just don't get?

Power Struggle

- Power Struggle, how might people describe you? What do you look like? What do you wear? What do you smell like? What feeds you and keeps you going? What do casualties do to keep you alive and happy? Where do you live? What does a day in the life of Power Struggle look like? What would make you no longer have a reason to exist?

Casualty of Power Struggle

- How did you become a Casualty of Power Struggle? When did you become a Casualty of Power Struggle? What keeps you a Casualty of Power Struggle? What benefits do you derive from interacting with Power Struggle? What are the costs of being a Casualty? What do you need from Power Struggle not to be the Casualty of Power Struggle? How else might I achieve satisfaction besides hanging out with Power Struggle?

Step Three—Open Interview Process *with Questions*

Instructions:

- At this point, any participant may ask questions of any entity.

- Questioners must continue to be in *a role*. It can be any role they choose: P, PS, or CPS.

- When the participants speak, they must identify themselves in one of the three roles: Power, Power Struggle, Casualty of Power Struggle.

- Anyone can answer the question, but must do so in a role.

Dialogue—What is our understanding of the three entities? In this phase, the group spends about 45 minutes to an hour in dialogue among the three groups: Power, Power Struggle, and Casualty of Power Struggle. Again, the instruction is given, "When you speak, you must be in role, until notified otherwise. When you speak, for example, say, (example) "As Power, _____."

Example:

1. A person who was in the Power Struggle has a question to ask as Casualty of Power Struggle.

2. Someone else in the room answers, speaking from the perspective of P, PS, or CPS.

Step Four—Shared Understanding

- Do we have a better understanding of Power, Power Struggle, and Casualty of Power Struggle?

- What is our understanding of Power, Power Struggle, and Casualty of Power Struggle?

- Closure—There is active reflection on the exercise, applying what they learned to their day-to-day work life.

Now that the organization has externalized their problem, they are ready to begin creating their new story where they, the heroes, defeat those problem characters.

Daphne DePorres may be contacted at daphne_udem@yahoo.com regarding this exercise.

need to externalize the problem in two ways: first, by addressing each individual's personal connections with abuse of power; and second, by externalizing both the personal and organizational experiences. She began in a small-group setting, where staff members were asked to give brief examples of how violence had touched their lives. This served to draw out a vast range of experiences as well as a range of emotions, in a very powerful way.

DePorres next helped the group to externalize their experiences of power abuse. The process began by viewing abuse not as something done by a person or persons ("my co-worker," "my boss," or "the administration") that was directed at me, the victimized employee. Instead, the problem was externalized. It became three new characters in the organizational story: Power, Power Struggles, and Casualties of Power Struggle (P, PS, and CPS). This allowed the organization members to address the problems, to "play with" the problem(s), without pointing fingers, without labels, and without the complex web of explosive emotions underlying these issues and enmeshed in both personal and professional/client experiences (i.e., without recreating the scenarios with which they were inundated daily as the essence of their jobs).

Now, instead of people drowning in problem-saturated accounts, the problem was externalized into separate characters. Now, the people of the organization could be the heroes. They could "play" with the problems and figure out how they might outsmart and defeat them.

In the proper restorying fashion, DePorres kept the focus on the organization's control of the story. She worked with organization members to design a theatrical exploration of organizational power abuses through the role playing of these three characters (P, PS, and CP). As a result of the exercise, participants were able to better understand and address the power dynamics at work, without denying emotions, yet without dysfunctional emotionalism.

PART V: DECONSTRUCTION AND RITZ HOSPITAL RESTORYING THEATRICS

Deconstruction is an important tool in the restorying process. Our workshop design for Ritz Hospital incorporated theatrics and deconstruction. Any (or all) of the first seven methods (below) help to understand and break the grip of the dominant story line. The eighth method leads us to a new story which is "resituated" and free of the old dualism. When resituation is accomplished, we can return to the restorying process. While a deconstruction cycle may be used almost anywhere in the restorying process, we find it most helpful during Steps 4, 5, and 6 (revise, strategize, and re-historicize).

Eight Story Deconstruction Methods

1. *Duality Search*—List terms that are bipolar opposites or express dichotomies (e.g., male/female, management/labor) and divisions in the organization (engineering/mar-

keting). For example, stories may be male- or female-centered and articulate more male or female images.

2. *Reinterpret the Hierarchy*—A story is one interpretation of an event told from one point of view. The dualities in a story can be explored to see if the terms are set in a hierarchy. For example, do the stories with male imagery dominate?

3. *Rebel Voices*—Stories will often leave out important voices or marginalize voices, giving them less power in the account. Whose voice is excluded or hierarchical, compared to others? Are there stakeholders who can not speak, such as women working in an overseas factory? Are there elements of the natural environment, such as trees or animals?

4. *Other Sides of the Story*—Stories always have many sides to them. A story can be retold from another viewpoint or told by a rebel voice that is usually not heard.

5. *Deny the Plot*—Stories are scripts with plots, recipes, and morals to toll. Plots include romantic, comedic, tragic, and satiric. Try changing the plot to see how the story shifts impact.

6. *Find the Exceptions*—What is the exception that breaks any rule, principle, or proposition in the story?

7. *Trace What Lies Between the Lines*—What was not said? *Is* there some writing on the wall no one is talking about? What is left out of the story that those in the know are filling in? Newcomers and new consultants may not be able to read between the lines.

8. *Resituate the Deconstructed Story into a New Story*—The point of doing the prior seven steps is to find a new story to enact. To resituate is to reauthor and rewrite the dominant story so that its hierarchy is not a trap, so that more views get included, and so that the plot can change, instead of just getting repeated.

Ritz Hospital Case

Characterize and Externalize

Ritz Hospital shifted direction dramatically 17 years ago. They managed to remain independent of the large hospital chains and still financially successful by being different and innovative. Ritz Hospital wants to stay ahead of the curve, to keep on being different and innovative. At the same time, Ritz wants to keep a strong sense of identity and values, of *who* and *what* Ritz is, to guide them into the future.

Sympathize

In the past, hospital-based health care was little more than charitable caretaking of those likely to die. As the recipients of charity, patients were expected to be silent and grateful for whatever care they got. The patient did not have a "voice" in the health care story; they were the "other," the "object."

Revise

About 17 years ago, Ritz Hospital put the patient at the heart of the organization, as the first priority. Patients had a voice, and their voice was heard.

Revise and Strategize: Questions for Deconstruction of Ritz's Present Story

• Who is on the bottom now? Who is marginalized in this story? (rebel voices)
• How can we remain small and stay independent? (dualism; deny the plot)
• What challenges and opportunities are we offered by new technology? (between the lines)
• What is our product? Can we offer an experience, not just a service? (resituate: not the well/ill dualism but a third alternative)

Story Deconstruction

To deconstruct a story is to discover the many other sides of the story. Part of that process involves taking apart the dualisms embedded in organization members' language (duality search). In our work with Ritz Hospital we asked participants to identify dualities. Their list included:

Access/cost	Doctor/patient	Patient/non-patient
Administration/staff	Male/female	Self-pay/third party pay
Cost/revenue	Money/public service	Sickness/health
Doctor/nurse		

Ritz had done away with most titles and positions and already had a reputation as a flatter, more customer-focused place to work. However, they still discovered places where hierarchy crept in. We used theatrics as part of our exploration of Ritz's dualism of administration/staff (listed above), and our process yielded the example with which we opened this chapter. Resituating that dualism eventually involved redefining the roles of administration and staff in relation to the client/patient and away from the old power struggles with each other. This incorporation of the client into the new story ultimately led to a redefinition of their product not as a service offered, but as a co-created experience.

We offer next a technique deeply rooted in the highly theatrical workshops of Augusto Boal (1979), which were themselves based on Paolo Freire's critiques of education. This activity uses methods such as stop-action theatrics to allow participants to artificially break down interpersonal and group events. Beginning with a series of scripted physical behaviors, each person experiences his or her own behavior, then sees the effect of his or her behavior on others, and then reacts to others' responses, in a chained sequence of scripted activities. These activities build from those designed to enhance simple awareness of self and others to the recreation of past events. The past is recreated as a living present, which is subjectively perceived by participants. This method is both social and liberatory. It emphasizes simultaneously the connectedness of individuals along with the freedom of each to act.

PART VI: MALBOGAT'S MANIPULATION-WALK WORKSHOP

We (David and I) invited Simon Malbogat to offer this introductory workshop on theatrics for organizational change for the Organization Development Division of the Academy of Management in Toronto in 2000 (Boje & Rosile, 2000). Malbogat is director of Toronto's Mixed Company theatrical troupe. This group, which performs all over the world, is devoted to using theatre for social change in corporations, community groups, and high schools. Simon Malbogat may be contacted at mixedco@echo-on.net or 416–515–8080 in Toronto, Canada, regarding this workshop. What follows is a description of the workshop, which was designed by Malbogat (2000) to address corporate power dynamics.

Phase I: Introduction

Malbogat begins with warm-up activities, first presenting his own enacting of a series of seven masks. Each painted facial mask has an expression, each expression is related to the seven forms of external manipulation (guilt, aggression, etc.). Malbogat identifies and then enacts each form, often directing his actions to one of the audience members, who may or may not respond. (There are also seven internal forms of manipulation which people do to themselves, but in the interests of time, these were not presented at this workshop.) In this initial phase, people become used to theatrical representations of behaviors, and see the behaviors (the masks) as separate from the person enacting them.

Phase II: Manipulation Walk

There are two phases to the Manipulation Walk: the Oppressed Walk and the Oppressors Walk. Here, Malbogat asks the participants to think of a time when they felt put down, disrespected, or manipulated. They are asked to walk around the room, using words and gestures in a monologue that acts out how they felt in this oppressed condition. They are encouraged to be expressive and cautioned not to injure themselves or others, nor to engage others in this monologue. After several minutes in this phase, action is stopped. Malbogat then asks participants to portray the person or persons who had been oppressing them in the previous walk example. For several more minutes, participants walk around as oppressors, and then action is stopped again.

Phase III: The Improvization

Now Malbogat divides the group in half evenly, and one half is asked to remain in their oppressor roles, while the other half returns to their oppressed roles. The oppressors are asked to remain still with hands raised, while the oppressed walk around and choose an oppressor with whom to partner. When two people agree to partner, the oppressor's hand is then lowered. When all have found partners, Malbogat asks for a pair to volunteer to demonstrate their interaction while the rest of the pairs observe. The demonstration pair begin spontaneously, each acting his or her private scenario and responding to the other person's actions if and as they choose. Frequently, tables are turned and the oppressed becomes the oppressor as the scene plays out. Then Malbogat stops the action and asks what the other participants observed. After brief discussion of the dynamics observed, each pair conducts its own improvisation for several minutes. Then Malbogat stops action for the final debriefing.

Phase IV: Discussion

Malbogat concludes with a whole-group discussion, inviting volunteer pairs to relate what happened in their scenarios. This discussion reinforces for participants what they have experienced: they are now more awake, aware, and aroused to action. Malbogat links their experiences back to the manipulation masks. They leave with a liberating understanding of the power dynamics of oppressors and oppressed as well as self-empowerment and self-disempowerment.

PART VII: PUTTING THESE CONCEPTS INTO PRACTICE

As with most powerful tools, these methods must be used with skill and caution. Narratives and stories are, by nature, richly contextualized and embedded wholes. Thus they elicit very rich responses from the whole person. This can mean less separation of personal and professional issues, more emotional involvement, and more powerful responses in general than approaches that may be predominantly intellectual in nature. Also, many activities described here, especially the theatrics, involve the physical body more than some other methods of organizational intervention. This physical involvement also serves to intensify responses and may evoke tears, anger, and other actions and emotions. At the same time, expect greater creativity, insight, depth of understanding, and immediate visible changes in behavior. We find these methods highly impactful, exhilarating, and effective.

Using narrative and theatrics places great demands on the consultant, challenging all your interpersonal and intellectual abilities. Prepare yourself by practicing some of these methods before adopting all of them. For organizations unused to such methods, prepare them with "warm-up" activities. Allow plenty of time for participants to translate what their bodies and emotions are telling them into thoughts and words, and ultimately organizational application. Remember also that with activities such as these, there may be profound effects that everyone experiences as profound but which may not ever be completely captured in words. Sometimes this is not necessary. A major benefit of theatrics is that some learnings may be applied instantly. New behaviors may be enacted and "played out" without over-intellectualizing analysis-paralysis. Further, even in inherently intellectual, abstract organizational change programs, small bits of restorying and theatrics may be used with stunning effectiveness.

We expect that you will find that many of your current organizational change consulting practices are rooted in, or already incorporate, narrative and theatrics. Those are the places to begin if you wish to expand your use of the methods we have briefly outlined here.

CONCLUSION

In summary, restorying and theatrics offer several fresh insights into the organizational change process, opening new opportunities for change. First, by viewing the organization as a narrative or story, we can use restorying to change the old story. Second, by externalizing the problem and locating it in the discourse as another character in the organizational story, we can address the problem without blaming, pointing fingers, and threatening the identity of self and other organization members. The problem no longer is "them," it is merely the problem. Third, theatrical methods allow us to "play" with organizational problems. We can role-play the externalized problem(s) to gain better understanding and control. Finally, when our new story is re-historicized and publicized, we take advantage of the contextual and embedded nature of narrative to elicit support for our new story.

We invite you to "play" with these narrative and theatrical methods for organizational change. Please contact us with your questions and comments as well as your insights from your own experiences in this area. Rosile and Boje may be reached through www.horsesenseatwork.com or New Mexico State University's Management Department (505–646–1201).

REFERENCES

Barry, D. 1997. Telling changes: From narrative family therapy to organizational change and development. *Journal of Organizational Change Management*, 10(1): 30–46.

Barry, D., & Elmes, M. 1997. Strategy retold: Toward a narrative view of strategic discourse. *Academy of Management Review*, 22(2): 429–452.

Boal, A. 1979. *Theater of the oppressed.* New York: Urizen Books; London: Pluto Press.

Boje, D. 1991a. The storytelling organization: A study of storytelling performance in an office supply firm. *Administrative Science Quarterly*, 36: 106–126.

Boje, D. 1991b. Consulting and change in the storytelling organization. *Journal of Organizational Change Management*, 4(3): 7–17.

Boje, D.M. 1995. Stories of the storytelling organization: A postmodern analysis of Disney as "Tamara-Land." *Academy of Management Journal*, 38(4): 997–1035.

Boje, D.M. 1997. Storytelling research in organizations. Presentation to Organizational Behavior Teaching Conference. http://cbae.nmsu.edu/mgt/jpub/boje/styrefs/index.html.

Boje, D.M. 1998. The Postmodern Turn from Stories-as-Objects to Stories-in-Context Methods Research Methods Forum (online), No. 3 (Fall). http://www.aom.pace.edu/rmd/1998_forum_postmodern_stories.html.

Boje, D.M. 1999a. Is Nike Roadrunner or Wile E. Coyote? A postmodern organization analysis of double logic. *Journal of Business & Entrepreneurship*, 2 (March): 77–109.

Boje, D.M. 1999b. Nike, Greek goddess of victory or cruelty? Women's stories of Asian factory life. *Journal of Organizational Change Management*, 2(8): 461–480.

Boje, D.M. 1999c. Lessons for theater: Beyond metaphor symposium. Tamara and other postmodern theatric(s). http://cbae.nmsu.edu/mgt/jpub/boje/theaterlessons/index.html.

Boje, D., Fedor, D.B., & Rowland, K.M. 1982. Myth making: A qualitative step in OD interventions. *Journal of Applied Behavioral Science*, 18: 17–28.

Boje, D.M., Luhman, J., & Baack, D. 1999. Hegemonic tales of the field: A telling research encounter between storytelling organizations. *Journal of Management Inquiry*, 8(4): 340–360.

Boje, D.M., & Rosile, G.A. 2000. Festival, spectacle, and carnival: Theatrics of organization development & change, ODC Symposium session #760 of the Academy of Management Meetings, Toronto, August 7.

DePorres, D. 2000. Unpublished Ph.D. dissertation, Pepperdine University.

Freedman, J., & Combs, G. 1996. *Narrative therapy: The social construction of preferred realities*. New York: W.W. Norton.

Kaye, M. 1996. *Myth-makers and story-tellers*. Sydney: Business & Professional Publishing.

Landrum, N.E. 2000. *A quantitative and qualitative examination of the dynamics of Nike and Reebok storytelling as strategy*. Unpublished Ph.D. dissertation, New Mexico State University.

Malbogat, S. 2000. Workshop presentation in "Festival, spectacle, and carnival: Theatrics of organization development & change." ODC Symposium session #760 of the Academy of Management Meetings, Toronto, August 7.

Parry, A., & Doan, R.E. 1994. *Story re-visions: Narrative therapy in the postmodern world*. New York: The Guilford Press.

Rosile, G.A. 1998a. The story of the scifi organization. http://cbae.nmsu.edu/mgt/jpub/rosile/scifiblkrosile/index.html.

Rosile, G.A. 1998b. Restorying and the case of the sci-fi organization. Academy of Management Presentation. http://web.nmsu.edu/~garosile/garscifiacademy.html.

Rosile, G.A., & Dennehy, R.H. 1998. Restorying for personal and organizational change. Proceedings of the Southwest Academy of Management, Dallas, TX, March.

Saner, R. 1999. Organizational consulting: What a Gestalt approach can learn from off-off-Broadway theater. *Gestalt Review* 3(1): 6–21.

White, M. & Epston, D. 1990. *Narrative means to therapeutic ends*. New York: W.W. Norton and Co.

Index

About the Contributors

TERRY R. ARMSTRONG has over 30 years of experience helping organizations manage change under numerous conditions. He has been involved in hundreds of change projects to include being a muticultural organizational development consultant to the Peace Corps, the U.S. State Department, the U.S. Navy, the U.S. Air Force, the Massachusetts Port Authority, the Florida Department of Transportation, and the Army Corps of Engineers. Internationally, he has consulted in Colombia, Ethiopia, Finland, Honduras, Mexico, Panama, Peru, Poland, Saudi Arabia, South Africa, Spain, and Venezuela.

ANN C. BAKER is an assistant professor in the School for Public Policy at George Mason University. She has extensive consulting expertise and experience with private, public, and not-for-profit organizations. Ann is the author of numerous publications on organizational conversation as a source of learning, multicultural learning, group dynamics, collaboration, and competency-based learning. She is currently writing a book, *Conversational Learning in the Knowledge Economy*, with David Kolb and Patricia Jensen that will soon be published by Quorum Books.

ANDREA B. BEAR is co-founder and president of Full Potential Organizations, LLC. She brings more than 20 years of leadership experience gleaned from a wide variety of positions—from operational to support—with several companies—from startup (including CNN) to institutional, high-tech to low-tech, and private sector to public sector (implementing various organizational change practices and initiatives). Andrea spent more than a decade in television news in positions ranging from executive producer to photographer. She was a founding producer of CNN in Atlanta in 1980, and while at an ABC-owned station in

Chicago she led a team, including Oprah Winfrey, to Ethiopia in 1985 to document the famine crisis.

DAVID M. BOJE, professor of management at New Mexico State University, has published numerous articles in *Administrative Science Quarterly*, *Academy of Management Journal*, *Management Communication Quarterly*, and other journals. He edits *Journal of Organizational Change Management* and is founding editor of *Tamara: The Journal of Critical Postmodern Organization Science*. He serves on the editorial board of *Academy of Management Review*, *Management Digest*, *Organization*, *Journal of Management Inquiry*, *M@n@gement*, *Organization Studies*, *EJ-ROT*, and *Emergence and Management Communication Quarterly*. Recent books include *Narrative Research Methods for Communication Studies* (2000) and *Spectacles and Festivals of Organization* (2001).

RICHARD E. BOYATZIS is professor and chair of the Department of Organizational Behavior at the Weatherhead School of Management at Case Western Reserve University. Prior to joining the faculty at CWRU, he was president and CEO of McBer & Co. from 1976 to 1987, and chief operating officer of Yankelovich, Skelly & White from 1983 to 1985. He is the author of numerous articles and books on behavior change, leadership, managerial competencies, and emotional intelligence.

KATHLEEN A. BREHONY is co-founder and executive vice president of Full Potential Organizations, LLC. She is an experienced organizational and personal coach, licensed clinical psychologist, sought-after speaker, and award-winning author of several popular books about change and consciousness, including *Awakening at Midlife*, *Ordinary Grace*, and *After the Darkest Hour*. All share a theme of the expansion of consciousness and the innate power in each of us to live up to our fullest potential. Kathleen has served as a management consultant to large and small, established and startup, private and public sector organizations for Arthur Young and Company (now Ernst & Young, LLP). She has more than 20 years in private psychotherapy practice.

JERRY W. GILLEY is a professor of human resource development at Colorado State University and was a principal at William M. Mercer, Inc. He has authored and co-authored 13 books and over 60 articles, book chapters, and monographs. His more recent books include *The Manager as Change Agent*, *Philosophy and Practice of Organizational Learning, Performance, and Change*, and *Organizational Learning, Performance, and Change: An Introduction to Strategic HRD*, which was selected the HRD Book of the Year (2000) by the Academy of HRD. He is editor of the New Perspectives in Organizational Learning Performance and Change book series for Perseus Publishing, and has been the director of the HRD Professors Network (ASTD) and a board of directors member of International Board of Standards for Training, Performance, and Improvement.

JAMES W. HANDLON is a senior vice president of corporate services at Digital Commerce–Powertrust in charge of strategic planning, business development, and product development. Jim received his MBA from George Washington University. After many years in consulting, Jim launched an Internet company. His interests include e-business development, shared services, and partner alliances.

ERIK HOEKSTRA is the director for people and organizational development for the Harbor Group, a management services holding company and consulting group. He holds a bachelor's degree in history and philosophy, an MBA in international management from The Rotterdam School of Management, and is a Ph.D. candidate in organizational learning at Iowa State University. He has served in various management capacities and was previously an instructor of marketing/management.

GIGI G. KELLY is an assistant professor at the College of William & Mary. She received her doctorate in MIS from the University of Georgia. She has extensive consulting experience in the areas of information technology and change management. Her research focuses on the integration of information technology and organizational change and has published articles in the *Journal of MIS*.

WILLIAM J. MEA is a commander in the United States Naval Reserve and was a manager at KPMG Consulting. He recently became a Deputy Assistant Secretary at the Department of Labor. Bill received his Ph.D. in psychology from Auburn University. He has experience working with several international e-marketplaces and his research interests are in supply chain optimization and change management.

KATHI MESTAYER, president, Mestayer & Associates, has assisted clients with a broad array of strategic and management issues, decision processes, and competitive strategies. Her projects include working with executives, elected officials, and other stakeholders on controversial regional public projects; designing and facilitating processes for strategic planning; and training executive groups on the effective use and leadership of teams and task forces. Kathi has developed and taught classes for national professional associations on managing public organizations, strategic outsourcing, and leadership skills. She is a trained facilitator and holds an MBA from the College of William & Mary.

SCOTT A. QUATRO is an instructor of management at Dordt College in Sioux Center, Iowa. An experienced human resource management and organizational development professional, Scott has been a senior consultant with a major management consulting firm and a human resources manager for a *Fortune* 500 retail company. His consulting and research work focuses on organization and job design, corporate culture, and spirituality in the workplace. He received a BA in English from Pepperdine University and an MBA from the College of William & Mary, and is a Ph.D. candidate in human resource development at Iowa State University.

EDGAR J. RIDLEY is president of Edgar J. Ridley and Associates, an international management consulting firm. An expert on symbolism and its effect on world cultures, Mr. Ridley has lectured at universities worldwide. He is the author of a trilogy beginning with *An African Answer: The Key to Global Productivity*, as well as *Symbolism Revisited: Notes on the Symptomatic Thought Process*. He is currently writing the third volume of the trilogy, *The Symptomatic Thought Process: Changing the Structure of Civilization*. Mr. Ridley has also been published in professional journals worldwide.

THEODORE L. ROBINSON III is a manager in the consumer and industrial markets line of business at KPMG Consulting. Trey received his MBA from Wake Forest University in addition to an undergraduate degree in chemical engineering. He has been a key member of teams launching several business-to-business enterprises. His research interests include performance management, digital marketplaces, and e-business strategy in traditional, brick-and-mortar organizations.

GRACE ANN ROSILE greatly enjoys narrative-based organizational consulting together with her colleague and husband, Dr. David Boje. Dr. Rosile is founder of Horse Sense at Work, a unique approach to consultation and management development which addresses the power dynamics of leadership, teamwork, and communication in the workplace through working with horses. Her articles have appeared in the *Journal of Applied Behavioral Science*, *Journal of Organizational Change Management*, and *Journal of Management Education*, among others.

LANE D. SAUSER is a certified public accountant and currently serves as the chief financial officer for the College of Agriculture and Alabama Agricultural Experiment Station at Auburn University. She earned her BBA and MBA degrees from Georgia State University and her doctorate in public administration from the University of Alabama. Dr. Sauser is a certified government finance officer and a certified government financial manager. In her role as consultant, she has assisted state and local governments to implement change in budgeting, financial management, and operations.

WILLIAM I. SAUSER, JR. is professor of management and associate dean for business and engineering outreach at Auburn University. He earned his BS and MS degrees in management and Ph.D. in psychology at the Georgia Institute of Technology. A former president of the Alabama Psychological Association and the Society for Advancement of Management, Dr. Sauser has consulted for a variety of private sector, public sector, and voluntary organizations on such topics as strategic planning, organizational change, and human relations in the workplace.

RONALD R. SIMS is the Floyd Dewey Gottwalld Senior Professor in the Graduate School of Business at the College of William & Mary. He received his Ph.D. in organizational behavior from Case Western Reserve University. He has more than 20 years of consulting experience with organizations in the private, public, and not-for-profit sectors. He is the author or co-author of 20 books and more than 75 articles, which have appeared in a wide variety of scholarly and practitioner journals. His most recent books are *Reinventing Training and Development*, *Accountability and Radical Change in Public Organizations*, *Keys to Employee Success in Coming Decades*, *Administration*, and *The Challenge of Front-Line Management* (co-edited with John G. Veres III), and *Organizational Success through Effective Human Resources Management*. Other forthcoming books include *Teaching Business Ethics* and *Managing Organizational Behavior in the New Millennium*. He has taught at the GE Management Development Institute in Croton-on-Hudson, New York. His research focuses on a variety of topics including organizational change management, human resources management, employee training and development, learning styles, experiential learning, and business ethics.

SERBRENIA J. SIMS is Director of Accountability, Assessment, and Grants Writing for the Williamsburg–James City County School System, in Williamsburg Virginia. She earned her BA and MPA degrees from Auburn University at Montgomery and her doctorate in education from the College of William & Mary. She has published a number of articles and books on a variety of organizational, training, and higher education topics. Her most recent books are *The Importance of Learning Styles: Understanding the Implications for Learning, Course Design, and Education* and *Total Quality Management in Higher Education: Is It Working? Why or Why Not?* both co-edited with Ronald R. Sims and published by Greenwood Press and Praeger Publishers, respectively. For the past three years she has taken her interest in individual change into the middle school classroom, where among other things she teaches science to seventh graders.